GOD
HAS SPOKEN

EXPOSITORY
PREACHING AND TEACHING

HEBREWS

Chang Soo Kim

i

The Bible Study Textbook Series

NEW TESTAMENT

The Bible Study New Testament Ed. By Rhoderick Ice	**The Gospel of Matthew** In Four Volumes By Harold Fowler (Vol. IV not yet available)	**The Gospel of Mark** By B. W. Johnson and Don DeWelt
The Gospel of Luke By T. R. Applebury	**The Gospel of John** By Paul T. Butler	**Acts Made Actual** By Don DeWelt
Romans Realized By Don DeWelt	**Studies in Corinthians** By T. R. Applebury	**Guidance From Galatians** By Don Earl Boatman
The Glorious Church (Ephesians) By Wilbur Fields	**Philippians · Colossians Philemon** By Wilbur Fields	**Thinking Through Thessalonians** By Wilbur Fields
Paul's Letters To Timothy & Titus By Don DeWelt	**Helps From Hebrews** By Don Earl Boatman	**James & Jude** By Don Fream
Letters From Peter By Bruce Oberst	**Hereby We Know (I-II-III John)** By Clinton Gill	**The Seer, The Saviour, and The Saved (Revelation)** By James Strauss

OLD TESTAMENT

O.T. History By William Smith and Wilbur Fields	**Genesis** In Four Volumes By C. C. Crawford	**Exploring Exodus** By Wilbur Fields	**Leviticus** By Don DeWelt
Numbers By Brant Lee Doty	**Deuteronomy** By Bruce Oberst	**Joshua · Judges Ruth** By W. W. Winter	**I & II Samuel** By W. W. Winter
I & II Kings By James E. Smith	**I & II Chronicles** By Robert E. Black	**Ezra, Nehemiah & Esther** By Ruben Ratzlaff & Paul T. Butler	**The Shattering of Silence (Job)** By James Strauss
Psalms In Two Volumes By J. B. Rotherham		**Proverbs** By Donald Hunt	**Ecclesiastes and Song of Solomon** — By R. J. Kidwell and Don DeWelt
Isaiah In Three Volumes By Paul T. Butler		**Jeremiah and Lamentations** By James E. Smith	**Ezekiel** By James E. Smith
Daniel By Paul T. Butler		**Hosea · Joel · Amos Obadiah · Jonah** By Paul T. Butler	**Micah · Nahum · Habakkuk Zephaniah · Haggai · Zechariah Malachi** — By Clinton Gill

SPECIAL STUDIES

The Church In The Bible By Don DeWelt	**The Eternal Spirit** By C. C. Crawford	**World & Literature of the Old Testament** Ed. By John Willis	**Survey Course In Christian Doctrine** Two Bks. of Four Vols. By C. C. Crawford
New Testament History — Acts By Gareth Reese	**Learning From Jesus** By Seth Wilson		**You Can Understand The Bible** By Grayson H. Ensign

GOD
HAS SPOKEN

EXPOSITORY
PREACHING AND TEACHING

HEBREWS

Owen L. Crouch

COLLEGE PRESS PUBLISHING COMPANY
P.O. Box 1132, Joplin, MO 64802

iii

Library of Congress Catalog Card Number: 83-71985
International Standard Book Number: 0-89900-197-1

TO

Lucille
James
Lorna

Table of Contents

Preface

Exposition involves discovering what an author says in the context in which he says it. It includes an explanation of what he means by what he says in the context in which he said it. Exposition demands that an expositor be true to the author's intent.

Exposition of the biblical text places on the expositor the responsibility of explaining the human author's message in its original environment. He also has the added responsibility of discovering and relaying that divine message embodied in the human situation. Exposition means that the teacher has implicit confidence that the word of God will meet universal human needs if and when it is explained in its native surroundings. God spoke to human need. An explanation in context of that which God has said will meet the need for which it was first given. The expositor does not have to manufacture "applications." When the text is clear to the human heart that heart will make its application to its own need. The Bible was given to reveal, not conceal. When the Bible is exposed it still reveals.

Within this book are expository helps on Hebrews. For the reader familiar with the Greek text it offers a diagram of the Greek text of the epistle. Also notes to help follow the diagram and its significance. To the reader not acquainted with Greek it offers the diagram in English. The notes will be of help to either Greek or English readers. But of real service to anyone, Greek, English, professional or layman, are the translations, outlines, and "Some Expository Thoughts." They aren't substitutes for faithful study. But they are stimulants to the mind.

This work is not designed solely for the professional preacher or academician though it can be of service to such students. This work has any serious student of the scriptures in mind. He who sincerely wants to know the message of Hebrews and whose desire is unquenchable may profit from the tools in this volume.

Pages xxiii through xxvi are worthy of special note. They present some statements relative to the nature of exposition. They give specific suggestions about methods of procedure. And they offer two examples of expository messages.

This effort is sent forth with the sincere prayer that God shall give it wings to soar beyond the limits that fear, prejudice, pride, or other human limitation that would shackle its usefulness.

Owen L. Crouch

May 2, 1982
First Christian Church
4800 Franklin Road
Nashville, Tennessee 37220

Introduction

"It pleased God by the foolishness of preaching to save them that believe." The apostle meant that it was the folly of the "thing preached," not preaching as a method. As a message the cross, to the wise-acres of this world, was and is foolishness. But no one is blind enough to insist that preaching as a device for propagating ideas is foolish. The advent of radio and television has not even dimmed preaching as a method. Politicians get elected by preaching their promises. Everything from automobiles to toothpaste is sold through commercialized mass preaching. And it is a fact, demonstrated in history, that the flame of reformation and revival have been fed by preaching. War and peace have often been the fruit of preaching. It is a sound, sensible way of spreading news, good or bad.

Through the centuries preaching has been determinant in the Christian gospel. Periods have appeared in which limited, specialized ministries have elbowed pulpit preaching aside. Sometimes ministries of charity, youth, music, administration, ritual, worship, have subordinated the pulpit as suspect, irrelevant to the demands of the harsh realities of current life. But preaching always outlives substitutes and recaptures its dominance in the propagation of the gospel.

Furthermore, expository preaching, while a less used manner, has always and everywhere been recognized as the finest for the expanding of knowledge of the word of God.

Let's not be misunderstood. Ninety percent of preaching is topical or textual. None should question this type as adequate for the saving of souls, the building of numerically large churches or inciting of social reforms. Any method that spreads Christian ideas is good and acceptable. One doesn't need to preach or hear expository sermons in order to save, serve or find full satisfaction in Christian fellowship in Christ. Yet, it still remains that expository sermonizing is Christian preaching at its best. No other method is equal for informing the mind, refining the heart, exciting the will to act, feeding the deeps of the soul, kindling the fires of imagination, broadening the knowledge of the scriptures, building character in the saints. Nothing surpasses it in the personal development of both speaker and listener.

If these be facts one can but wonder why ninety percent of preaching is not expository? Whatever the reasons, they lie beyond the purpose of this study. But among the reasons is the lack of helpful literature that teaches what it is and how it may be done. Hopefully, the following pages will help in some way to fill that lack.

In this project it is not presumed that this is the way expository preaching "ought" to be done. The only claim is that this is the way one man has done it. And that it has been done with some measure of favorable response.

WHAT CONSTITUTES A SERMON?

The essential elements which make up a sermon are:

1. Topic
2. Text
3. Introduction
4. Proposition (theme)
5. Body (structure)
6. Conclusion

Whether a message be topical, textual, biographical or expository any sermon includes these elements. Some students give other names to these ingredients. There may be some overlapping in the use of terms but by whatever name they are called these basics may be found in any sermon.

The *topic* announces what the author-preacher presumes will attract attention. It declares either directly or obliquely the idea or ideas that will be developed in the message. It announces that which the public may expect if it should hear or read the sermon.

The *text* grounds the message in the Judeo-Christian heritage. It gives to the discourse a biblical setting; it flavors the sermon with the color and taste of the Christian writings; it enhances the communication with whatever inspiration and authority the Bible may carry to the listening audience.

The connection of the text to the sermon determines what the classification of the message is. In the topical sermon the text may or may not have some bearing on the content of the message. The topic is the chief burden. The text is only an appendage, useful to give biblical standing. In a textual sermon the text is definitely attached to the message. It may range from merely being a motto of the idea to the forming of the structure of the sermon. In some fashion or other the text furnishes the frame for the sermon. But in exposition the text *is* the sermon in a very vital sense. The content, structure, theme; all the basic material is the warp and woof, the very fabric of the entire message. Even the context in which the text arises plays a vital role. The bones and the meat on the bones come out of the passage chosen to be exposed. It is the most purely biblical of any form of preaching.

An *introduction* is the porch, the entrance to the house. It is to arouse interest, unite the minds of the listening people and suggest what is to come. When people assemble, their minds are as varied as the number present. The introduction must capture these rambling minds and point them toward a single goal and channel them into that direction which the message and messenger choose. It must say to the listener, "This is the way we will travel and you're going to be excited at what you discover."

The *proposition* specifies exactly what the messenger is trying to prove, develop, explain, affirm or answer. It may or may not be expressed in so many words. But at all times it should be present. If it isn't written, at least it should be in the preacher's mind as he prepares and delivers the sermon. If a fellow doesn't know where he is going, he won't get there. When making a proposition one is merely choosing to achieve a particular goal.

Some sermonizers draw a distinction between theme and proposition. They may be different in that theme is more of a general idea, less specific. The theme could be "faith" but the proposition, "one must have faith in order to please God." The proposition includes a theme although a theme is not necessarily a proposition. But for our purposes here proposition is treated as being one of the basic elements in a sermon. In our useage proposition includes theme. It's the specific, concrete goal toward which all else drives and from which all else derives.

The *body* constitutes the larger part of the sermon material. It includes the structural outline and all the facts plastered to it. The body develops the proposition by furnishing evidences that shoulder the idea of this basic thesis. It encompasses any and all illustrative, clarifying observations which help picture the point of the sermon.

A broad variety of sources supply data for filling out the meat for the skeleton. Personal habits and practiced skills enter into the body of a message. Alert observation as one lives from day to day offers much matter for the discourse. Wide reading from the arts and sciences is a rich spring from which may pour tributaries to the water of life. Filled with the fruit of such study the sermon will become alive to human interests and needs. The Bible itself can be like gold to a prospector. It makes both sermon and sermonizer richer in the use. If introduction is the appetizer and conclusion is the dessert, then the body is the main course. If we expect the famished hearts of God's people to be healthy in spirit then they must be fed well-balanced meals of nutrients. This is what the body of a sermon proposes to offer.

The *conclusion* is not only the termination but, from the standpoint of securing a decision, the most important portion. Assuming that it has a legitimate proposition, every sermon moves toward getting the listener to decide on some action. It may not be evangelistic so as to secure a conversion. But it seeks to stir a person to decide something. Thus the conclusion is designed to arouse the emotions and challenge the will to act. One should never act simply because his emotions are touched. But on the other hand one will never act until his emotions are awakened. As the body of the sermon has enlightened the mind the conclusion fires the will by provoking the emotions. It is here that the speaker makes his approval to move the listener to action. He must not manipulate but he does persuade. The conclusion draws on the preacher's highest motives and finest skills. There will be occasions when the circumstances of the moment will dictate a conclusion. But for the most part it is well to think it out in advance.

WHAT CONSTITUTES A LESSON?

What, if any, is the difference between sermon and lesson, between preaching and teaching? And we have in mind *expository* sermon or lesson from biblical literature. Sermons and lessons have some elements in common. In such points they identify and overlap in form and function. But they differ in certain ways and it's these differences that make of one a "lesson" and the other a "sermon." If the same man who delivers a sermon in the pulpit walks from that pulpit into a neighboring classroom to teach a lesson what is he to do differently? Particularly if he is dealing with the same passage? Does any difference lie in the place, the listeners, the purpose, the techniques? Or is the line between the two overly-drawn by the hair-splitting of minds which live in the clouds instead of on the solid earth of daily realities? In Mark 1:14 it is said that "Jesus came preaching. . . ." In Matthew 5:2 we read that Jesus "having opened his mouth was teaching them. . . ." And he proceeds with what history knows as the *Sermon* on the Mount! Was he teaching or preaching or both?

The fact that such a question is raised implies that *some* kind of distinction exists. But it also implies that they have points of similarity. What are the similarities? First, the content of the material is the same. Exposition means *to explain*! There is no difference in the basic material used in lesson or sermon. Furthermore, both, at least ideally, seek to explain the *author's* point in whatever passage is used. He who hears sermon or experiences a classroom lesson wants to know what the author of the text says, why he says it, and the reason it was included in the book, essay, poem or narrative. The listener may even want to know why the author introduced this point at this place in his book or essay. Preacher or teacher is not creating new material. He is explaining the significance of someone else's creation. Therefore, he's morally obligated to teach or preach that which the author says and means. As teacher-preacher he may desire to use the author's thought in application far beyond the author's intent. But he is obligated to find that author's purpose as a base from which to go "beyond."

And what of the differences? Wherein does sermon differ from lesson? It may be oversimplifying yet there is certain truth in saying that a sermon "proclaims" while a lesson "informs." This certainly is not to say that proclamation is necessarily absent from teaching or that information is lacking in preaching. But a sermon does proclaim while a lesson may or may not. A lesson's chief purpose is more that of investigation and declaration of what is discovered. The lesson leads the student through facts in order to arrive at sound conclusions. A sermon is proclaiming of news; it is announcement of something that has happened that has important bearing on the hearer's life. Furthermore a sermon involves an attempt to persuade to action in view of the news announced. A lesson is an inquiry into material to arrive at judgments without necessarily any effort at persuasion. A lesson is to stimulate a love for the truth; a sermon arouses the hearer to obey the truth proclaimed.

Other divergencies also exist. A sermon is usually more formal in pattern. Even though not written out in manuscript form a sermon is more rigidly structured. A lesson, though it may and surely ought to be carefully planned, is more flexible, less fixed in its development. Historically, in a sermon there is *no* opportunity for the audience to participate verbally in the development of the message. The people are passive or must wait until later to respond in word or life. But in the lesson feedback from the audience is not only possible but in most instances encouraged and welcomed. The lesson lends itself more to sharing than does the standard sermon. But one should observe that this audience participation places an added responsibility on the teacher and his lesson. He must channel the feedback. And when class participation wanders, as often it will, down blind alleys and irrelevant topics, it's the task of the teacher to rescue the meandering discussion back to the main artery he has prepared.

Last, yet in no sense least, the sermon is designed so as to lead the worshiper to a confrontation with God. In some aspect or other the conscience must be touched, the emotions aroused, the will stirred. In a study group in which a Bible lesson is presented the object is enlightenment about God and about God's Word. Both the written and personal Word, that is, Jesus Christ the living Word! A lesson brings illumination about life, the community of the church, the biblical ethics and morals that govern Christian action. One preaches to a worshiping congregation; one teaches a people who are searching the word for God's ways with men.

The passage forming the basis of both sermon and lesson are exactly the same. Study materials may be largely the same. But the approach in handling the material will be different. Immediate goals are different. Hence methods will vary. And so far as actually teaching or preaching is concerned the skill with which either teacher or preacher executes his task will vary with individuals. Dedication to learning not only content of the Bible but also the techniques of the two functions will determine how well either task is done. No substitute for dedication and hard work has ever been discovered. James' exhortation, "be not many of you teachers . . ." (James 3:1) is not to discourage people from an active ministry. It is to remind of the serious responsibility that rests on anyone who stands behind pulpit or podium to represent God's word, whether teaching or preaching. One of the finest ways to keep faith with that responsibility is through exposition of the biblical text. When the word reaches with clarity the heart of man it will bear fruit unto salvation.

EXPOSITION: WHAT IS IT?

Sweeping aside all dust and debris exposition simply means *explanation*. If the demands of the situation call for it exposition may include answering three questions. What is it? Why is it? How do you do it? To an aborigine of the back country in Australia who has never seen an ice cube one would have to answer, "What is it?" The why and how might or might not need answer depending on whether the natives decided they wanted ice or not. One may "explain" what, why and how to build a bridge, make a salad or fly to the moon. But the bottom line in exposition is to "explain."

In dealing with preaching or teaching the Bible we start with a paragraph. But at this point a decision must be made as to whether we are to prepare to preach a sermon or get ready for a Bible study class. Let's first be concerned with sermon. A specific question must be answered. What *is expository preaching?* In answering it would be well to eliminate a few misconceptions. When we clean out cobwebs we clear away confusions. Faulty ideas, though honestly held, create complexities. They bewilder the mind leaving it uncertain what it is expected to learn.

As it relates to preaching, expository preaching is *not* the exegetical verbalizing of successive verses of scripture. Surely exposition does involve "explaining" but merely to exegete verses is hardly of itself preaching. A dictionary will define exposition as "detailed explanation." But a detailed explanation of a passage of scripture is not an expository sermon. True, it is based on sound exegetical work but vocally reciting the meaning fails to fit the measure of a sermon. Expository preaching is the organizing and delivering of a *sermon*. The materials of a good meal may be abundant and well stored on shelf and refrigerator but until a cook opens the cans, thaws the meat, follows the recipe, cooks and tables the combinations it isn't a meal. Thus with one who would serve the bread of life to his hungry people. By exegetical toil the divine chef is thawing out the meat, getting ready the vegetables and flavoring the food. But they must still be arranged so as to be dished out, attractive to the appetites of the guests, before it is a meal for the souls of men. It must be organized and temptingly arranged to be an expository sermon.

Neither is expository preaching the search for and delivery of "applications" which are "revelant" to modern life. That statement is subject to misunderstanding. Certainly scripture must find its application in the lives of real people. If it doesn't apply and has no relevancy what is the value of preaching of any kind? But merely making an application, real or imagined, isn't exposition. When the apostle writes in Ephesians 1:18 of ". . . the hope of his calling . . ." the speaker might "apply" the idea of hope as referring to our confident expectation that heaven awaits faithful believers. The Christian certainly has such a legitamate hope. However, the "application" ignores and even actually defeats the idea which the apostle publicized at the time when he penned these words. Such an application is not an exposition of the meaning of the text in its context. That which the apostle divulged was God's hope in calling us into his service, not our hope of getting a heavenly inheritance as true as that is. Not until an author's original truth becomes unveiled is an application of the author's idea possible. How can we apply something that we do not yet know?

Expository preaching means more than just explaining. Words, phrases, clauses, sentences are building blocks. They go to make up the completed building but they are not the structure. Without lumber, nails, sand, cement, bricks, mortar, plumbing and wiring there can be no house. These things must be put together into an architectural unit before they become a house. Materials assembled, no matter how essential, don't constitute a house. So it takes more than words, phrases, clauses, sentences and paragraphs, even when explained, to make an expository sermon. They must be put together in a symmetrical whole to make a message.

What is an expository sermon—expository preaching? It bears repeating that in the broad field of literature such as newspaper, magazine, short story or novel, exposition simply means to explain. This sounds very much like what the expository preacher seeks. And there are points of common interest. But the content of what the instruction is about and the goals are different. Of necessity words and phrases etc. need explaining. But until they are assembled in logical array there is no expository sermon. Furthermore, the form and arrangement must sustain a convincing biblical proposition. And that proposition in some specific way should contain the fundamental idea of the ancient author.

Thus far we have seen that one goal of Bible exposition arrives when the author's original point becomes clear in the mind of him who listens. Most surely illustration and application must become involved. But until the biblical author's own idea is made clear all that the Spirit hoped to reveal through the text is smothered. In its most limited, refined and purest sense expository preaching embraces the point the author made *and nothing other*. As stated, this entails quite a limited definition of exposition. However, within that limited sense, this is an unalloyed description of Bible exposition.

In thus defining expository preaching it is not to be supposed that if five different men selected the same paragraph as basis for their sermons each of the five resultant sermons would be precisely the same. Each sermon would bear the distinctive imprint of each of the five preachers. Topic, proposition, arrangement, style would alter from man to man. In fact, even the same man preaching from the same paragraph but in different situations would come up with two distinctive sermons. But in every instance the point of the sermon will be the point of the author of the text. It may be restated, modified, abbreviated, lengthened or otherwise dealt with but the pith of the message will be found in the biblical author's idea. Furthermore, the material of the sermon draws directly from the content of the biblical text. Any material other than the text will be for illumination of the passage under discussion. In expository sermonizing the student doesn't have to search for material. He has to evaluate, select, eliminate and arrange the abundance at hand.

A SAMPLING

No better way has been found to teach than to furnish examples. So at this point let's investigate an expository effort based on Hebrews 1:1-4. Research precedes all else. We assume that the student has already informed himself of the needed introductory problems of Hebrews, particularly the situation and purpose for which the book was written. There follows a careful analysis of the text. Turn to page 4 for the diagram of our chosen passage. If you use the Greek, well and good. But if not study the English portion of the diagram. Also examine the translation and outline appearing on pages 2 and 3. A reading of *SOME EXPOSITORY THOUGHTS* on pages 6 - 13 will be suggestive. Other research in commentaries will be advisable to the limit of available time and library.

The topic and outline of pages 2 and 3 can very well serve the framework for an expository message on the topic GOD SPOKE! The skill of the preacher will be tested as he manages to pare the points suggested and the mass of material at hand. Or he might prepare two or three sermons using one of each of the three major points suggested. It should be observed that the outline is really a reflection of the diagram. That "God spoke" is from the one independent clause of the sentence. The time, methods, fragments (or unity) of his speaking are suggested in the dependent modifiers hanging from the main clause. And from the word "Son" on to the end all ideas describe the person and work of that Son. From the study of introductory problems we have learned that the purpose in writing the book is to show the *superiority* of God's speech in the "Son" versus his revelation in "the prophets" of Old. With that in mind we present a digest, howbeit a full one, of a sermon with the topic of:

Who Is Worthy to Be Worshipped?

Introduction: The word "worship" is the same root as "worth." Who or what has the inherent right to primary, absolute, worth? Whoever is of highest value is worthy of worship! Read the text!

The Body: Who is more worthy than this Son in whom Eternity spoke to us in Time? Could anyone abandon trust in such a princely person? Who would quench the rays of a noonday sun for the feeble beam of a flashlight? If the ship, Queen Mary, is crossing the Atlantic is anyone abandoning that floating palace for a rowboat to sail the turbulent sea? Yet this is what those to whom this epistle was written were doing? The Son had steaks for a banquet but they were returning to the bare bones from which the meat had already been cut. They were shifting from the freely sacrificed blood of Christ to the forced blood of dumb bulls. They were substituting make-believe for the real, the picture of Christ for the person of Christ, shadow for substance.

But we do the same! Don't we make more of what the eye sees, hands handle, tongue tastes and ear hears than that which is experienced by faith? We prefer a house in the wooded park over one in our Father's heaven. A rest in the Carribean more than God's rest that "remains for the people of God." We'd rather have peace with the Russians than peace with God through Christ. Would we exchange the Son for gold, power or comfort? Is *he* of supreme value?

Of highest worth? Is there anyone more worthy of worship than He? Consider seven facts from the text.

First, God spoke in this Son "whom he appointed heir of all." Besides the built-in right by being a son *this* Son was "appointed" heir. He's positioned as inheritor of the cosmos. From the distant star-cluster to the warm heart of the tiniest child—it belongs to him. If there be any value 4 in kings or culture, nations or peoples, man or beast, fish or fowl, matter or spirit, *he* is the "appointed heir." "All things have been created through him and unto him" (Col. 1:16). He is first and final cause; the reason why all that is *is*; why all that happens *happens*! He who had "no place to lay his head" is heir of all places, people and things.

Second, God spoke in this Son "through whom he made the ages." He frames all the unfolding epochs of time. The ages of history are not a patchwork of unrelated revolutions of meaningless bloodshed. Each successive age, every tributary stream of history is being woven according to pattern. The Son of God is the master weaver who takes each human, every crimson strand of man's history and weaves it into the design of redemption. He steers the slow- 5 moving epochs to that "far off divine event toward which all creation moves." Of every nation of men he "has determined its appointed seasons (epochs) . . ." (Acts 17:26). He's the tailor by whom the pattern of history is cut and by whom the pieces are sewn to form the beautiful design of redemption.

The text next describes this Son as "being the effulgence of his glory." One Easter morning before the sun leaped from behind a near-by mountain range stood a group of worshippers. No one yet could see the sun. But they knew it was there. Like jet streams fingering across the vault of heaven its rays of golden light were scattering in all directions. They dobbed the blue canvas of sky with yellow tints of fiery colors. What these rays were to the unseen fireball Jesus, the Son, is to the invisible God. He is the "irradiation of God's glory." Jesus cried, "He that has seen me has seen the Father" (Jn. 14:9). And John witnesses, "No man has seen God at any time; the only begotten Son who is in the bosom of the Father, he has declared him" (Jn. 1:18). We know that God in his highest heaven weeps in perfect human sympathy because we see Jesus sobbing with the sisters at the grave of Lazarus. Indeed, he is "the effulgence of God's glory."

A fourth fact: the Son is "the express image of his substance." He is more than the radiating ray of light, he is the very ingredient of the sun itself. He is the "stuff," the elemental essence of the light. As the imprint of the metal die produces itself on a blank coin, so Jesus is the exact engraving, the precise etching, the detailed sculpturing of the image of God. He's the divine substuff, the pith and marrow, heart and soul, germ and core of the divine reality. He's the "express image" of God's foundational fabric. "He called God his own father, making himself equal with God."

A fifth fact reports an uncommon idea. The Son "upholds all by the word of his power." The Son supports the orderly universe in which the stars fly their courses with mathematical precision. He does more than just sustain "all things." He "carries" them to a purposeful end. He nourishes plant and animal life and coordinates them with wind, rain, stream, storm, golden sunset and flashing lightning. Stars shine, volcanos erupt, men live and die, empires rise and fall because the Son "bears all things by the word of his power" to the end of man's fulfillment of his purpose on this globe.

The sixth fact of the text touches human tragedy at its most tender point of pain: "having made purification of sins. . . ." The inflamation of sin hurts man most. Purification implies dirt; dirt needs removal. The dirt is embedded in the conscience; the edgy, disquieting sense of estrangement from God. The fretful feeling of alienation in a hostile world. I have become evil, resentful—toward God and 9 man. And my conscience senses the moral evil of what I've done and become. What can ever change this inner bleeding of the conscience? I've soaked it with drink, burned it with passion, bathed it in parties, outshouted it in the athletic arena, dulled it with charitable work, shot myself with the opiate of a plush home, richly adorned car, elegant clothes, prestigeous profession, and an affluent life style. Facing the mirror of eternity in my naked soul these false priests and illusive idols fail to uphold me. My conscience unsheaths its cutting edge and cleaves between the veneers with which I have carefully covered my ego. It declares, "You are guilty." And I know that time and eternity cannot change that fact. No pangs of remorse can recast the reality of my sin.

Somebody other than I must relieve this awesome sense of wrong. I need a physician to diagnose my disease, a nurse to cool my fever, an orderly to clean up my filth, a loved one to take me back to the home of my early purity. All this the Son does as priest. He is a priest with the purity of God, the permanency of eternity, and sympathy with 10 suffering man. The Son has achieved the "purification of sins." Christ can not change the fact that I've sinned. But he dissolves the effects of my wrong; he alters the consequences of my sin. He makes me feel clean and pushes me along the pathway of purity. Christ is my highpriest, the only abiding, purifying priest in all my human experience.

The seventh statement proclaims the Son "sat down in the heights on the right hand of the majesty." Thus our priest sits as king sharing the throne of God. And there our sovereign waits until all enemies are conquered; physical, moral, spiritual, men, devils; in this world or that to come. Christ is king! to whom we have committed our lives, our homes, our time, our all!

Conclusion: Is not this Son of supreme worth? The universe is his house, his heritage. He radiates the image, character, essence of God. He shoulders creation like an Atlas and carries it to its appointed destiny. More than mystical mumblings of robed priests he cleans the stain of sin. He rules from the highest throne of kingly authority. He's the highest peak of God's revelation to men; the maximum answer to man's abysmal, bottomless need.

Whom do you worship? Who is worthy of supreme value? Only you can give answer! The choice rests in your hands.

THE SAMPLE ANALYZED

From the bottom of page xxii to the top of page xxvii a sample sermon appears. Even if there were an "ideal" expository sermon no claim is made that this is such a sermon. But it is a real sermon delivered to a living audience. It fits the pattern of exposition as described on pages xviii - xxi. We examine the sermon in some detail.

The message consists of thirteen paragraphs each of which is numbered on the margin. Though abridged in essence it is the message as delivered. Each paragraph is designed to effect a point as the thought moves to its climax.

We proceed by pointing out what each paragraph is designed to do.

In delivery the *Introduction* was more expansive than here. But the idea is to relate the term "worth" to "worship." Hopefully this would arouse curiosity. It also suggests the idea of the supreme worth of the Son which is developed in the full message.

The Body of the sermon has ten paragraphs. The first shows the lack of logic on the part of one who abandons the best for a second-rate substitute. It includes also two closing sentences which show that the first readers were being tempted to do that very thing. Paragraph three (2nd in the body) attempts to relate our practice to theirs. This makes the listener aware that the sermon has a meaning to moderns.

Paragraphs four through eleven present seven specific points that reveal the sublime greatness of the Son. Each paragraph finds its core idea from a specific clause in the text. Paragraph four presents the Son as "heir." Five lifts him up as "agent" of creation and the ages. Six and seven combine to display the Son as having the nature of God; he is the "effulgence" and "express image." Number eight declares Son to be him who "bears" all to a designed goal. The most prominent teaching of Hebrews deals with the priestly function of the Son. He purifies the putrid! So as this sermon develops, a bit more attention goes to the sixth of the seven descriptive ideas. Two paragraphs (9-10) are given to that idea. The entire of paragraph nine attempts to get the hearer to face the fact of the impossibility of getting the sin-stained conscience at peace with itself. Paragraph ten presents the Son as the one who gets that priestly work done for me. Paragraph 13 gives a brief snapshot of

Son as sovereign king.

The *conclusion* might have been handled in a number of ways. The method used here represents an attempt to restate in staccato summary form the peerless characteristics of the Son! The whole design of the sermon is to show the Son as incomparably superior to any conceivable rival to loyalty. He, therefore, is alone worthy of worship. The final paragraph, number 13, is a challenge to make a personal decision.

This is not the only way to handle this text as an expository message. But it is one way. Regardless of the method adopted or how the material of the text is organized the author's point of Son's superiority will rise to the fore in some way or other. To bring the author's point to bear on the conscience of the listener is expository preaching.

PREPARING AN EXPOSITORY SERMON

1. Select a passage. If possible make a translation. Otherwise, compare a minimum of three English versions.
2. Analyze (diagram) the text. This helps visualize the author's thought. Often it furnishes an outline which may form the basic structure for the sermon. At least it helps to grasp the chief ideas as well as the subordinate and supporting thoughts.
3. Restudy the text making written notes of all points that seem to be significant. Make notes of anything that may contribute to the proposed sermon. On this note-making don't discount anything no matter how unlikely it seems.
4. Make an outline. Include major points and any subordinates which seem pertinent at the moment. This

outline may be altered as work proceeds. But an outline, written or unwritten, should be made. This helps in being specific as to the proposition which the sermon intends to develop.

5. Read exegetical commentaries. This helps test one's own ideas and will suggest other reflections that have been overlooked. Don't be restricted to one commentary. Use two or more. They serve as checks to one another.

6. Write the sermon. Through the above process more than enough material has been assembled. But any material from general reading—history, literature, art, current events, etc. may be drawn on, limited only by one's collecting and filing methods. Such material should be used as it relates to the author's point being developed. By association many specifics which go into the sermon will materialize as the work proceeds.

7. Whether one writes out the sermon or makes full notes the same procedures will produce an expository sermon. The student must never forget the purpose for which the Bible book was first written. He must keep aware of the immediate context not to mention the general context in terms of geographical, social, cultural, legal, linguistic or any other factor out of which the Bible book arose.

PREPARING AN EXPOSITORY LESSON

In preparing a lesson follow the first five points as in the preparation of a sermon. But then the teacher will take note of material from the text not used in a sermon. He will want to give attention to teaching techniques which will stimulate class participation. Prepared projects, questions to stimulate thought, personal examples, visual aids and such like will serve that end. Actual preparation is not too different between preparing sermon or lesson. Differences lie in the situation of class environment, delivery, and/or class sharing.

THE BIBLE

Genesis
Exodus   Leviticus   Numbers
Deuteronomy   Joshua   Judges
Ruth   Samuel   Kings   Chronicles
Nehemiah   Esther   Job   Psalms   Proverbs
Ecclesiastes   Song of Solomon   Isaiah
Jeremiah   Lamentations   Ezekiel   Daniel
Hosea   Joel   Amos   Obadiah   Jonah   Micah
Nahum   Habakkuk   Zephaniah   Haggai
Zechariah   Malachi

Matthew   Mark   Luke   John   Acts   Romans
Corinthians   Galatians   Ephesians
Philippians   Colossians   Thessalonians
Timothy   Titus   Philemon   Hebrews
James   Peter   letters of John
Jude
Revelation

EXPOSITORY SERMONS

A word contributes to the meaning of a clause. Each clause advances the meaning of a sentence. A sentence offers something vital to the purport of the paragraph. The paragraph is a major unit of thought and can stand by itself. But it is vitally connected to the message of the whole book. Hence the pith of the paragraph must be clear if we are to understand the meaning of the paragraph, not to mention the book.

In expository sermons the unit to be used as a text must first be chosen. The sermon will then make clear the thought in *that unit* whether it be word, sentence or paragraph.

THE POINT OF THE PARAGRAPH

Expository sermons are frequently associated with a paragraph as the base unit of thought. Yet one may preach an expository message from a single word. However, not in isolation from its context. The point of the word *as it contributes to its context* makes the sermon expository. So with a clause or sentence. Exposition lies in *the point which the sentence offers to its context.* This is true as well with the exposition of a paragraph. Exposition makes *the point which the paragraph makes* in the total structure of the book involved. The material, theme and proposition is guided by the context.

Bible
↑
book
↑
paragraph
↑
sentence
↑
clause
↑
word

Paragraph

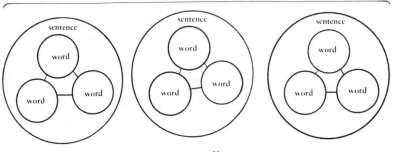

THE DIAGRAM

When an author projects his idea in an organized form he creates a sentence. When a reader envisions the author's thought he recreates the author's idea. This is communication. At the bottom of the communication is sentence analysis. The author assembles the building blocks, words, phrases, clauses in various combinations. They follow a *pattern* dictated by logic, style and accepted norms of speech. If communication is to take place the reader must *analyze* the author's construction of thought.

The term "analysis" stems from the preposition ἀνά *up* joined to the verb λύειν *to loose*. Analysis reduces the sentence to its words, phrases and clauses including a critical scrutiny of each of these parts in its relation to the whole. Analysis "loosens up" a sentence into its constitutional elements.

When analysis is objectified in the form of a written diagram it pictures relationships. A diagram images the sentence. It meets the eye, stirs the imagination, objectifies the logic by visual impressions. Diagram dramatizes ideas, makes prominent what is prominent, subordinates what is dependent. It even points up any obscurities, ambiguities, or confusions in an author's thought. In spite of certain limitations diagramming remains a practical working tool for the expositor. If we would trace an author's thought we must *re*trace the author's thought. The discipline of the diagram offers the finest map available for guiding over the devious paths of the thinker whose thought has been put to paper.

Parts of Speech

The elemental parts of speech number eight. If ABC's are basic to constructing words then parts of speech are essential in clear communication. Is it too simple to say that parts of speech are indispensable to speech? One could as well speak without parts of speech as he could work mathematical problems without the multiplication table.

Noun means name. A noun is the name of a person, place or thing. A *man* must be begotten again. The word "man" is a noun.

Verb means word. In the course of history *verb* came to be limited to that word which expresses action, being or state of being. "I swim" affirms action; "I am" expresses being; "I hurt" asserts state of being.

Pronoun is a word "for" (pro) a noun. It's used instead of a noun. A pronoun may be personal: I, you, he. It may be demonstrative: this, that. It may be relative: who, which, that. It may be interrogative: who, what. It may, with adjective force, suggest quantity: much, little, enough; or number: many, few, all; or order: former, latter; or distribution: each, either, any.

Adjective means to "add to" and refers to that class of words that are added to nouns to describe or define them. Adjectives are used in one of two ways: as attributes or as predicates. In "the red man" red is an attribute; it describes without affirming. In "the man is red" red is the predicate. It *affirms* something about the word it modifies.

Adverb means "added to the verb." An adverb is a word added to describe, limit, or intensify a verb. However, in the development of language adverbs also came to modify adjectives or other adverbs. What you do, do *quickly.* "Quickly" modifies "do" by telling *how.* In the sentence, "What you do, do *very* quickly" "very" is an adverb modifying the adverb "quickly."

Conjunction means to "join together." It is a word used to connect words, phrases, clauses or sentences. They are of two classes: coordinating conjunctions join members of equal rank. The boy *and* girl are of the same family. Subordinating conjunctions join elements of unequal rank. *If* he loves me he will keep my commandments. "If" is subordinating; it joins a dependent clause to the independent, "he will keep etc. . . ."

Preposition is a word that defines relationships between nouns and other words in the sentence. It helps link its object to some other word. The moon rose *before* midnight. "Before" relates its object "midnight" to verb "rose." Prepositions also clarify or intensify verbs. When so used they are adverbial in function. He climbed *up*. "Up" sharpens the idea of "climb."

Interjection comes from Latin "to throw in between." It's a word thrown in to express emotion; it has no grammatical relation to the rest of the sentence. *Bah*! That's nonsense!

The Mechanics of the Diagram

The actual diagram is not so confusing as it may seem. After all there are only eight parts of speech and each has a specific role to play. Putting them down on paper so the eye may see the relationships is what's involved.

Subject, verb, and object (if any) or predicate nominative (if any) go on a base horizontal line.

| he | helps | angels |

xxxx

"He" is subject because it's the person about which the sentence is speaking. "Helps" is the verb, the action which is stated about the subject. The object to which the help extends is embodied in "angels." A small vertical line intersects between subject and verb. A small upright line above the horizontal line separates verb from its direct object. This is the basic of a diagram of simple sentence or clause.

God | is \ Father

"Father" is predicate nominative. The slanting line indicates that "Father" refers back and identifies with the subject "God."

Adjective and adverb modifiers are placed on lines slanting down from the basic horizontal line.

God | spoke | word
the high | often | his true

"The" and "high" are adjectives modifying "God." "Often" is adverb modifying "spoke." "His" and "true" are adjectives limiting "word." A simple sentence may have more than one subject and/or more than one predicate. They are called *compound*. When such compounds appear they are diagrammed on a bracket joined by an appropriate conjunction.

apostle | preached | gospel
the pure and | taught | the of redemption
prophet | clearly | word
the true | | the pure

In the diagram at the bottom of the previous page there is a compound subject and a compound predicate. They are each joined by conjunction "and." Each of the verbs has a direct object, "gospel" and "word." The definite article "the" appears four times each time as an adjective modifying a noun. The word "true" is adjective and the word "pure" also. They are placed on a slanting line beneath the word each modifies. The term "redemption" is a noun linked to "gospel" by the preposition "of." It actually describes the "gospel" as being a redemption kind of gospel. So it is adjectival in function. One should observe that a group of words without subject or predicate is called a "phrase." And any phrase, thought of as a single unit of expression, is to be treated and diagrammed as either noun, adjective, or adverb. In the above example "of redemption" is used as adjective. It describes "gospel." "Clearly" is an adverb.

Sentences are divided into one of four classes. They are: simple, compound, complex, compound-complex. A simple sentence has one independent clause. All the above are simple sentences.

A compound sentence has two or more independent clauses, those that would be complete if any of them stood alone. A sample is: "I am the vine, and you are the branches."

A complex is a sentence with one independent and one or more dependent clauses. A dependent clause is a group of words having subject and predicate yet cannot stand alone. Here is sample: "If a man abide not in me, he is cast out."

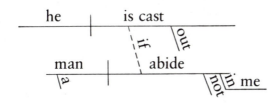

"if a man abide . . ." is dependent. If left alone it doesn't make a complete thought. "He is cast out" could stand alone for it contains a complete thought. As in phrases, so in clauses, each can be envisioned as a unit of thought. So it will be either noun, adjective or adverb. The "if" clause here is adverb; it states a condition. Conjunction "if" goes on a broken slanted line attached to the base horizontal line. "In me" is adverbial indicating *where*.

A compound-complex sentence has two or more independent clauses of equal rank plus one or more dependents. "Life was that which became in him and the life was the light of men." This compound-complex sentence may be diagrammed as follows.

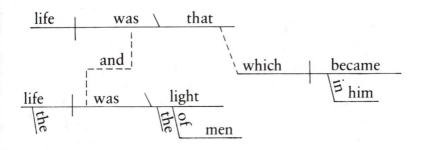

Three clauses appear in the above sentence. Two are independent and one is dependent. The first has "life" as subject, the copula "was" as verb, and the demonstrative pronoun "that" as predicate nominative. It is placed on a horizontal line with the upright intersecting line between subject and verb. The slanting line between verb and predicate nominative points back to the subject to indicate that the "that" identifies with the subject. The second independent follows the same pattern of subject, copula verb and predicate nominative "light." The definite article "the" modifies "life" and "light." The prepositional phrase "of men" describes the noun "light." It is adjectival in function. The dependent clause is: "which became in him." Subject is the relative pronoun "which" with verb "became." It is joined to the word it modifies "that" by a slanting broken line. It is adjective in function because it describes the "that." Telling *where* it "became," therefore adverbial, is the prepositional phrase "in him."

There are other structural arrangements to diagramming than here set forth. However, these cover the basics. Infinitives (verbal nouns), participles (verbal adjectives), appositional words and phrases, complements, genitive absolutes are matters with which the student will want to become familiar. But the above explanations lay a foundation. Other items may be observed as they arise in the actual diagrams from Hebrews. For the most part an infinitive is placed on a pedestal and the entire phrase treated as a noun. Being verbs they may take cases as any other verb. Participles, being dual in nature (verbs *and* adjectives at the same time), will be placed half on a slanting and half on horizontal line. Appositional words will be placed within parentheses next to the word to which it is in apposition.

INTRODUCTION

Because of the differences between Greek and English some difference between English diagram and Greek will have to be observed. For example, the Greek often contains the subject of finite verbs in the verb endings. But in English the subject is usually a separate word. Thus in the Greek diagram the symbol (X) appears often where the subject would appear as a separate word in an English diagram. Three items are placed within parentheses in the diagrams of this text. (1) Appositionals, (2) subjects, and (3) words or phrases not stated but implied from the context.

Remember! What one can conceive and believe he can achieve!

A Translation
Hebrews 1:1-4

In many parts and in many methods God, of old, having spoken to the fathers in the prophets, upon the last of these days spoke to us in (one who by nature is) son, whom he appointed as heir of all, through whom also he made the ages, who being radiance of his glory and stamp of his essence, and consequently bearing all by the word of his power, having made cleansing of sins, sat down at (the) right of the Majesty in (the) heights, having become by so much better than the angels by howevermuch as he has inherited (a) superior name than they.

AN OUTLINE OF HEBREWS 1:1-4
GOD SPOKE

Introduction: The need for God to speak to his creation. The need lies both in him and in his creation. As father he *must* speak; as creatures men *must* hear!

I. God spoke earlier. vs. 1

II. God spoke later. vs. 2

III. God spoke fully and finally. vss. 2b-3

I. GOD SPOKE IN AN EARLIER REVELATION. vs. 1
1. In a variety of parts, methods, times, places.
2. To various generations, "the fathers."
3. In *persons* suited for divine speech; "the prophets."

1

II. GOD SPOKE IN A LATER REVELATION. vs. 2a
 1. Upon the occasion of "these last days."
 2. To "us," one generation in one locale at one time.
 3. In the person of him who by his nature was "son."

III. GOD SPOKE FULLY AND FINALLY. vss. 2b-4
 1. He spoke "in (one who by inherent nature is) *son*."
  (a) He is heir apparent of all creation.
  (b) He is agent through whom all creation came.
  (c) He took his seat as reigning king.
 2. The nature and work of "son" reveals him as superior!
  (a) He is the radiance and express image of God. vs. 3a
  (b) He sustains God's creation. vs. 3b
  (c) He functioned as priest, having "cleansed sin." vs. 3c
  (d) As son he is superior to angels through whom God spoke in his earlier revelation. vs. 4

Conclusion: A full and final revelation in such a person is inherently authoritative.

SOME EXPOSITORY THOUGHTS ON HEBREWS 1:1-4

Although Hebrews 1:1-4 entertains but one independent clause it bears two cardinal ideas. The vital certitude is: "God spoke." The manner in which he spoke is: "in son." It's a classic periodic sentence. The author might well have presented the ideas in two separate sentences. But he didn't! He chose to channel both in one beautifully balanced sentence. The independent element sustains the fact that God

2

spoke. That 55 of 72 words tell of the person and work of "son" shows the importance of the manner in which God spoke.

That "God . . . spoke" is a fact. How could he be Creator, not to say "Father," and not speak? For heaven to remain silent after creating man "in his own image" would turn God into a demon. That is especially true when we note the sinful, hurting condition into which man has fallen. The very idea of God's being "good" necessitates that he "speak" to his creatures. And the very fact they are "fallen" makes it even more imperative.

But God had to accommodate his speaking to the level on which humanity lives. That necessitated a bit by bit, piece by piece, line by line revelation. During the childhood and "teen" age portion of human history God couldn't speak to men as spiritually mature. Of "old" God did speak. But he spoke to selected people who were segregated in location and social-religious contexts. The Hebrew "fathers" were a "chosen" people designed to hear God's speech. Yet even they were only prepared to receive the speech of God piecemeal. The very fact that the divine voice came in "many parts and many manners" implies that God's utterance was incomplete. A part is less than the whole. Besides, the manner in which God spoke in the "old" time had to alter, shift, and change depending on the situation in which various of the "fathers" found themselves. As a first grade teacher changes his method with a precocious child from that with a slow learning child so God used a different method in a Jeremiah than a cheating, stubborn Jacob. Time, place and person altered both content and manner of God's fragmented speech. His older revelation was "perfect" at the kindergarten level, yet the fact that it was at such a level meant it was incomplete. It was imperfect in content from the standpoint of what humanity needed to hear. The full oration would come later in "the fulness of time."

But in due time God declaimed his full address. That was "at the end of these days." When the rivers of history came together and became the ocean of universal humanity, at "these end times" then "God spoke in son." At one time, in one person, at one place, to one humanity God spoke his one perfect piece. Once, fully, finally, and for all he spoke his ultimate revelation. In fact, so great and effective was God's speech, so perfect was his method of speech, so definitive was the content of his speech, nothing more could be said. Though later generations of men have tried to improve on God's speech in "son" they have only succeeded in garbling his message and clouding his revelation. "God, having spoken in various tid-bits, finally, fully and completely spoke in *son*."

The preposition ἐν ("in") appears twice in verses 1-2. The translators come up with different results in their efforts to render this plain little word. "By," "through," "in the words of . . ," are samples of how they recast "in the prophets" and "in son." For the most part they overlook the fact that the author is not speaking of the *agents through which* God spoke but the manner *in which* he brought his message to humanity. The simple root idea of the word is: a "point within which." A simple uncomplicated idea. If we give the word its plain meaning of "in" it is quite suggestive.

In the earlier revelation God spoke "in the prophets." In his final revelation he spoke "in son." It was in the prophet Isaiah that God spoke, not just Isaiah's book. It was in the person of his son that God spoke his messaage, not in anything that son wrote. As a matter of fact we have nothing that Jesus wrote. "The Word became flesh," not a book! God spoke in persons not just pages. He spoke in spirits of men not just libraries, literature, or letters. When Hosea found that his wife, Gomer, had children by adulterous relationships he was heartbroken. But the experience through which he was dragged by her unfaithfulness opened up to him the vastness of God's love for his people. God spoke his word of love "in" Hosea, his marriage, his heartbreak, his efforts at Gomer's rehabilitation. God spoke similarly "in" all the prophets.

And certainly that can be said for Jesus, God's son. As already noted Jesus wrote nothing, at least nothing that had been left to us. Once he stopped and wrote something in perishable sand. Life speaks to life in life. Eye to eye, face to face, person to person in God's ultimate method of speech. He speaks in historical events in which *people* are involved. Their joys and sorrows, their defeats and victories, their loves and hates, their battles, struggles, trials and temptations. In this idea lies the necessity of the Incarnation! God HAD to become a human in order that he might communicate himself and his message to humans. If one is to communicate to a human he must talk in human terms. And to talk in human terms he must *be* human. "The Word became flesh (human)."

This idea is pregnant with meaning. God's "word" is still best communicated "in" life, person to person. No denying that God gets something across to men by the written word. God spoke through Hosea's *life*. And God's message to and through the prophet's life was then written

5

down in a book. What we have in the book of Hosea is therefore a part of God's speech. However, that doesn't take away from the fundamental fact that before the written word was the life lived. God spoke *in* the prophets" says the author of Hebrews. That is, in the person of the prophet. And that remains still the primary and best method that God has of getting his message across. Aside from the fact that an unbelieving world doesn't read the written word the most readable word from the Lord is the life of a redeemed soul. If "what you do speaks so loud that I can't hear what you say" is true, then what you do is the most effective means of God's speaking today!

Another point of grammar over which some translators stumble is the ἐν υἱῷ ("in son"). The Greeks had no indefinite article "a" while the definite article "the" does not appear in the Greek text of Hebrews 1:2 with the word "son." The author doesn't say "a" son. "A" wasn't a part of the vocabulary. The "son" was not "a" son as though he were one among many. The author chose not to say "the" son as pointing out the prominent, one-of-a-kind son, even though that might well be true. Nor did he say "his" son, though that too is obviously true. In contrast to all these translations the author said that God "spoke in son." The absence of the definite article calls attention to the inherent quality, the innate nature of this one in whom God spoke. By the absence of the article our author is giving pointed testimony to the fact that God's speech came in one who in his innate nature was of the "stuff" of which sons were. He was of the same cloth as God; he was deity, as much so as God himself. Being himself deity he was of course of a nature in which God could personally say that which he wanted to say. Remember, speech is most forceful when it is given by life against life, person to person. Therefore, one who is in essence deity, while at the same time being human, is fully equipped to communicate perfectly the revelation of God. It's the divine nature of this son that our author emphasizes by the absence of the definite article.

This son is "heir" of all creation. The son was the final cause, the ultimate purpose for any creation at all. Every intent of God in creating finds fulfillment in this son. He has been "appointed heir of all." It's his by God's design in creation! No father ever made better provision for a son than God did for this son!

This son is the *agent* (2c) "through whom he made the ages." "Son" was not only present *at* creation, he was actively involved in the creating processes. "All things came through him and without him not one thing came which became" (John 1:3).

What the son is in himself unfolds in 3a, "Being the radiation of his glory and the imprinted stamp of his essence." As a mountain spring is the source of the mighty life bearing river so God is to the life-radiating, light-shedding quality of "son." What the light ray is to the central sun so "son" is to God. Furthermore, he is the "express stamp of his essence." The son once said, "He that has seen me has seen the father" (John 14:9). Christ is God's speech "seen" and God's essence comprehensible to man.

3b says "son" is the sustaining power in creation. Creation is not just something which happened in ages past, it is an ongoing process. And as "son" was involved at creation he shoulders the ongoing forces within creation. He furnishes the coordinating, cohesive energies which make this

7

a universe instead of a chaos. He "bears all things by the word of his power." A sparrow does not fall without his concern. Nor does the bird fly without his involvement. He carries all things toward their designed goal.

In his earthly experience this son effectively performed the function of high priest. "Having made cleansing of sins." Other priests offered sacrifices but both priest and sacrifice were not effective. The priest himself was sinful and his sacrifice in no vital way reached the conscience. But this "son" was sinless. He was a living, personal, willing sacrifice that could pierce and arouse the sinner's conscience. Man's sin finds relief in son's death on the cross followed by resurrection.

Because of God's concern for his sin-laden creatures he had to deal with the problem of sin. It must be eradicated. It's guilt must be removed and its consequences eliminated. This took sacrifice. Since there was no one else it had to be God's sacrifice. So God "spoke" in the person of this exalted "son." The vital thing he said was spoken in the cross—the death that transpired there and the meaning of that death! In order for God to reign over his creation man must be "cleansed" from the guilt, power and consequences of sin. Having done that at calvary "he sat down" as reigning king, henceforth to direct the campaign against sin and to await his final triumph over it!

In view of what an exalted person this "son" is, who or what could be "superior" than he? No man or angel surpasses him in quality of nature or in efficiency and extent of his work. The rest of the book of Hebrews is given to show this majestic superiority of "son" as he towers high over all other agents, divine or human. So, verse four turns from the introduction of the theme to the development. Having, by his redemptive sacrifice, become so much better than angels, this son "sat down." Angels were one of the most exalted of God's agents of speech in the older revelation. This "son" is "better" by any measure-able scale. Therefore, give heed to what the son says and does. Such a one, as God's ambassador, carries the weight of absolute and final authority in the life and death issues facing mankind. If the son be Lord, be obedient to his Lordship! And certainly don't abandon him for lesser angels or sinful priestly substitutes. The "son" is ultimate, final, complete, perfect! Abandon him and there's nothing or no one to whom to turn!

Hebrews 1:1-4

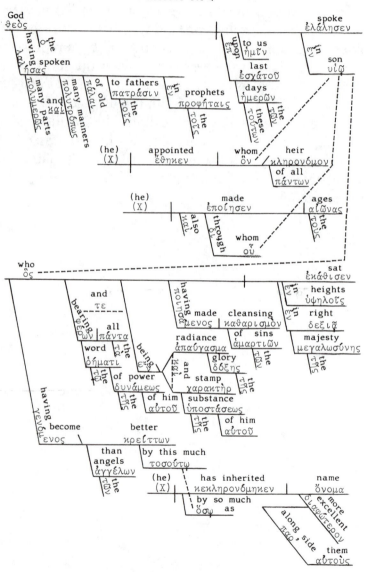

THE DIAGRAM OF 1:1-4

The Greek text of this sentence presents it as complex in structure. The one independent clause says, "God . . . spoke." The fact that he spoke in an earlier revelation is briefly professed in the aorist circumstantial participle λαλήσας (having spoken) with its modifiers. That took only ten words. The five adverbs or adverbial phrases modifying this participle tell five things about this earlier speaking. (1) Variety of parts (2) manners (3) time ("of old") (4) to whom ("fathers") and (5) in whom ("the prophets").

The remainder of the sentence tells of God's later, final speech. *To whom* he spoke comes out in the personal pronoun ἡμῖν ("to us"). *When* he spoke to us develops in the prepositional-adverbial phrase "upon last of these days." Then comes the weighty ἐν υἱῷ ("in son") which the rest of the sentence describes.

υἱῷ has three adjectival relative clauses flowing from it. If we count ἐν υἱῷ then 55 words of the total 72 deal with this "son." He must be important in God's speech to men. The first relative says, "whom he appointed heir of all." κληρονόμον is objective complement. It completes the object ὅν. God did more than just "appoint him." He appointed him "heir." The second relative sets the son forth as the agent "through whom" God "made the ages." διά with genitive is a normal way of expressing indirect agent.

After the first two relative clauses relate what God did to and for "son" the third relative divulges what the "son" himself did; "who *sat*. . . ." Four accompanying particulars describing this son (ὅς) are set forth in four circumstantial participial phrases: "bearing . . . being . . . having made . . . having become . . ." φέρων (bearing) and ὤν (being) are linear action presents describing what he was doing and his inherent nature when he "sat down." That is, he was "sustaining all things" and he was "being (the) radiance of his (God's) glory and stamp of his substance." ποιησάμενος is aorist reflecting punctiliar action. It looks to the antecedent point at which the son performed the priestly sacrifice of cleansing, that is, the cross. The participle suggests cause. "Because he made cleansing for sin he sat down" as king to reign. Having done in one act the work of priest he took his seat as reigning king. And of course, the fact that he was God's speech to mankind made him also prophet, speaker for God.

All this descriptive material related in the first three of these circumstantial participles puts him in a position of being "better" than others who went before. So γενόμενος followed by comparative κρείττων tells us "having become better. . . ." Ablative ἀγγέλων is the object of comparison, "better than the angels." Just how much better is introduced by the quantitative demonstrative τοσούτῳ followed by its correlative ὅσῳ. Perfect tense κεκληρονόμηκεν that "son" not only at a point "did inherit" but also the inheritance became permanent. "He inherited a better name and he still has a better name. The exalted degree of greater excellence is amplified and emphasized by the added comparison διαφώτερον followed this time by accusative αὐτούς with παρά to give the standard of comparison.

Judging by this description of "son" in whom God spoke, *he* is not only important but what he says should be heeded.

A Translation

Hebrews 1:5-14

For to which of the angels did he ever say, "You are my son, this day I have begotten you."? And again, "I shall be as father to him and he shall be as son to me."? But whenever again he brings in the first born into the habitable earth, he says, "And all God's angels are to worship him." And on the one hand he says of the angels, "the one making his angels winds and his official ministers (a) flame of fire." On the other hand, of the son (he says), "Your throne, O God, is unto the age of the age (forever) and the sceptre of uprightness is the sceptre of his kingdom. You loved righteousness and hated lawlessness; on account of this God, your God, anointed you with oil of rejoicing beyond your partners."

And —

"You, Lord, at the beginnings founded the earth, and the heavens are the works of your hands. They shall perish, but you are abiding; and all shall grow old as a cloak, and as a mantle you will roll them up, and as a cloak they shall be changed. But you are the same and your years shall not fail."

But to which of the angels has he ever said, "Be sitting at my right until ever I put your foes as footstool of your feet."? They are all ministering spirits, are they not, being sent forth for service on account of the ones being about to inherit salvation?

OUT OUTLINE OF HEBREWS 1:5-14
THE SON SUPREME OVER ANGELS

Introduction: The Son, "a more excellent name (person)" than any lesser servants or idols. In the Old Testament; among Gentiles; or modern scientifc technologists.

I. SUPERIOR AS "SON." vss. 5-6
1. Christ is *son*; not creature, slave or ministering messenger.
2. Psalm 2:7 unfulfilled until Jesus came.
3. II Sam. 7:14 unfulfilled until Jesus came.
4. No angel or mortal addressed as "son."
5. Deuteronomy 32:43. Angels prompted to worship the Son.

II. SUPERIOR AS SOVEREIGN OVER MORAL UNIVERSE. vss. 7-9
1. Psalm 104. His angels, temporary winds and fire.
2. Psalm 45. Sovereign over moral universe hence eternal.
   (a) His rule based on "uprightness."
   (b) Christ's historical experience; he "loved righteousness."

III. SUPERIOR AS CREATOR. vss. 10-12
1. Psalm 102. An exile's trust of the Creator.
2. The "stable" creation is transient and temporary.
3. The Son, agent of creation, is eternal.

IV. SUPERIOR AS SOVEREIGN OVER SERVANTS. vss. 13-14
1. Psalm 110. Joint rulers on the divine throne.
2. Kings rule; servants run!
3. Angels function as messengers, not rulers.

Conclusion: It's wise to worship the Son, not his servants.

SOME EXPOSITORY THOUGHTS ON HEBREWS 1:5-14

The seven quotations from the Old Testament in 1:5-14 have force because of the prophetic quality of events in Hebrew history. Five of the quotes are directly from the Psalms. II Samuel 7:14 furnishes one. The other, though not in the Hebrew of Deut. 32:44, is in the Vatican text of the Septuagint.

After the introductory charting of the chief ideas of the letter, the author's first point presents the superiority of the Son over angels. Angels played a prominent part in Old Testament events. Abraham's search for a wife for Isaac looked to angelic help. To his servant the patriarch reminded that the God of heaven "will send his angel before you, . . ." (Gen. 24:7). This is typical of these divine messengers as servants guiding the unfolding purpose of God through its human channels. According to Jewish tradition the law was ministered by angels. Galatians 3:19 reflects this belief that the law "was ordained by angels through an intermediary." And Stephen in his stern philipic against the "stiff-necked people" who opposed Christ referred to the law as given by angels; "you who received the law as delivered by angels and did not keep it" (Acts 7:53).

As angels were intermediaries through which the old covenant was ministered so were lesser powers supposed to mediate the speech of the gods to Gentile peoples. Fire, wind, sea, storm, grain, valley, mountain, and forest were inhabited by demonic spirits and superhuman powers. So thought the nations. In modern times of sophisticated enlightenment and materialistic skepticism men have substituted scientific technology for the living God of the Bible. As an idol men now bow down to science. Such gods are self-sufficient. They make useless the rituals of religion or rites of less enlightened ages. Sin has no place in a world of relative, constantly changing moral values. As much as ancient idols were, these modern gods are the creations of man. Hebrews 1:5-14 encompasses them in its breadth of view. Creation will be "rolled up as a garment." But the eternity of the Son shall outlast all these lesser "gods" either ancient or modern, primitive or sophisticated. "You are the same and your years shall not fail." The world and its gods are for time; the Son is for eternity. Hence he is better in moral quality, greater in mighty power, and superior in spiritual assets.

Superior because he is "son."

To one who senses the vitality of the "living God" the trivia of man's foolish fumblings with his idols is dwarfed when contemplating the exalted Son. In him we touch reality. Christ is *Son*! Not creature, nor slave, nor ministering messenger.

The second Psalm reflects God's victory over massed enemies. But the Psalm doesn't find an adequate fulfilling in any of David's successors. Solomon, Rehoboam, and certainly no combination of rulers under the divided kingdom ever realized "the ends of the earth" as a possession. Therefore, it remained for some other One to fulfill the prophetic heritage. The only thing that the external, national, political kingdom did was to furnish the frame in which God could place his divine picture of redeeming purpose.

When David purposed to build a temple for the Lord the prophet Nathan brought God's message to the shepherd

16

king. David would not be allowed to build a house for God. Indeed, it would be the other way around. God would make of David a house. He would bring forth from David's loins a son who would build "a house for my name." "But," says God, "I will establish the throne of his kingdom (his house, his dynasty) forever. And I will be father to him and he shall be son to me" (II Sam. 7:11, 13f.). Once again we face the fact that nothing in succeeding history ever adequately brought to realization this promise of God. No earthly king satisfied the terms of the prediction. Solomon's temple was destroyed. At the Captivity the kingdom passed from David's line. Men were forced to look for a "seed" apart from any mere earthly ruler. According to the Hebrew author that seed was the "Son" who actually realized the full meaning of "I will be father to him and he shall be son to me."

No earthly mortal was ever designated "son." The rhetorical question remains unchallenged, "To which of the angels did he ever say, 'You are my son, today I have begotten you.'" But Jesus was "designated son of God in power according to the spirit of holiness by his resurrection from the dead" (Rom. 1:4). Though Jesus' eternal relationship to the Father remained unaltered, yet his resurrection from the dead designated him as "son" with the prerogatives inherent in life. By the resurrection he became known as the "resurrection and the life" the demonstration and agent of all sonship.

True, no angel ever heard himself addressed as "son." Besides, all angels have been exhorted to worship the Son. The 32nd chapter of Deuteronomy gives a recital of the prophetic meaning of Israel's early history. The prophecy comes to a climax when God unsheathes his "glittering sword" and his "hand takes hold on judgment." In the

Septuagint version verse 43 exhorts "all the angels of God are to worship him." The same idea is reflected in Psalm 97:7 though "gods" appears instead of "angels." But it's a similar idea. Subordinate beings are urged to worship the exalted God of justice. All inferior powers, honored by the nations of men, are to acknowledge the absolute sovereignty of the Lord God. Such acknowledgment finds its fulfillment in the praise of angelic hosts to Jesus, the son of God. At his birth! Yes! But more fully before the universe of created beings "whenever he *again* brings the firstborn into the inhabited, world" of redeemed men. At the consummation of human history, when Jesus returns on the clouds of heaven, when the redeemed are caught up into final glory, the chorus of angels are impelled to prostrate themselves in worship of the redeeming Son.

Is not the object of worship, the Son, greater than those who worship him? Why fall back to the lesser when the greater has come? Or why pay sacrificial homage to any creature of man's conception? Can the technology of a space age heal a broken heart standing by an open grave? Or break that universal curse of death? "*This* is my beloved son. Hear you *him!*"

Superior as ruling sovereign

The transient, ephemeral character of the serving angels contrasts with the permanence of the sovereign Son in 1:7-9. The author sustains his point by two Psalms.

The 104th Psalm portrays creation as a garment of God. All natural creation is God's servant. Clouds are his chariots, winds his messengers, consuming fire his concierge. Creation is more than a finished act. Preservation is continuing creation so it's still going on. And God is involved in the process. This is the Psalmist's view. The author of Hebrews picked up this point. Where men only view wind and fire, material objects, in these "natural phenomena" God is engaged in the person of his ministering servants. That which "appears" as wind and fire are actually forms his angels assume as they minister to human destiny.

But the main point is the mercurial mutability of angels. They are meteoric, momentary, evanescent, transitory. In Jewish tradition angels were so ephemeral that they only lived as they ministered. They were "new every morning." For the author to make his point, that need not be true. But that many Jews believed it furnished the idea of the transitory nature of angels. If angels themselves weren't transitory their service was. They were as real but also as temporary as the winds. They were as fleeting as fire. As soon as wind or fire have done their appointed tasks they disappear. Such is all creation. Having served a function it is not further use to God or man.

But not so is the moral universe over which the Son rules. Materiality is temporal; morality is eternal. Material changes; purity is permanent. That which is carnal is corruptible; that which is spiritual is incorruptible. Angels stand before the Son awaiting assignments to serve. The Son sits to reign, assigning his attending ministers to errands of service.

The 45th Psalm sings the marriage song of a king. The Psalmist addresses the king as "God." Hebrews applies this to the Son. "Your throne, O God, is enduring as an ageless thing." It is not short-lived or fading; it is immutable, changeless, permanent, eternal. It runs on "into the age of the age."

This durable quality of the King-Son has a basis in something that makes it durable. The kingdom of the Son is based on "uprightness." It stands on the solid foundation of right, truth, goodness and justice. The king who exercises his rule on these principles will necessarily be eternal for they are eternal. Falsehood and deceit are illusory. In this world they *seem* to prevail and to be permanent. But even here eventually they break under their own weight. And when one views them from the vantage point of eternity they are more transient than angels.

In his earthly career Christ "loved righteousness and hated iniquity." When tempted to compromise with evil his peremptory remark was "Get behind me Satan." When faced with wrong, compromise was intolerable. In fact, that was his choice in Gethsemane. He adopted death rather than yield to wrong. The "will of God" was his meat and drink even at the cost of life. How could he be anything other than eternal with such "uprightness" the basis of his throne? So serve the sovereign, not the servants.

Superior as Creator to creation

The author's next quotation is from Psalm 102. It's a complaint of an exile. He suffers under the judgment of God on Israel, particularly as it has fallen on him. But it is a song of hope sung on the eve of his restoration to Zion. God as Creator guarantees the care of his creation, especially his people as chosen to fulfill his redeeming will. On the permanence of God as Creator the Psalmist rests his hope. God supervises his people and therefore in spite of judgment, in spite of the brevity of life, God will bring to fulfillment his purposes in the Psalmist.

The point here (1:10-12) is similar to that just preceding. But another emphasis is apparent. From man's point of view nothing is more stable than the created universe. We can count on mountains, stars, earth and seas. Yet these are but functional parts of the clothing of the Creator. They will wear out whereas the wearer will go on and on. Suits and dresses grow threadbare and new ones replace them. But not the wearer. He lives on. Just so is the Creator in relation to his creation. As clothes are rolled up and discarded so the heavens and the earth shall wear out and "be changed." But God shall go on forever and his "years will not fail." From creation past "at the beginning" to consummation in the future "you are the same."

The author of Hebrews is treating the Son of God himself. It was this Son who was the agent at creation "through whom he made the worlds." Angels were but spectators at the world's shaping. But as the divine agent of creation the Son was as eternal as God himself. The Son was himself involved in the creating process. Both angels and creation were inferior to the divine Son. "They shall perish." That is, they shall be transformed from one shape to another. But the Son is "the same." He goes on forever as creating, sustaining person.

If the Son as Creator is superior to material creation and angels are but adoring spectators at the marvels of creation, then nothing on the earth beneath or in the heavens above should take the Son's preeminent place. Who would adore a suit of clothes in place of the one who wears it? That would be as foolish as desiring rags instead of riches. One chooses a "thing" for a function but he chooses a "person" for fellowship. God's creation serves human needs in this temporal order. But God is more than a "thing" to be used. He is for adoration and fellowship.

Superior as sovereign to servants

In the earlier quotations the eternity of the Son is the emphasis. In this last quote the Kingship of the King stands paramount. The conflict between good and evil is under review.

The 110th Psalm pictures a session in the throne room of a king. A joint ruler sits on the throne at the right of the king. They contemplate the conquest of enemies by a vast volunteer army "in holy attire." God spoke unto the Psalmist's Lord, "Sit on my right hand until I make your enemies as footstool of your feet." The author of Hebrews identifies this joint ruler of God's as the "Son" of 1:1. God never addressed an invitation to sit as reigning king to any angel. Only to the Son! Hence the Son is superior!

Kings sit on thrones to rule. Before kings servants stand waiting to serve. Kings command; servants obey. Kings rule; servants run. As ruling sovereign the Son sits. The king's angelic messengers constantly are on the run for they "are ministering spirits sent forth to do service for the sake of those about to inherit salvation."

As a matter of fact the sovereign son exercises much of his authority through these serving messengers. Hebrews 1:14 gives a positive affirmation that angels play a vital role in the redeeming process continually going on among men. And in behalf of men, those men "being about to inherit salvation." As God, in the form of one of his angelic ministering messengers went down to the cesspool of Sodom and Gomorrah, so these divine messengers have been racing here and there throughout history at his behest. And according to Hebrews it is for the same purpose as for Lot. To rescue men from the folly of their own making. That is, to save them out of their sin. An angel prompted

Joseph to recognize and honor Mary's virginity. They protected the baby Jesus from the murderous wrath of Herod. They supported Jesus in the onslaughts of Satan in the wilderness temptations and came with strengthening ministrations in his Gethsemane agony. They helped in physical difficulties by "rolling away the stone" that announced the risen Christ. They stood by Paul to give encouragement in the darkest storm on board a ship at sea. They maneuvered the release of Peter from jail and directed the apostle to the household of the first Gentile convert to Christ. Over 250 biblical references give support to this Hebrews' statement that angelic messengers are ever at work serving the providential needs of redeemed people. They may "appear" as winds or fire or any other such "natural" phenomenon. Hebrews insists that they are "official ministers" of God serving human redemption. God has at his service for man's saving innumerable servants appearing in countless forms. His methods amaze even the elect of God!

But in the main point of this whole series of quotations is to reassure the wavering Hebrews that it is wiser to worship the exalted Son than to fall back to the lesser agents of God as great as they are. Cling to the reality; don't return to the shadow. Hold tight to the substance. Even though you can see it with the eyes, don't revert to the ephemeral. Worship the Son, not his servants. "Let no one disqualify you, insisting on . . . worship of angels" (Col. 2:18). It is Christ "in whom are hid all the treasures of wisdom and knowledge" (Col. 2:3).

Hebrews 1:5-6

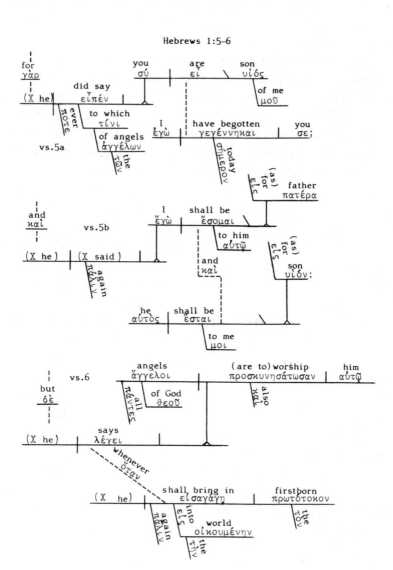

24

THE DIAGRAM OF 1:5-6

The development of the discussion of Hebrews 1:5-14 involves the quoting of seven passages from Old Testament scriptures. As arranged and punctuated in the Nestle's text these embody eight separate sentences. Three appear on the facing page. Most of the *substance* of the author's contention comes out in the quotations. They appear as clauses, subordinate to the "he says" or some such expression of the introductory independent clauses.

Verses five through six contain three complex sentences. Verse 5a embraces three clauses one of which forms the independent "he did say." A temporal negative idea is gained by ποτε, "ever" coupled with adverbial phrase. "to which of the angels." "To which of the (single specific) angels did he ever say. . . .?" As direct objects of εἰπέν are two noun clauses quoted from Psalm 2:7. "*You* are my son," "this day *I* have begotten you." Contrasting pronouns σύ and ἐγώ are quite emphatic both as words distinct from the verb endings as well as by position. Present tense εἶ speaks of a continuing state; perfect γεγέννηκαι looks to a specific point the effect of which continues into the present. Adverb σήμερον stresses some definite critical climax of recognition. See Acts 13:33, Rom. 1:4.

The independent clause of the complex sentence of verse 5b is elliptical. The subject and verb must be supplied from the context. They are borrowed from 5a, "He said," The two dependent noun clauses serve as direct objects of the main verb. They are quotes from II Samuel 7:14. Each of the dependents has a prepositional phrase introduced by εἰς as predicate nominative. In this context the "for" may be rendered "as."

Verse six structures another complex sentence with "he says" furnishing the independent element. Direct object of λέγει is the noun clause reflecting ideas from Deuteronomy 32:43 and/or Psalm 89:27. "All angels of God also are to worship him." The aorist imperative προσκυνησάτωσαν is better translated "are to worship" rather than "let them worship. . . ." The angels are not "permitted" to worship the Son; they are commanded. ὅταν performs as a temporal relative conjunction introducing an adverbial dependent, "whenever he shall bring into the world. . . ." πάλιν is a temporal adverb "again." It probably refers to the Christ's final entrance into the world at the consummation of history.

πρωτότοκον is worthy of special attention. It appears also in Rom. 8:29, Rev. 1:5, Col. 1:15 and 18. The author chose this word rather than υἱός here because it emphasizes the unity of the whole creation in him, especially of the son to all human creatures. In his having been "begotten" and his death, resurrection and exaltation he represents the whole human race. "The patristic commentators rightly dwell on the difference between μονογενής, which describes the absolutely unique relation of the Son to the Father in His divine Nature, and πρωτότοκος, which describes the relation of the Risen Christ in His glorified humanity to man." (B.F. Westcott, *Epistle to Hebrews*, pg. 23). As the "first-born" he represents the greatness and destiny of all mankind.

Hebrews 1:7-9

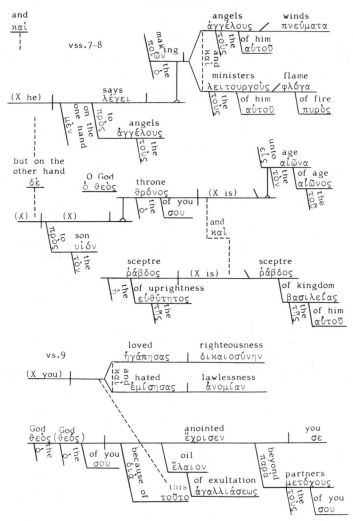

THE DIAGRAM OF HEBREWS 1:7-9

Taking verses 7-8 as one sentence it would be classified as compound-complex. The "he says" of the first independent clause by implication is repeated in the second. These two parts of the sentence are at once joined together while set in contrast to each other by the μέν . . . δέ, "on the one hand . . . but on the other hand."

The contrast continues. In reference to whom "he" spoke is presented by the πρὸς phrases, "of the angels . . . of the son. . . ." *What* he says, in the first clause, is set forth by the noun-object phrase introduced by the attributive participle ὁ ποιῶν, "the one making." This participle has direct objects ἀλλέλους "angels" and λειτουρλοὺς "official ministers." The objects are completed by objective complements πνεύματα "winds" and φλόγα "flame." The phrase would read, "the one making his angels (messengers) winds and his ministers (a) flame of fire."

Two noun clauses form the direct objects of the implied λέγει of the second main clause. "O God, your throne (is) unto the age of the age (forever)" and "the sceptre of uprightness (is) his kingdom's sceptre." The second ῥάβδος is predicate nominative. Though it lacks the definite article it may be translated "the sceptre of his kingdom." The genitive βασιλείας makes it definite.

The diagram treats ὁ θεὸς as vocative. It is from Psalm 45 in which the poet describes a royal wedding in which the king is addressed as *God*. Some scholars shrink from identifying an earthly king with the deity. They treat this as a predicate "your throne is God forever." This is possible. But it really is addressing the king in his Messianic role and there should be no hesitation of using the vocative.

Since the diagram can't have it both ways we decide for vocative.

Verse 9 embodies a complex sentence. It has one independent clause from which stems an adverbial dependent clause of cause. The independent has a compound predicate, "you loved . . . and hated." There's a decisiveness about the aorist tenses in these verbs. The tense fits the idea that love for righteousness and hate for lawlessness were definitive determinations.

διά with accusative introduces the basis on which a given action takes place. Here "because" you "loved . . . and . . . hated . . ." "God, your God, anointed you. . . ." Accusative ἔλαιον is a second accusative after "anoint." It could be viewed as a second object. The diagram positions it as an adverbial accusative, "with oil." Genitive ἀγαλλιάσεως tells the *kind* of oil ("of gladness"). Here παρά with accusative μετόχους is one way of showing comparison or contrast, "alongside" (beyond) your partners."

A word about ἄγγελος frequently translated "angel." It really means "messenger" and probably would be better rendered by that English term. The association of *angel* with halos, wings and femininity is misleading. Whatever forms they assume the function of biblical "angels" is that of "ministering servants." According to Hebrew tradition angels live only as they serve or minister. They are actually messengers doing service for God in behalf of men. In this context their temporary nature forms a perfect contrast to the permanent exalted place of the "Son."

Hebrews 1:10-13

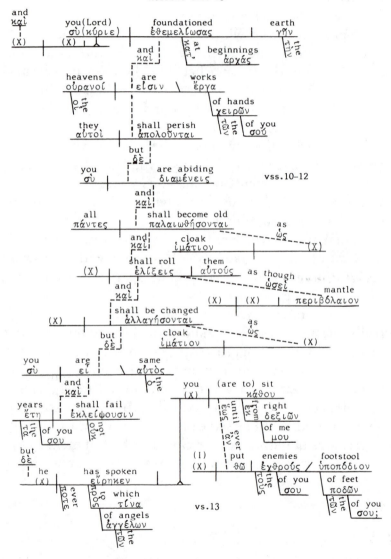

vss.10-12

vs.13

30

Hebrews 1:14

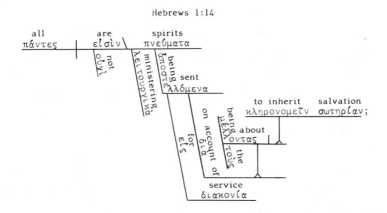

THE DIAGRAM OF HEBREWS 1:10-14

On this and the preceding page three sentences appear. That of 1:10-12 is complex with the independent clause implied by the context. This main clause, "'he' (or 'it') says," is followed by nine noun dependent clauses. Each serves as an object of the understood verb "says." From three of these object clauses hangs an adverbial clause. Two are comparison introduced by ὡς = "as." One is inaugurated by ὡσεὶ = "as though." It is concessive.

Verse 13 embodies an interrogative complex sentence of three clauses. The adversative conjunction δὲ sets the thought of this sentence in contrast to the idea in the last two clauses of the preceding sentence. There the eternal abiding change-lessness of the Son was asserted, "you are the same and your years shall not fail." "*But*" (δὲ) to which of the angels has he ever spoken . . .?" The perfect tense εἴρηκεν gives stress to the fixed nature of what "he has spoken." What he said still stands!

κάθου represents a noun clause, object of εἴρηκεν. It is present imperative. It is God's assignment to the Son to

31

"keep on sitting." The adverbial clause heralded by ἕως ἂν is temporal, "whenever." The time during which the Son is to keep on sitting is "until whenever I (God) put your enemies (as a) footstool of your feet." ὑποπόδιον is an objective complement that expresses that which God will make of the Son's enemies.

In spite of appearances verse 14 is a simple sentence. It has but one clause, "all are not spirits. . . ." It is a negative interrogative expecting "no" for an answer; "all are ministering spirits are they not?" The present circumstantial participle "being sent" (ἀποστελλόμενα) describing "spirits" is linear action; "being sent from time to time as human need arises." εἰς with accusative expresses purpose. διά with accusative expressed grounds on which or cause. The articular attributive participle μέλλοντας has for its object the infinitive phrase "to inherit salvation."

A Translation
Hebrews 2:1-4

On account of this (the Son's superiority and the angel's redemptive service) that we be heeding carefully the things which we've heard is necessary that we not be swept past them. For if the message having been spoken through angels became firm so that every overstepping of legal restraint and every failure to hear got an exact punitive return, how shall we escape, having carelessly neglected so great a salvation? And this salvation, having been personally preached at the first by the Lord, was confirmed to us by those who heard. Furthermore, God joined his testimony with theirs by means of signs, and wonders, and various dynamic powers and distributions of the Holy Spirit as measured by his will."

AN OUTLINE OF HEBREWS 2:1-4
IT PAYS TO PAY ATTENTION

Introduction: Life rewards concentration on the task at hand. No bonus is granted for careless neglect in any field of endeavor.

I. A FOUR-FOLD TESTIMONY vss. 3b-4
   1. Old Testament prophetic testimony. "God, having spoken . . ."
   2. The Lord's personal testimony. ". . . spoken by the Lord . . ."

    3. Apostles' testimony. ". . . confirmed by those who heard . . ."

    4. Testimony of the Spirit. ". . . signs, and wonders, and various powers, and distributions of the Holy Spirit . . ."

II. THE LOGIC OF PAYING ATTENTION. vs. 1

    1. We've personally heard the testimony once. It makes sense to pay attention and give heed.

    2. The inherent danger in drifting.

    ". . . lest we be swept away from them . . ."

III. THE CERTAINTY OF THE CONSEQUENCES. vss. 2-3a

    1. Under the older, lesser angelic revelation punishment followed inevitably and fitted the crime exactly.

    2. Is God more lax under the greater revelation? Is he not just as moral under the Son's greater grace?

Conclusion: Hear and heed the Son and live. Neglect and die!

SOME EXPOSITORY THOUGHTS ON HEBREWS 2:1-4

Ninety percent of retail products are not bought. They're sold! That's the conclusion of sales organizations and people. Whether through mass media, special promotion, or hard-nosed door to door selling, most things are sold, not bought. We may be convinced logically of our needs and wants but someone tips the scales and *persuades* us to buy. That goes for everything from a ball point pen to a thousand acre ranch.

But once what I purchase is in my possession then it's my responsibility to keep it, service it, use it in the pursuit of life's goal. It's possible to lose it! By failure to preserve carefully my vested interest I can forfeit my possession. And sometimes quite quickly. Life grants no bonus for careless neglect in any field of activity. On the contrary concentration at the task before me is the price of preservation of possessions. And that's true whether those possessions be material or of the spirit. The athlete on the field of competition loses because he takes his eye off the ball. The artist in the studio fails to paint the masterpiece because his mind wanders, his heart wavers, his hand slips. In other words, he doesn't pay attention to the task in front of him. The business goes bankrupt because the president becomes absorbed in his golf score more than his sales force. He neglects the soul of his operation. It pays to pay attention.

The fullness of the testimony

In Hebrews 2:1-4 the author attempts to "sell" his product, the retention of faith in Jesus the "Son." This is his sales talk to those who were tempted to return to the nostalgic glory of Old Testament ritual. And to the fellowship of visible, colorful, friendly, priests who were helpful in present problems.

He reminds his readers that "God spoke." He spoke "in the prophets." He spoke through angels, his "ministering spirits." God went into detail, line upon line, precept upon precept to make his redemptive purposes clear to "his people." The whisperings of God's voice through the Old Testament centuries led men to expect God's full-toned speech in the "age to come," the age of Messiah.

35

Then God "spoke in one who was Son." In fact, God's word was personally delivered "at the first the Lord" Jesus himself. In sermon, parable, miracle, and demonstration of life, Jesus spoke face to face with men. He taught the purpose and meaning of life as men can find it in the kingdom of God. Then God climaxed his speech in Jesus by the demonstration of the cross. Crucifixion is God's method of rule, the very fabric of any successful human life. Successful from the divine standpoint.

God's revelation was "confirmed to us by those who heard" the Lord Jesus speak "at the first." This is the apostolic witness. They heard, saw, handled and examined the Lord, the living "Word" who became flesh. They ate and drank with him, watched him die, experienced him alive after the cross, and told of his continuing presence by means of the Spirit. These were the men who experienced the power of Pentecost. They were men who spoke in languages they had not learned; men who, when threatened, prayed and "the place where they were gathered was shaken and they were filled with the Holy Spirit and spoke the word of God with boldness" (Acts 4:31). These men did not travel alone nor did they invade a city or country single handed but always "in power and in the Holy Spirit and with full conviction" (I Thess. 1:5). They were bouyed up and carried along by strength from on high and powers beyond the human. God was their personal partner in the gospel venture. He "jointly witnessed with them both by signs and wonders, and various kinds of powers and distributions of the Holy Spirit along the standard of his will." Signs point the way to a necessary goal. Wonders penetrate the calloused, encrusted heart and stir to reformed renewal. Various kinds of powers enable one to meet life's problems head on and resolve what otherwise would defeat us. Such powers grapple with sin in us and lead to certain triumph. And God constantly distributes his Holy Spirit in infinite ways as we each need His special guidance. He is both guide and "Comforter." God's witness in us to us and for us ties together all who have brought his will to us; the prophets, the personal Son, the accumulated testimony of the apostles. How can we neglect God's purpose and plan of redeeming love when we consider the fullness of his testimony?

The logic of paying attention.

If careful attention is disregarded, with the passing of time the freshness and thrill of new faith wears thin. While the showroom smell of a new car still lingers, oil can be overlooked, gas can be ignored, tires can be run too low of air. Before long rust and road grime not only disfigure but they begin their deadly corroding effect. The car is ready to be discarded before we would like.

Such can happen to faith—and often does. It's for this reason the author of Hebrews exhorted that "we must pay the closer attention to what we have heard. . . ." If he were a car dealer he would exhort us to "read the manual." Learn what makes things run smoothly. Learn about air pressure, oil filters, spark plugs. One's faith can not exert its proper power without close attention to "what we've heard." The forgiveness of guilt, the power of the new birth, the joy of Christian fellowship, the reading and hearing of "the apostles' teaching," the power of personal prayer, the cultivation of the presence of God's Holy Spirit, the love, the grace, the mercy and patience of God with my stumbling faith—these and much else must maintain the fragrance of our first faith. But they will not come naturally or easily. They require daily effort and constant attention. In a world of carefree evil it makes sense to keep faith fresh and "new each morning." If one pays close attention to the market value of his real estate and regularly services his car he certainly knows the value of servicing his faith and keeping close tab on the vitality of his convictions. "An ounce of prevention is worth a pound of cure" is nowhere more applicable than in the matter of one's relationship to God in Christ. Give heed to "the things that have been heard."

Danger of drifting is always present. "Lest we drift away" is the way the English states the danger. The Greek text is more urgent; "lest we be swept past. . . ." It takes no action on my part to drift. The currents impelling us downstream are viciously strong. We don't drift so much as we are driven by the power of currents of which we are unmindful and so unheedful. To flow with a crowd is easier than to row against the current. I can dream if I drift. I must toil if I row. I can float downstream but I must swim upstream. If the goal is upstream I must be alert to wind and current lest I be swept downstream. If you would reach the upward goal be alert to the downward draft. If you want to rise up, don't drift down!

The certainty of consequences

Consequences of human behaviour are inevitable. Seed in the Spring means harvest in the Autumn. "If the word having been spoken through angels became firm. . . ." This is the form of logic the Hebrew author uses. His use of "if"

38

does not imply doubt. It is historically true and absolutely certain that the word of the angels' revelation was firm. Divine punishment, though never vengeful, was sure, certain, and immediate. "Every transgression and disobedience received a precise retributive result." On a national scale the Babylonian Captivity was the classic example. "Have you not brought this on yourself by forsaking the Lord your God?" (Jer. 2:17). The Psalmist contemplated the fate of the wicked man. "Truly thou dost set them (the wicked) in slippery places. Thou dost make them fall to ruin. How they are destroyed in a moment, swept away utterly by terros" (Ps. 73:18-19). When the sister of Moses raised her voice in rebellion against the Lord's leader, "the anger of the Lord was kindled . . . behold, Miriam was leprous, as white as snow" (Num. 12:9f.). Korah the son of Izhar rebelled against Moses' leadership. With the swiftest of judgments "the ground under them split asunder, and the earth opened its mouth and swallowed them up, with their households and all the men that belonged to Korah." Under this lesser angelic revelation God's judgment followed swift and sure.

Is God less moral under the Son's revelation than that of angels? True, he has provided a Saviour, a way of escape for all who look to the Son. But he who neglects that Son, who grows careless and takes for granted the mercy of the Lord suffers consequences. Grace does not repeal retribution; it overcomes it when we don't neglect grace. The wrath of God is as righteous and sure as it ever was under the older covenant. If *they* did not escape judgment under the lesser how can *we* escape under the greater? The Son is the means of escape. If we neglect the Son, there is no escape! If men find retribution when they rebel against law will they not find greater retribution when they rebel against grace? If it's sin to disobey abstract law is it not sin to disobey the person of the Son? To sin against law is bad. But to sin against the Lord is worse.

"Watch! For you know not the day or hour!"

Hebrews 2:1-4

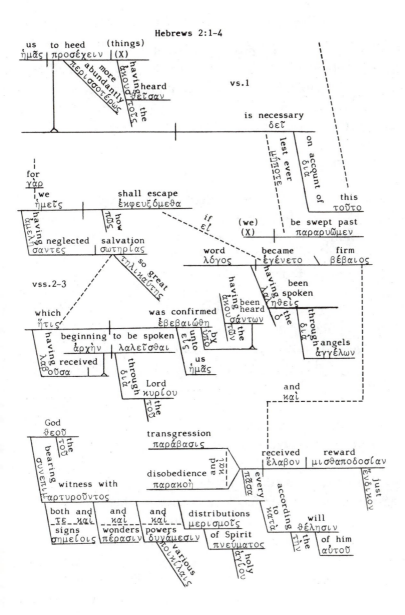

41

THE DIAGRAM OF 2:1-4

This paragraph admits of two sentences. However, the genitive absolute of verse four is so "loosely attached" that it almost performs as a separate unit of thought.

Having one clause the sentence of verse one is simple in structure. The word δεῖ = "it is necessary" signifies a *logical* necessity. It has for its subject an infinitive phrase, "to heed more abundantly . . ." προσέχειν is present active infinitive with accusative of general reference; "to heed in reference to us" but more smoothly "that we heed. . . ." Object of the infinitive is understood "things." Modifying this "things" is the attributive aorist passive participle translated, "the having been heard things." The prepositional phrase διὰ τοῦτο is used as an adverb expressing why or the grounds on which the necessity is based; "because of this." The "this" connects back to the argument of 1:5-14. "On account of the Son's superiority to angels therefore that we give more abundant heed . . . is necessary."

Verses 2-4 embody a complex sentence with one independent idea, "How shall we escape . . .?" The pronoun ἡμεῖς is emphatic. The sentence is a rhetorical question expecting a negative response, "We can't!" The aorist circumstantial participle "having neglected" is conditional in force, "if we neglect." The aorist tense treats the neglect as a thing done, sealed and clinched, an accomplished disposition. The adverbial εἰ clause is in fact a first class conditional assuming the condition to be true. "If the word . . . became firm and it did. . . ." The subject λόγος has the attributive aorist passive participle λαληθεὶς limiting it, "the having been spoken word." διὰ with genitive expresses the agent through which the word was spoken.

It's an obvious reference to the use of angels in giving the law at Sinai. Another first class conditional is added, "if every transgression and disobedience received . . . and it did. . . ."

παράβασις is literally a "stepping alongside" and signifies an overstepping of prescribed boundaries; it's like a foul ball. παρακοή means "hearing alongside." That is, not paying attention to what is said and so hearing something that wasn't even said. Thus one disobeys that which actually is said.

The dependent clause prefaced by ἥτις is adjective describing σωτηρίας, "which salvation was confirmed. . . ." The aorist circumstantial participle modifying ἥτις presents the manner in which the salvation was confirmed, "having received a beginning to be spoken. . . ." Note the present passive infinitive with accusative of general reference ἀρχὴν λαλεῖσθαι. Those who confirmed are set forth by ὑπό with ablative of aorist attributive participle, "the ones having heard."

Though genitive absolute of verse four is not a complete sentence, it does add a thought to that about confirming. "God bearing witness with" these others who confirmed. And he did so in a four-fold variety; "by signs, wonders, various powers, and distributions of gifts. . . ."

This paragraph is a tightly packed arrangement of thought. It's an exhortation appealing from the lesser to the greater. If that by angels is firm that by the Son must be more so.

A Translation
Hebrews 2:5-18

For not to angels did he subject the coming world concerning which we are speaking. But one somewhere testified saying, "What is man that you remember him? Or son of man that you visit him? A little you made him lower than angels. With glory and honor you crowned him; all things you subjected under his feet.

For in the "subjection of all things" to him, he left nothing unsubjected. But now we do not see the "all things" yet subjected. But we do see Jesus, the one having been made lower as to little, because of the suffering of death crowned with glory and honor, in order that by God's grace he should taste death for all. For it was befitting him, because of whom are all things and through whom are all things, leading many sons unto glory, to perfect the leader of their salvation through things suffered. For both the one sanctifying and the ones being sanctified (are) all of one; for which reason he is not being ashamed to call them brothers, saying, "I will declare your name to my brothers; in the midst of (the) assembly I will praise you." And again, "I will trust on him." And again, "Behold, I and the children which God gave me."

Since, then, the children have shared in blood and flesh, he also similarly partook of the same that through death he might render inoperative

the one having the power of death, that is, the devil;
and that he might set free however many by fear
of death were liable to bondage through all of life.
For surely not to angels is he helping but rather he
helps Abraham's seed. Whence he was being obliged
to be made like his brothers that he might become
merciful and faithful highpriest in the matters that
relate to God, that he might expiate the sins of the
people. For in that in which he, having been tried,
has suffered, he is able to come to the aid of the
ones being under trial.

AN OUTLINE OF HEBREWS 2:5-18
DESTINY THROUGH DEFEAT!

Man's measure of "success" is not God's. With God
man is saved through suffering; man gains his promised
destiny through defeat!

I. MAN'S DESTINY FULFILLED IN JESUS. 2:5-9
  1. The "world to come" not created for angels. vs. 5
  2. It was made for man. vss. 6-8a
  3. Finally fulfilled in Jesus. vss. 8b-9

II. MAN'S DESTINY FULFILLED THROUGH
   SUFFERING. 2:10-18
  1. The Son and his brothers. vss. 10-13
    (a) The bond between them declared. vs. 10
    (b) Their origins in a common father. vss. 11-13
  2. The Son became human. vss. 14-15
    (a) To achieve full fellowship with brothers. vs. 14a

    (b) To vanquish the prince of death. vs. 14b
    (c) To set brothers free from fear of death. vs. 15
  3. The Imperative of the Son's humanity. vss. 16-18
    (a) The domain of his work—mankind. vs. 16
    (b) The reach of his work—redemption. vs. 17
    (c) For the effectiveness of his priestly function.
    vs. 18

SOME EXPOSITORY THOUGHTS ON HEBREWS 2:5-18

God's measuring rod for "success" is different than that of man's. Heaven's viewpoint of "victory" is not earth's. God believes in being a "winner" but his idea of "winning" is at variance with human notions. By way of example take the sports arena. More particularly basketball. In the final minutes of a game with a team one or two points behind the skillful player is sent into the game with explicit instructions to commit a foul in order to "win" the game. In other words violate the stated rules in order to get the larger point-score. From God's viewpoint the deliberate commitment of a foul is itself a confession of defeat. In economic relationships the making of a profit is the measure of success. Yet from God's point of view a profit at the expense of the integrity of the soul is failure, not success. God says, "My thoughts are not your thoughts, neither are your ways my ways" (Isaiah 55:8).

A stumbling block to faith for the early Christians was the death of the Christ. Why the necessity of death of *God's* Son? Death, especially as a criminal, was a sign of defeat, not victory. Could not God, who holds all power, find some other way than humiliation and death to win man's salvation? Death is so irrational and absurdly illogical! Yet from God's point of view Christ's death was the sign and measure of victory over the world, the flesh and the devil. The reasonableness of the death of Christ is the burden of 2:5-18. The author shows that it is fitting, logical, and effective for man's redemption.

Human destiny fulfilled in Jesus

God created man "in his own image" and placed him in a most delightful world. Man was to enjoy a divine nature, human dignity and universal dominion. It was "not to angels" that God subjected "the coming world." It was only to humanity!

The facts of history didn't mesh with the promised destiny. The frightful failure of man to attain "dominion" over creation, not to mention over himself, made the divine promise at creation a sheer travesty. Yet God's promise stands unchanged, immutable. At the masthead of history the promised destiny stands, "let's make man in our image." Man was and is the object of God's creative grace, not angels or angelic beings of any description. Man inherited the divine nature. He was endowed with noble dignity. He was promised unbounded dominion! Angels may be privileged to stand in the presence of God, they may be honored as messengers of God's mercy and grace, they may enjoy celestial ambrosia but they were not created "in the image of God." They're not divine in nature. Neither do they enjoy the heights of human dignity nor the privilege of being sovereign kings. "The world to come" was for man not angels. Angels were made to serve; man to rule.

In moral and spiritual virtue he is to rule over himself. He's to rule over all creation, ". . . over the works of thy hands . . . sheep and oxen . . . beasts . . . birds . . . fish . . . whatever passes along the paths of the sea" (Ps. 8:7-9). Man was fashioned after the pattern of God himself. He was but "little lower than deity" for he was divine in design.

Hebrew thought developed the concept of "the coming age" or "the world to come." This didn't refer to "heaven." It referred to the age of Messiah. In New Testament terms it would be the "kingdom of God" or the "Christian order under the aspect of a moral organized system" (Wesct. p. 42). It was in fact the state of things intended at creation. It was the time, condition, or era in which God's creative purpose would be fulfilled in man. It would be that age in which man arrived at the destiny to which God pledged him. In experience man would be an authentic "image of God,"—in nature, dignity and dominion all God expected. The Psalmist made clear that God intended that "nothing" be left "unsubjected to him (man)."

But reality doesn't respond to promise. "Now we do not yet see all things having been subjected" to man. History furnishes a trail of blood testifying to "man's inhumanity to man" Disease, hunger, pestilence and plague walk unchecked making the beauty of God's earth a living hell. Hate, greed, violence, war and death make of this earth a garbage dump of rotting, festering, burning discharge of castoff rubbish. Man's experience testifies: "their worm dies not, . . . their fire is not quenched." "We see not yet all things subjected. . . ."

Yet, in spite of man's collapse as a sovereign, his coarse vulgarity, his degenerate divinity "we do see Jesus . . . crowned with glory and honor. . . ." This Jesus "became a little lower than angels." Deity in nature, in degree and time he became limited by the bounds of "blood and flesh." The human race, as represented in this man Jesus, fully realized the glory, honor, and boundless dominion God pledged at creation. Though man never did, man in Jesus did subject "all things." Jesus, by his conquest of moral wrong, his overthrow of death, demonstrated his dominion over "all things," physical, moral and spiritual. And what he did has had a permanent effect. The victory is a thing of the past. Its finale is yet to come. The Son of Man, the Son of God, Jesus of Nazareth fulfilled in his person the promised destiny designed by the Creator.

Man's destiny fulfilled through defeat.

The classic reversal is the victory of Jesus by means of his "defeat" on the cross. The "victory" of the world and the devil, such as it was, took place at calvary. This is the limit of the devil's success. Put the good Man, the divine Son to death. Eliminate him in pain, shame, weakness, disgrace of a criminal's execution. Death row is not the world's view of a throne room from which to redeem. Nor is the cross or electric chair the human idea of a king's throne! Yet these devices of defeat God restyled into tools of triumph. Death, the ultimate consequence of sin, is the devil's last straw, the world's topmost power. Yet the death of Jesus on the cross is the sceptre of Christ's glory. The empty tomb is the throne room from which he came to exercise his royal dominion. Isn't this what the Hebrew writer says? "Because of the suffering of death" Jesus "was crowned with glory and honor." Nor was it an accidental entrapment by which he died. It was by "God's grace" that he "tasted death for every man." Though human beings must answer for their part in the death of the Christ, it was by God's gracious design that Jesus died. At bottom the death of Christ is the work of God, not man. "No man takes my life . . . I lay it down of myself."

Death adorns the divine Son as jewel-bedecked robes enhance a king. "It was fitting" for God to perfect his Son through the things he suffered as man. As creator and shaper of human destiny what could be more divinely suitable than to suffer in behalf of his creatures? Especially to save them? It's more appropriate for an army captain to *lead* his men into the fire of the enemy than to *send* them. To save his sons it's fitting for a father to plunge into a burning house. Certainly as becoming as to rely on professional firemen. So it is that Messiah's death, rather than "foolishness" actually is seemly in a God who loves. The crimson beauty of a rose is not diminished because it shows up on a thorny bush. Nor is the death of Jesus crackbrained because it's brutal, cruel or criminal. Though unexpected, the suffering of the cross is superb in prudence and matchless in redemptive power. Indeed Christ's suffering is "the power of God and the wisdom of God." What is more divine than power and wisdom?

Through suffering Christ became "perfect" as a saviour. By virtue of the fact that men are a family of sinners, brethren in corruption and violence, Christ was impelled to become one with them—one amidst their sin but not in their sinning. He must join men in their humanity. A lifesaver at a beach resort cannot save struggling swimmers by shouting instructions from the shore. If he would rescue drowning men he must plunge into the water, survive the storm, take hold of the sinking men, and drag them to safety. A saviour riding on a white horse was the visionary wish of an oppressed people. But considering the corrupt condition of the family of brothers, to deliver from one oppressive tyrant only to transfer them to another was to be no saviour at all. To be a "perfect" saviour he must deliver from the sin which makes any political or social system an oppression. Hence, to be "perfect" he must identify with the lost as one with them.

Besides full fellowship with his brothers, Christ humbled himself to die for two basic reasons. First, he thus could vanquish death. To set free imprisoned men one must hold the key that unlocks the barred door that makes of life a prison. If men are to be set free from death Christ must destroy death. He must go to the prison where the prisoners are. And he must go with the authority and power to open the gates. A deliverer must go *inside* the prison walls with power to bring the prisoners out. The author of Hebrews declares that all this Christ did. "Since the children have shared in blood and flesh, he similarly partook of the same that through death he might render inoperative the one having the power of death, that is, the devil." The devil has always used death as a means of enslaving God's children. By his dying Christ rendered death ineffective to enslave men. By dying and rising from the grave the Son wore death out. He unmasked it for what it is, a weak, impotent, illusive threat; not a permanent coma of oblivion. Death is a supreme lie; it wears a false face. By his death Christ stripped the falseness from it. Through death Christ outplayed Satan's trump card.

Furthermore, by his death Jesus neutralized the *power* of death. Fear of death sabotages the rapture of living. It's fear of death that perpetually gnaws at the core of man's soul. Christ's victory removes this gnawing anxiety. I am free to enjoy the ecstacy of living. Because he rose I shall rise. Though I face death I'm free from the paralyzing fear of death.

The necessity of the Son's humanity

Though Son of God, until he served as sacrifice and priest Christ could not complete man's destiny. "He was under a continuing moral obligation to be made his brothers." He *had* to become human. In order to serve sick people's needs a doctor must go where sick people are. For the Lord to be merciful he must live among those who need mercy. How can he be trusted unless he lives with those who search for one worthy of trust? Because he became man men could know mercy! Because he became human, human beings found trust to be a viable option. Because God became human we know he *is* merciful; God *can* be trusted! And Jesus *could* extend mercy and *be* trustworthy! In healing man's broken relationship with God the Incarnation became necessary that Christ might become "a merciful and trustworthy high priest in matters that relate to God."

Besides this, his ultimate aim in becoming human was that he might "expiate the sins of the people." Sin blocked the free fellowship between man and his father-creator. An impassible gulf separated. No man could bridge that moral abyss. Since sin began in human history the need for expiation has been present. A redress of man's moral defeat must be obtained. Not that God's love ever ceased. But moral wrong in the soul of man dams up the flow of that love. It cuts the source of life. Expiation doesn't act on God but on that in man which alienates from God. So Christ became human that he might remove the cancerous sin that eats at the vital flow of divine life toward man. Christ died that he might "expiate the sins of the people." He became both priest and sacrifice that he might remove all barriers between me and God.

In his humanity Christ passed through trials enabling him to rush to my help in my trials. "Having been tempted he is able to help the ones being tempted." He who has never stumped his toe is little moved by the tears of him whose toe is bleeding. He who never has been lost overboard at sea cannot enter into the panic, fright, and terror of such vast loneliness. He who would enter into the ordeal of the sufferer must himself suffer. He who is coming out of prison can better support and succor him who is going in. God found it imperative to become human in order to taste the pain of trial. That God in his Christ should suffer in order to save is not foolishness and it should not be a stumbling block. It should have been expected. What is human foolishness is God's wisdom; what is a stumbling block to man opens God's door to man's salvation.

The suffering of Christ was imperative. It's for man, not angels; it's the power of redemption, not weakness. It makes the priestly function effective for the hurt of humanity. Because Christ suffered he is able to save me in my suffering.

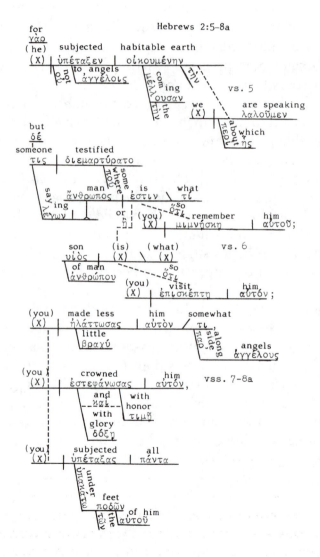

Hebrews 2:5-8a

54

THE DIAGRAM OF 2:5-8a

With 2:5 the author returns to an extension of his argument that the Son is superior to angels. It is a complex sentence. "He subjected the coming habitable earth" is the independent element. The dependent clause describing οἰκουμένην is adjectival. It identifies the "habitable earth" as that world "about which we are speaking." This physical, temporal order of the world is administered by angels (cf. Deut. 32) but not this Christian order, this kingdom of God, this new Israel, this "age to come" about which "we are speaking" in this epistle. The "coming age" was an expression then current, signifying the age of Messiah. Such a moral order is administered by the Son, not angels.

The sentence of verse six has five clauses. It is complex in form. The main clause says, "Someone testified. . . ." The manner in which he testified is seen in the circumstantial present active participle "saying." Two noun clauses, objects of λέγων, tell *what* he says. The first of these noun clauses, "What is man," sprouts a dependent adverbial clause, "so that you remember him." The second object clause, "(What is) son" also is supported by a ὅτι result clause. These two adverbial clauses might be classified as noun clauses in apposition to subjects ἄνθρωπος and υἱός. But the diagram prefers the adverbial result idea, a loose causal idea.

Verse six suggests the frailty of man. The awesome size of creation dwarfs man. And even more amazing, man receives the attention of the Creator of such a vast creation! God never created man only to abandon him. On the contrary, he "remembers" him and "visits" him. The author has thus prepared his readers for his next idea: how God has enobled man.

Verses 7-8a contain a compound sentence of three independent clauses. They embody three eminent features with which God has adorned man. First, when placed "alongside angels," God has made man "a little less somewhat" than such heavenly beings. In other words, "practically divine in nature." The clause obviously takes its starting point from "in our image" of Genesis 1:26. It is to be noted that some renderings use "God" or "deity" rather than "angels." But history never really revealed the fulfillment of this promise of creation until the appearance of the Son.

The next of the three clauses refers to the essential elegance of character of man coupled with a display of dignity, a dignity that makes the inward essence outwardly manifest. δόξα means *glory*, or *essential nature*. τιμή means *value*, *price*, *honor*. God gave man a glorious quality of being. And a value beyond any material measure. Yet, here too, man never fully realized such high expectations until the Son of Man trod this earth and ascended to sit at God's right hand.

"You subjected all things under his feet." This clause indicates man's destiny of dominion. Man was created to rule. Genesis is still coloring the mind of the author. And though man's dominion is obviously crippled almost beyond recognition he was originally made to rule "all things." The object πάντα includes all the physical plus himself, and any hostile powers that might rise to oppose.

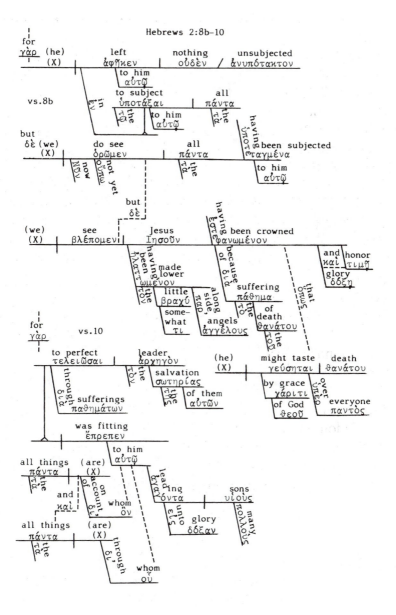

Hebrews 2:8b–10

57

THE DIAGRAM OF 2:8b-10

The conjunction γὰρ introducing verse 8b connects to the idea in verse five. When God subjected the "coming age" to man rather than to angels it was to be complete and universal. Since ἐν τῷ and infinitive is a phrase rather than a clause the sentence of verse 8a may be branded as simple in form. The only full clause reads, "For he left nothing unsubjected." The verbal ἀνυπότακτον, "unsubjected," acts here as objective complement filling out the object οὐδὲν. In translation we may treat the infinitive phrase as though a temporal subordinate clause, "when he subjected to him all things." The aorist tense ὑποτάξαι looks to the historic point when God decreed that all things be subjected to man.

Verses 8c-9 frame a compound-complex sentence. The first independent clause says, ". . . we do not yet see all things subjected. . . ." The second says, ". . . we do see Jesus having been crowned. . . ." Each clause has a perfect participle in indirect discourse with verbs of perception. In the first ὑποτεγταγμένα is supplementary to the main verb while as adjective it fills out the idea in the object πάντα. Note that the participle in indirect discourse is used here where a *real experience* becomes involved. The infinitive or ὅτι would have been used had this been only "intellectual apprehension, opinion, or judgment" (ATR Hist. Gr. pg. 1041). ἐστεφανωμένον functions in its clause in the same way; "we do see that Jesus has been crowned." The perfect tense brings to the fore the abiding result of the action. The Jesus is *still* a crowned man!

The perfect participle ἠλαττωμένον is circumstantial. It's an added predicate description but, unlike ἐστεφανωμένον, it could be removed from the sentence without "bleeding it to death." διά with accusative gives the causal basis on which Jesus was crowned. The clause advanced by ὅπως expresses purpose, "in order that." The reason why Jesus went through the death followed by crowning as king with glory and honor was "in order that" he "might, by God's grace, taste (experience) death for everyone." The purpose clause refers to the *whole* idea, not just the participle, "having been crowned," or just the phrase "because of death." The death of Jesus without the crowning was just another death. Nor would there have been a coronation without the death. Together they were "in order that."

Verse ten is a complex sentence. Stripped of all appendages the main clause reads, "To perfect was fitting. . . ." Subject of the verb ἔπρεπεν is the aorist infinitive τελειῶσαι, to perfect. διά with the genitive tells the means through which the perfecting was accomplished. The sufferings were many (plural) but the aorist in the infinitive views the perfecting as a point reached.

The dependent clauses are connected to the αὐτῷ (to him) in the independent clause by διά with relative accusative ὅν expressing "on account of whom." διὰ with the relative genitive οὗ expresses agent, through whom. While present circumstantial participle ἀλαλόντα refers to αὐτῷ it gets its accusative case from the understood accusative of general reference with infinitive τελειῶσαι.

Hebrews 2:11-13

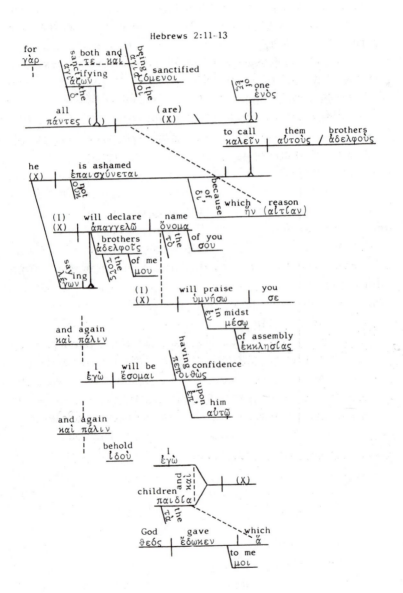

60

THE DIAGRAM OF 2:11-13

Does 2:11-13 contain one or three sentences? If the last two quotations (Isaiah 8:17 and 18) are viewed as direct objects of present participle λέγων, then we are dealing with only one sentence, a complex with several dependents clauses. But the diagram arranges the material in the form of three sentences.

The first is complex. The independent clause states, "All are of one. . . ." The prepositional phrase ἐξ ἑνὸς is a predicate nominative referring back to the subject "all." The ablative calls attention to the origin. The Son and all sons have a common father hence are one family. The subject "all" has in apposition to it the compounding of two attributive participles, "both the one sanctifying and the ones being sanctified. . . ." The present tenses ἁγιάζων (active) and ἁγιαζόμενοι (passive) remind us that sanctifying is an ongoing process and not just a completed act. Sanctification is a continuing, increasing dedication to holy ends—in the individual and the community of Christians.

The first dependent clause is launched by διά with accusative ἥν. It is adverbial expressing the basis on which the idea in the clause is true. Because Jesus and Christians are "of one" paternal origin they are brethren. And Jesus "is not ashamed to be calling them brothers." ἀδελφοὺς is objective complement. ἐπαισχύνεται is present passive indicative with strong negative οὐκ. The fact that the many brothers are sinners doesn't change the reality of the common origin of the Son and sons. They are brothers and he continues (present tense) to be unashamed of the family relationship.

Two noun clauses appear as objects of circumstantial participle λέγων. They are quotes from Psalm 22:22. The first gives biblical support to the author's reasoning that the Son and sons are brothers of one father. "I will declare your name to my brothers." The second tells how the king, who suffered so much in the earlier part of the Psalm, now shares songs of praise in common with the brethren assembled for worship. He's one with them. "I will praise you in the midst of the assembly."

If we take 13a as a separate sentence it is simple in structure. After the author's introductory "And again" it is another quotation from the Old Testament; "I will trust upon him." πεποιθώς is perfect active participle of πείθω, persuade. Used intransitively it means to *trust, have confidence*. In conjunction with future ἔσομαι it forms a periphrastic future indicative perfect meaning, "I will have confidence." Amid painful judgments the prophet, when God was "hiding his face," declares his unwavering confidence in the Lord. The periphrastic adds striking emphasis. ἐγώ adds to the emphasis.

The final sentence (or clause) is another quote from the Old Testament (Isaiah 8:18). The sentence is complex in form. The subject of the main clause is compound, "I and the children. . . ." The verb must be supplied from the context, ". . . (are of the same family). . . . A dependent adjective clause "which God gave . . ." describes and identifies "children" as being the gift of God.

Hebrews 2:14-16

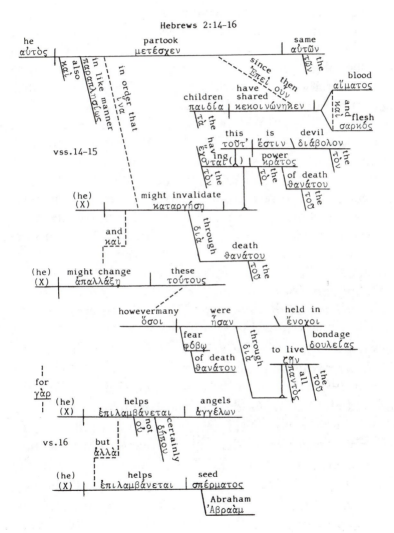

THE DIAGRAM OF HEBREWS 2:14-16

One independent followed by four dependent clauses tags the sentence of 2:14-15 as complex. "He partook the same" is the affirmation of the independent clause. αὐτῶν is direct object of μετέσχεν, a genitive after a verb of sharing. One reason lying back of his partaking of "the same" is expressed by the adverbial clause, "Since, then, the children have shared in blood and flesh." The perfect tense κεκοινώνηκεν reaches back to the beginning of humanity at creation and moves the action (sharing) up to the present moment, "to share and still share. . . ." "Blood" and "flesh" are genitives as direct objects following a verb of sharing.

The ἵνα clause performs the role of purpose hence is adverb in function. In fact, it actually launches two purpose clauses; that "he might invalidate," and that "he might change (set free). . . ." The verb translated "invalidate" is a compound word consisting of the preposition κατά, *down* and verb ἀργέω, *to non-work*. The word at bottom means to work something down until it won't work, this is, to destroy by using it up or exhausting its power. The aorist tense here would suggest the effective conquest of the devil's use of death as a means of controlling and enslaving the created children of God. The Son conquered by wearing death down to nothing; he wore death out until it lost its effectiveness any more. διά with genitive θανάτου proclaims the agency "through which." The phrase controlled by the articular attributive present participle ἔχοντα functions as noun, direct object of the verb "might invalidate." The expression τουτ' . . ., "that is the devil" is in apposition to the participle and specifically identifies precisely who "the one having the power of death" really is.

The verb of the second purpose clause ἀπαλλάξη means to *change* or to make other than. In this instance to make those in bondage other than what they are would be to "set free." Its direct object τούτους is described by an adjective clause, "however many were liable (held in by) to bondage." The subject ὅσοι is a quantitative relative pronoun. Again we note διά with genitive but this time with present active infinitive ζῆν, *to live*. The infinitive is in a fixed case form but is nevertheless genitive. Its present tense emphasizes the continuousness of life as indeed the notion native to the root idea "live" (Aktionsart) is a linear concept. The διά here denotes "through" in the sense of "extending clear through the living of life." It's a very vivid picture! Instrumental case φόβω means "with fear," that is to say, "fear" was the means (instrument) by which the devil plied his power. Genitive θανάτου identifies the "kind" of fear, the "fear of death."

The sentence of verse 16 is compound with two independent clauses joined by strong negative conjunction ἀλλά, *but*. First comes the negative, "he is not helping angels" followed by the positive giving a very pointed contrast, "but he is helping the seed of Abraham." Ἀβραάμ is genitive case specifying what "kind" of seed it is that he is helping. It's "*Abraham's seed*" not any other kind of seed. The genitives ἀγγέλων and σπέρματος are direct objects after a verb of helping (sharing).

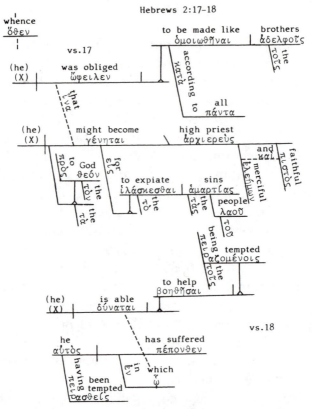

Hebrews 2:17-18

2:17 frames a complex sentence. Imperfect ὤφειλεν reflects a constant obligation on him who would perform the work of priest for the "brothers." Object is aorist infinitive ὁμοιωθῆωαι which, has instrumental ἀδελφοῖς for its object. ἵνα announces a purpose clause. εἰς and present infinitive "to expiate" introduces another purpose idea. Article τὰ modifying the πρὸς phrase is an adverbial accusative, "as to the matters pertaining to God."

The sentence of 2:18 classifies as complex. ἐν ᾧ ushers in an adverbial clause of cause. It declares *why* "he is able to help the ones being tempted." Point action of aorist circumstantial participle πειρασθείς presents the decisive fact

66

of his trials. Present of attributive πειραζομένοις points to the repeated trials of those he came to help. It suggests also a distributive idea.

A Translation
Hebrews 3:1-6

Whence, holy brothers, partners of a heavenly calling, concentrate your minds on the apostle and high priest of our confession, Jesus, being faithful to the one having made him to be apostle and high priest, as indeed (was) Moses in his (God's) house. For this (one) has been deemed more worthy than Moses according to as much as the one who built it (the house) possesses more honor than the house. For every house is built by someone. Moreover, the one having built all things (is) God. And, on the one hand Moses (was) faithful in his (God's) whole house as servant for a testimony of the things which shall be spoken, as, on the other hand, Christ (is) faithful as son over his (God's) house; whose house *we* are, if unto the end we tightly hold firm the bold confidence and the boast of the hope.

AN OUTLINE OF HEBREWS 3:1-6
THE HOUSE OF GOD

No house springs up of itself "for every house is built by someone." A house reflects the creative imagination of its architect, the determination of the builder. "The one who built all things is God."

I. THE HOUSE OF GOD. vss. 3-4
   1. God wanted and conceived a "house," a "holy temple," a "people for his own possession," a dynasty, a royal household of holy people.

68

2. God established Moses and Jesus builders of his house.
   (a) Moses was the lesser on two counts:
      (1) He was a part of the material, a "living stone"—as are we!
      (2) He worked as "servant," a hired hand—as do we!
   (b) Christ greater than Moses.
      (1) He's the builder; the master-mason of living stones.
      (2) He's the son, not servant; architect, not carpenter.

II. CONSIDER THIS JESUS, THE BUILDER. vss. 1-2
   1. Apostle of our confession. Sent on ambassadorial mission.
   2. High priest of our confession. To purify from sin.
   3. "Faithful" to God who made him apostle and high priest.

III. THE HOUSE WHICH JESUS IS BUILDING. vs. 6
   1. "Whose house *we* are!" The Christian community of brothers. "Partakers of a heavenly calling."
   2. The condition. "If we hold fast. . . ."

   Hold the mind on Jesus; keep the heart on the Christ —this is our staying, stabilizing power.

SOME EXPOSITORY THOUGHTS ON HEBREWS 3:1-6

No house ever springs up of itself "for every house is built by someone." That is true whether it be a house made of mortar and stone in which human beings dwell or a legislative body of elected representatives. Or even a dynasty, a line of descendants viewed as a single family. Every "house" of any kind is "built by someone." It is someone's idea implanted in an outward pattern.

Furthermore, every house echoes the inventive inspiration of its architect and builder. It's the final form of the first vision of the imagination of an artist. Morever, a house represents the persistent determination of someone to see it through to the end. A house is the embodiment of hours, years, even centuries of unending labor that refuses to quit until the last shingle is on the pinnacle.

This is preeminantly true of God's house. God has a house. He has labored through centuries to build it. He designed it, patiently watched over its every detail, sent builders at each stage of construction and insured its completion by sending his Son who in fact had oversight from beginning to end.

But what, why and where is the house of God?

The house of God, its builders

God wanted a "house." Not one made with man's hands for what man or group of men could build a house that could contain the Eternal? Besides, God, who is spirit does not dwell in *places*. Nevertheless, God desired a "house." The kind of house God wanted is intimated in his word "let us make man in our image." He sought a family of human beings sufficiently like himself that they could be the "people of God." As Spirit he would dwell in spirits, not boxed into places. Upon Israel's escape from Egyptian bondage God designated that multitude as "my own possession among all peoples . . . a kingdom of priests, a holy nation" (Ex. 19:5f.). The New Testament authors

70

declared Christians to be "a chosen race, a royal priesthood, a holy nation, God's own people" (I Peter 2:9).
Speaking of the expanding church Paul declares, "the whole
structure is joined together and grows into a holy temple
in the Lord; in whom you also are built into it for a dwelling place of God in the Spirit" (Eph. 2:21f.). No one can
doubt but that God desired a holy dynasty, a royal household of deified people.

In his exhortation the author of Hebrews uses four terms
that reveal his sense of the "people of God" being the house
of God. They are: "brothers," "holy," "partners," and
"heavenly calling." Believers are brothers, knit together in
a divine family. They are holy, not because any are personally perfect but because Christ himself has made them
holy, set them apart for sanctified ends. They are partners
because they all participate in the realities of redemption
brought to them in Christ. And they are participants in
a heavenly calling because God has called them from heaven
and to heaven as the issue of their redemption in Christ.
Such a holy family of heavenly participants is the temple
of God, his house, his "habitation in the Spirit." The
"people of God" is where God dwells among men. Such is
the house of God!

Two builders

Like any builder God used skilled people to build his
house. He employed human architects, draftsmen, and
laborers. Two stand prominent, Moses and Jesus. God
"made" both the lawgiver and Saviour to be vital builders
in the history of his house. Moses towers high above all
Old Testament laborers. He was the greatest of lawgivers.
His code embodies the standard of morals, ethics and

religious regulations which made of Israel a community rather than a mob. His laws yet form the basis for modern civilization. Standing at the headwaters of a long line of special servants of God, he was prophet par excellence. As prophet he served as pattern of *the* prophet-Messiah who "was to come." And when occasion demanded he played the part of priest standing as intermediary between sinful Israel and God's judgmental wrath. In tradition and fact none were greater than Moses.

But great as he was Moses was lesser than Jesus on two counts. He himself was part of the house on which he was builder. He was a "living stone" cut from the same quarry as all the stones which go to make up God's house. Indeed, as are all who choose to be built into the temple of God. The magnificent marble which adorns the banquet hall of heaven's temple, dazzling as it may be, is still but part of the building. It's less than he who builds.

Furthermore, Moses worked as a "servant," a hired hand, an employee. He must take orders and follow the design of him who "builds all things," even God. In this respect Moses was like all who serve at the most menial tasks in the developing temple of God. We are servants, not sons!

But Christ is greater than Moses. He's the builder, the master-mason of all the "living stones." He cuts, carves, polishes, and puts in place each stone so it may give its greatest splendor to the final result. Besides, Jesus is son of God not a slave in God's house. He's not a part of the building; he's the builder. And it goes without saying that the builder is greater than the thing built. Is not the farmer greater than the seed he plants or the crop he harvests? As the sculptor is sublimer than the statue he carves, or the singer than the song, so Jesus, the builder, is greater than Moses, a part of the thing built. All men are important. All bear some of the image of God. But as important as a man may be he is less significant in the total building than Christ the builder. Under any descriptive figure of speech Christ is superior than any man. Even looking on Christ as a "stone" in the building, he has "become the head of the corner." By any measure Christ is the greatest, he who has the preeminence over men and angels. The son is greater than the servant.

Consider this Jesus

The text of 3:1-2 labels Jesus with three epithets. He is the "apostle and high priest of our confession." He is also "faithful." The word "apostle" means messenger; one sent off on a special mission. He is an ambassador, carrying in his mission the authority of him who sent him. He exerts the full weight of his master on those who benefit from his mission. As a matter of fact he has power of attorney; legally he is one and the same as his sender. So, as apostle, Jesus was sent on a mission of redemption. In what he said and did he represented God to man. The night before his cross he prayed, "I glorified you on earth, having accomplished the work which you gave me to do" (Jn. 17:4). He declared to Pilate, For this was I born . . ." (Jn. 18:37). So, he confessed having a specific mission in the world. Indeed, the apostleship of Jesus is a major part of "our confession." He came to save sinners. This was his mission of mercy in our behalf. When we waver and doubt, when the storms blow heavy and hard, when our grasp of salvation begins to slip, turn the mind to Jesus, consider carefully Jesus as God's envoy of salvation to us.

Hold the mind also on Jesus as high priest. As apostle he represents the power and authority of God for men. But in the same person we have an effective representative of our sinful selves before God. He is our high priest. Ladened with guilt what can men do in the highest court of heaven? Stained and calloused in conscience where can man find relief without a priest? Christ's mission as apostle was to do the work of high priest. To remove the guilt and relieve the conscience. This high priestly work of Jesus is also a major point in "our confession." When the paralysis of doubt comes, when the freezing blight of uncertainty descends, then consider with care the high priestly work of Jesus. Without Jesus as priest there is no light at the end of the tunnel, no star in the midnight darkness of human misery. Guilt will disappear, weak conscience will grow strong, the stain of sin will be expunged by our high priest, Jesus. Consider well this high priest.

Consider that he is "faithful." He is trustworthy; we can count on him. In a world of disrupted promises and broken contracts consider how reliable is the pledged word and work of this Jesus. He has given his word that he has power on earth to forgive sin, that he can and will break the hold of death, that there is salvation for the sinful, and life beyond death. He is "faithful" as God's apostle to man and man's priest before God. Trust him and live; doubt him and die! This is our choice!

The house which Jesus is building

The Hebrew letter says, ". . . whose house *we* are, . . ." We whose faith is rooted in "the apostle and high priest of our confession," even Jesus, *we* are the house of God.

Moses was faithful over a house of God. God had said

74

of Moses, "he is entrusted with all my house." This "house" was the "people of God" under the old covenant. Israel was God's house. But it was only after agonizing years and the severe judgment of Babylonian captivity that the "house of God" could be pried away from places and outward symbols. When the Jerusalem temple was demolished in 586 B.C. Yahweh no longer had a *place* where he could "dwell." This forced people to worship in groups wherever they could. Patterns of behavior, standards of admission were developed. In the outgrowing synagogue these patterns survived the return of the outward temple. They formed the framework on which the New Testament church patterned itself. And Jesus promised that he too would "build my church." Thus the concept of the new "people of God" being the house of God came to maturity. Paul could say to the church, "You know, don't you, that you are God's temple and the spirit of God dwells in you?" (I Cor. 3:16). The same author calls the church "the household of God" (I Tim. 3:15). And Peter speaks of believers as "living stones . . . built into a spiritual house, a holy priesthood to offer spiritual sacrifices acceptable to God through Jesus Christ" (I Peter 2:5). It seems obvious that the author of Hebrews has a similar view of the living church as the point of God's residence in this world of sight and sound. He affirms, ". . . whose house are *we* . . ."

That the church of God is the house of God, his dwelling place in this world, is an important fact. But people seem reluctant to grasp the idea. Men do not assemble *in* the church. They assemble *as* the church. God still does not dwell in temples made with man's hands. But he does dwell in the house which his son built, "whose house *we* are."

But there is a condition attached. "Whose house are *we*, *if* we hold fast our bold confidence and the boast characterized by hope firm unto the end." These early Hebrew Christians were on the verge of forfeiting all the advantages that God's "apostle and high priest" had brought into their lives. They were about to fall back from fulfillment to prophetic promise, from substance to shadow, from the graduating senior class to the elementary kindergarten. So the author urges on his readers this warning. In human beings, whose very moral nature involves choices, the personal result in each human life must entail an "if." Even when the appeal stems from an overpowering attraction of divine love, in a moral being the will must be freely exerted. Thus it is that believers must be persuaded to retain their bold confidence. They must not surrender their hard won hope. God *will* fulfill his promise. No disappointment or open opposition can change that fact of faith.

Be firm unto the end. Christ, the son, is superior to Moses the servant. God is among you, in you, and with you. Our "confession" contains the revelation of God's apostle. And it offers forgiveness through the ministry of our God-given high priest. Besides, you can count on Christ. He is "faithful" to him who appointed him as apostle and high priest. That's why we can rely on his promise. Be holding fast to faith firm unto the end until in the end faith will hold you fast.

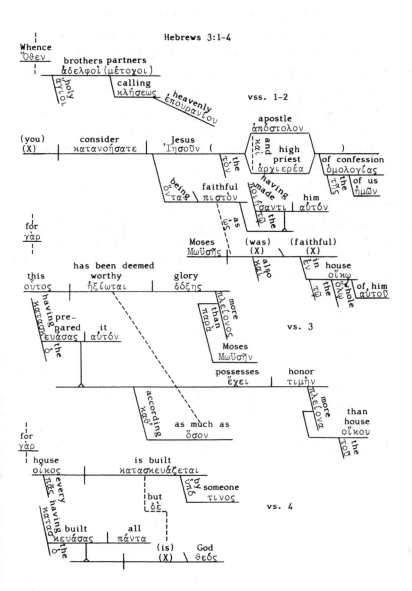

Hebrews 3:1-4

vss. 1-2

vs. 3

vs. 4

77

THE DIAGRAM OF 3:1-4

The complex sentence of 3:1-2 connects with the preceding idea by a strong "whence" or "from which." What follows, logically flows from the fact that Christ became human, suffered, and thus is able to fulfill our human needs. A vocative "brothers" amplified by "holy" indicates our sanctified destiny more than individual purity. As a family of brothers the appositional "partakers" suggests a sharing in some objective reality. That is defined by "heavenly calling." Quite an extended address!

The main clause exhorts, "consider Jesus." *What* we're to consider about him is in a compound apposition "apostle and high priest." *That* about his apostleship and high priesthood which we should consider is expressed by present active circumstantial participal "being faithful. . . ." The *standard* by which his faithfulness is compared shows up in the adverbial ὡς clause, "as Moses was faithful. . . ." The point action of aorist κατανοήσατε does not deny that we repeatedly hold our minds on Jesus but it does emphatically urge that a determined decision be settled on. Such definite determination will shore up wavering faith of unstable souls.

The form into which verse three falls is also complex. It has one independent element, "this one has been deemed worthy of glory. . . ." The perfect tense ἠξίωται proposes the permanency of Christ's glory more than the historic point at which the glory became his. His glory is an abiding reality, not just a past conferral at a point in history.

παρὰ after comparative πλείονος followed by accusative Μωϋσῆν presents the degree of glory with which he has been forever endowed. The same comparative in the independent clause is followed by ablative οἴκου to express degree. Also note genitive δόξης appears as object of verb of mental action ἠξίωται whereas accusative τιμὴν is object of ἔχει in the dependent clause. This dependent clause is an adverbial idea of comparison introduced by the phrase "according (to this measure) as much as." ὅσον is a quantitative relative pronoun suggesting how much. Subject in this clause is aorist active attributive participle κατασκευάσας, the one having prepared. Its direct object αὐτόν is masculine agreeing in gender with οἴκου but translated "it."

Verse four embodies a compound sentence of two clauses. "Every house is built by someone" and "the one having built all things (is) God." Linear action present κατασκευάζεται contrasts with point action participle κατασκευάσας. The present calls attention to a distributive notion, "everyone, this one, this one, and this one. . . . It also implies a continuous process of building. The aorist offers the fact as fact that God builds "all things."

The term "house" as used in these sentences quite obviously refers to something more than a house of stone and mortar. During the Babylonian captivity the Jews had to get along without a temple. God had no *place* in which to dwell! The Lord *had* to live elsewhere than in a house made with men's hands. Groups of people began to assemble for prayer and exhortation. This *community* of levitically "clean" people became thought of as a temple of God. So the "house of God" was a community of people.

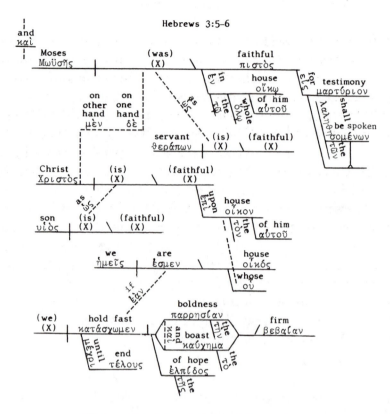

THE DIAGRAM OF 3:5-6

This is compound-complex. The independent ideas are sharply contrasted by μὲν . . . δὲ. "Moses was faithful . . . Christ is faithful." They were equally faithful. The contrast is the *position* in the house, one a "servant," the other "son." θεράπων is one who *freely* serves, nevertheless, a servant with no inheritance. "Son" is heir, therefore greater. The adverb ὡς introduces two comparative clauses. οὗ brings in an adjective idea identifying "whose house." Pronoun ἡμεῖς is very emphatic, "whose house *we* who believe in Jesus are." "We" are the covenant "people of

God!" ἐάν is 3rd class conditional leaving open whether we will or won't hold fast. Aorist tense κατάσχωμεν reflects the idea of clutching tightly, grasping firmly. It was a decisive act done once-for-all. Certainly we would continue to hold. But the aorist fixes attention on the decisive, effective act of grabbing hold.

A Translation

Hebrews 3:7-19

Wherefore, just as the Holy Spirit says, "Today, if you will hear his voice, don't harden your hearts as in the embitterment, according to the day of testing in the desert, where your fathers tried (me) in testing and saw my works forty years. Wherefore, I got angry with this generation and said, 'They are always deceiving the heart!' But they did not get to know my ways. So I swore in my wrath, 'If they shall enter into my rest, (I am not God).'"

Be taking heed, brothers, lest ever (an) evil heart of unbelief shall be in any one of you so as to apostasize from living God. But be exhorting yourselves daily while it is called 'Today,' that no one of you become hardened by the deceit of sin. For we have become partners of the Christ, if indeed we hold fast the fundamental assurance firm unto (the) end, while saying, 'Today, if you will hear his voice, don't harden your hearts as in the embitterment.'"

For who, having heard, got embittered? Yea! Did not all the ones who came out of Egypt through Moses? But with whom did he become angry forty years? was it not with the ones who sinned, whose carcases fell in the desert? But to whom did he sware (that they were) not to enter into his rest if not the ones who disobeyed? And we see that they were unable to enter because of unbelief."

AN OUTLINE OF HEBREWS 3:7-19
A PATTERN OF APOSTASY

In a world such as ours apostasy is an ever-present threat. Many siren voices allure us to turn from our commitment of faith.

I. PATTERN OF APOSTASY. vss. 7-15
  1. The "fathers" tested God. 8
  2. God gave extensive evidence for forty years. 9-10a
  3. Human hearts "deceived . . . they knew not my ways." 10b
  4. The Divine reaction. 11
    (a) God's wrath.
    (b) Refusal of entrance into the divine rest.

II. CAUSE OF APOSTASY. vss. 16-19
  1. Though escaping Egypt, the people "got bitter." 16
  2. The consequences: a whole generation died. 17
  3. Failure to enter caused by unbelief. 18-19

III. CURE FOR APOSTASY. vs. 14
  1. Partners with Christ. vs. 14a
  2. Steadily "holding fast." 14b

IV. EXHORTATION TO AVOID APOSTASY. vss. 12-13
  1. Watch *your* heart—that's personal. 12
  2. Mutual support—that's social. 13a
  3. Do this daily—be constantly alert. 13b

While it is called, "Today." Procrastination is Satan's best weapon.

SOME EXPOSITORY THOUGHTS ON HEBREWS 3:7-19

In a world in which evil intimidates good and Satan enslaves God's creation the threat of apostasy is ever present. Too many siren voices sing their alluring tunes for anyone to take his relationship to God for granted. Past confession is no guarantee of present obedience. Former faith doesn't discard today's doubt. The tragedy of yesterday's saint being today's sinner has repeated itself too many times through history for anyone to treat lightly personal Christian faith.

Joe Doe had devoted Christian parents. From the Beginners' through High School he enjoyed exposure to Christian teaching from dedicated saints. Even college experiences deepened his Christian faith. As deacon, elder, teacher, counsellor and friend he was idealized by a growing band of believers. He was "pillar of the faith" furnishing strong pattern for oncoming young believers. As husband and father he showed the whole community an exemplary pattern of behaviour. But there came a change. Joe Doe's children married and moved away. His wife died. Someone overlooked him, misinterpreted his motives. Besides, he hungered for the warmth of an understanding companion. Joe began to miss church occasionally. After a year he disappeared entirely from the congregation. Then one day the police called his oldest son. Joe Doe was found dead in a house of prostitution. Is the story overdrawn? With the exception of the name it is a recitation of a factual experience. How often does such a story happen? Who knows?

Secret doubts are kept secret. Works of darkness are

done in darkness, especially those of saints. They are covered over with a thick blanket of conformity. Apostasy is not the abnormal but the normal human experience. Abandonment of Christ and his church is more frequent than church rolls indicate. The record of the soul is kept in the heart of God—even more than in the mind of the apostate himself. For who cannot but rationalize his own behaviour and justify his own faithlessness?

The historic pattern of apostasy

The history of the people of Israel not only offers a pattern for faith it furnishes a prototype of apostasy. A forsaking of faith that repeats itself over and over. It was at Massah in the desert when Israel was parched with thirst that the people "tested" God. They rebelled against Yahweh and pricked Moses into arranging a "proving" of the Lord. "Your fathers tested me by contending with me in the wilderness." This is the classic example of repudiation! The religious and psychological principles involved in all apostasy the people of Israel displayed in the sandy wastes of Sinai.

Apostasy is never caused by want of evidence of God's presence or blessing. "They saw my works forty years." The marvel of the Red Sea escape, the gushing water from the desert granite when Moses bludgeoned the rock at Massah, the defeat of Amelek at Rephidim when Aaron and Hur held up the wavering hands of Moses,—these and myriads of other such "signs" evidence the presence of the living God to lead, support, defend and bless a people seeking a homeland with its promise of peace, rest and security.

And have we not shared in even more of God's providences? Prophet, apostle, and 2000 years of Christian history have multiplied examples of God's rescuing his people from crisis after crisis. Though Christian people have suffered through fire, famine, poverty, sickness and death as is the common lot of all humanity yet God has seen them triumphantly *through* such distresses, not overpowered by them. And when occasion merited *from* them! We do not lack evidence that God "works all things for good."

But Israel "deceived" its heart. They "knew not my ways." In spite of evidences or blessings self-willed people find ways of self-deception. They rationalize and do what they want. To "know the way" from New York to Boston does not mean the ability to locate the highway on a road map or to know its numerical symbol or the terrain over which it stretches. To "know the way" is to travel on it. To know God's ways is more than to have erudite information about his laws; it's to experience them, to do them, to struggle in life's conflicts with them as the norm of behaviour. Israel had cerebral apprehension without day-to-day obedience. They preferred intellectual perception to participation in God's moral absolutes. They were self-deceived; they "knew not his ways." How many have followed in their train?

And how does God act in view of such action? "As I sware in my wrath, if they shall enter into my rest, (then I am not God)." God does not get "mad." His anger is not reckless, rash, impatient pique. When a man leaps off a New York skyscraper God isn't mad at him. But his divine wrath takes effect in a crushed, broken body. To such defiance of physical law death is the expression of God's wrath. The same was true with Israel. God's wrath is the reaction of a righteous, moral God to any immoral, disbelieving disobedience to divine moral law. The consequence was death! Death for an entire generation. As sure

86

as God is God no man can enter into God's rest when he ignores the moral absolutes that are rooted in God's righteous nature. So Israel did not enter! Such is the pattern of apostasy in history.

The cause of apostasy

It's an "evil heart of disbelief" that lays the groundwork for falling away. Who got "bitter" and "rebelled" against Moses and God? And "to whom did he sware that they should not enter into his rest, but to those who were disobedient?" The author adds a companion idea, "We see they were unable to enter because of disbelief." Disbelief is not a matter of the mind; it's an act of the will. This is apparent from the author's joining "obedience" in verse 18 with "disbelief" in verse 19. To obey is to believe and to believe is to obey. And they did neither. As a consequence they became apostates while still moving among the people of God's promise. It's a paradox of the wilderness that men could disobey (another term for disbelieve) amid the forty years of witnessing the marvels of God's leadership. Sustained by manna, entering into conscious covenant contract they knew they were "the people of God" yet they "disbelieved." In the crises they failed to trust! Hence they "disobeyed."

The cure for apostasy

To suggest a cure for apostasy seems a contradiction. The idea implies a decisive repudiation. Yet provision is made for preventing final treason. In fact the epistle is designed to help avoid the pattern of Israel's rebellion. What was their salvation?

87

Verse 14 advances two counsels. The first is a statement: "We have become partners of the Christ." The proverb "a chain is no stronger than its weakest link" is reversed by the person of Christ. In my partnership with Christ, from weakness I'm made strong. I participate in his strength. That is particularly true with the chinks in my spiritual armor. Three times Paul petitioned that he be relieved of the painful, humiliating "thorn in the flesh." Three times God refused but not without promise, "my grace is sufficient for you, for my power is made perfect in weakness." Paul's bouyant response was, "For the sake of Christ I am content with weaknesses, insults, hardships, persecutions, and calamities; for when I'm weak then am I strong." The purpose of partnership is mutual support. It's when I exercise my partnership with Christ that I am strong at my point of doubt, disbelief and disobedience. Trust in Christ staves off apostasy. A viable partnership with Him eliminates the danger.

But that partnership is conditional: "if" I hold fast "firm unto the end" the underlying "essence" of him whom I trusted when I launched this Christian journey. When the end matches the beginning then temptation to apostasy has been conquered. *Any* deviation is a danger inviting defeat!

Exhortation to avoid apostasy

The text offers three admonitions. First, "take heed lest there be in any one of *you*. . ." *You* watch *your* heart. If I'm to guard against my being an apostate the place to begin is with *me*. That's very personal. Attention to someone else's danger can quite possibly cause me to lose my balance and fall into the same stormy waters that endanger my troubled friend. *I* must be strong. A life guard who has become anemic or lost his skill cannot save himself nor a drowning swimmer. It's wise to "take heed to thyself."

But as much as for myself my own strength is for the sake of someone else. The text urges that we "exhort one another. . . ." This is our obligation as a society of people who travel together. When we share in weakness we multiply our strength. When we identify in troubles we increase our prospects for victory. One stick by itself won't create a fire but many sticks together can heat a whole house. Mountain climbers link themselves together that none shall be lost should any stumble. We need each other for any one of us to be saved from apostasy. Indeed I must "take heed to myself" and then share strength with another.

This is to be done "daily." As long as it is called "today" must I "take heed" to myself and "exhort one another." Satan has no better weapon than "wait until tomorrow to do what is right." If it's right it's right right now! Tomorrow is too late! Therefore, take heed today! Exhort today! For "today is the day of salvation." *Now* is "the acceptable time."

Hebrews 3:7-11

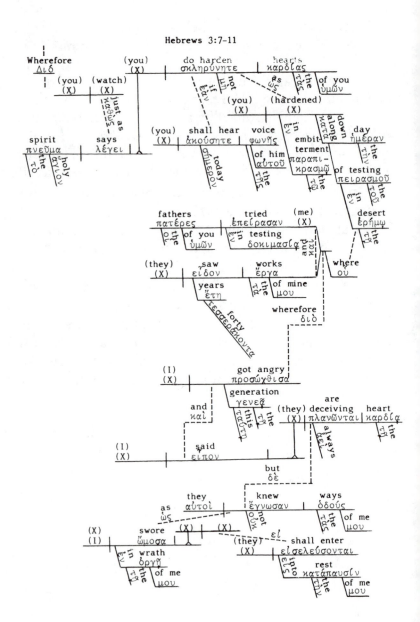

90

THE DIAGRAM OF HEBREWS 3:7-11

A diagram is an attempt to pictorialize in an eye-catching form the flow of thought in a sentence. The consistently logical author doesn't write with a diagram consciously in mind. Both logic and clear thought make diagramming easier. But neither are called in just for the sake of diagram. Hence there are times when a diagram must be tentative, even arbitrary, in the way in which it pictures thought. This is especially true when an author inserts a quotation from another author. So it is in Hebrews 3:7-15.

In Nestle's text 3:7-11 is punctuated as one sentence. But *as* it appears in the text there is *no* independent idea. The sentence begins with comparative adverbial clause controlled by καθώς, "just as the Holy Spirit says. . . ." The substance of what he says is pictured in twelve dependent clauses. But no independent idea appears in verses 7-11. So the diagram must borrow the independent exhortation "you watch" or "you be taking heed" from βλέπετε of the sentence of 3:12-15. The sentence is an urgent exhortation, "you be watching just as the Holy Spirit says." In formal structure this is a complex sentence.

First comes the noun clause, object of "says." "Do not harden your hearts. . . ." From that stems two adverbial clauses. (1) "as you hardened in the embitterment . . ." (2) and the third class conditional "today, if you hear his voice. . . ."

Two adjective clauses follow. They describe "desert" (ἐρήμῳ) in terms of certain circumstances which occurred in that desert of trial, "your fathers tried (me)" and "they saw my works forty years." ἔτη is adverbial accusative expressing extent of time.

91

The next two clauses, "I got angry" and "I said" state additional details that happened while Israel was in that desert. God "got angry." προσώχθισα is ingressive aorist suggesting that God entered into anger out of which arose a threatening statement. So God "said." εἶπον is also aorist that suggests the critical urgency of what God says. The content of what he says is introduced by the noun-object clauses "they always are deceiving their heart" and "they didn't get to know my ways."

The adverb ὡς inserts an idea correlating the disbelieving, disobedient hearts of the Hebrews with God's oath, "as I swore in my wrath. . . ." Precisely *what* God swore in his wrath shows up in a noun clause, not stated but plainly implied by the context. *Something* has to be supplied by the reader or the author's idea is left hanging in the air. Whatever we supply is supported by the εἰ (if) clause, a first class conditional, "if they shall enter." The very absence of a stated conclusion (apodosis) gives even greater force to what the reader supplies to the stated condition (protasis). Whatever is supplied must be very strong. In our translation we have filled out the oath with "I am not God." So the sentence says, "If they ever enter into my rest (and I'll assume that they will) then in that case I am not God." Such a sentence is the strongest kind of statement that indicates that the unbelieving, disobedient will never enjoy the blessings of God's rest.

Hebrews 3:12-15

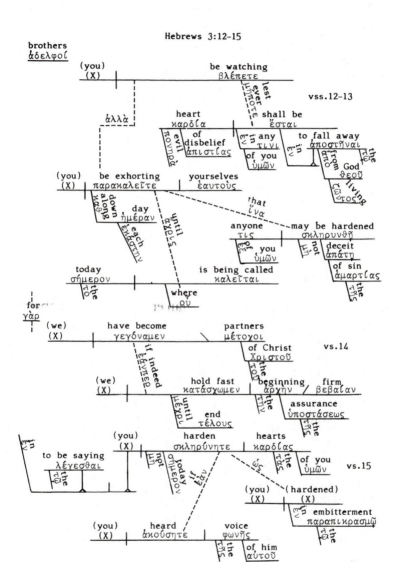

THE DIAGRAM OF HEBREWS 3:12-15

A diagram helps unravel an author's thought. He has compacted his ideas in a closely knit fabric of words, phrases, clauses so related as to articulate a message. To a kindred mind a diagram images the relationships and un-weaves the warp and woof of the sentence. The sentence of 3:12-13 has five clauses. The warp is formed by two independent exhortations both of which use linear action present imperatives. "Be watching (continuously) . . . be encouraging one another (continuously). . . ." The woof threads into the textile of the sentence three subordinate clauses.

Stitched to the first of the independent clauses is the negative purpose clause, "lest ever (an) evil heart of dis-belief shall be. . . ." Such an adverbial idea lends support to this first exhortation by proposing the reason why the readers should "be watching" so alertly and continuously. Instead of an expected subjunctive the negative purpose appears with μήποτε and future indicative ἔσται. The use of indicative after a verb of apprehension suggests that the clause has almost an independent force. "You be watch-ing; perhaps in one of you shall be an evil heart of disbelief." The seriousness of such disbelief is urged by the genitive ἀπιστίας. It was a rebellious disbelief, not just passive un-belief. Also is added the strong aggressive adjective πονηρὰ, *active* evil. The ἐν with aorist infinitive labels the disbelief as to how wicked it really is; "in falling away from living God."

The second independent exhortation presents an insistent supplement by use of the climacteric conjunction ἀλλὰ, "yea, be exhorting yourselves. . . ." The purpose of such constant encouragement follows in the adverbial ἵνα clause, "that anyone may not be hardened. . . ." In terms of time, the extent to which such self-stimulation should continue finds utterance in the adverb clause ushered in by ἄχρις οὗ, "until which point *today* is being called." In other words, as long as time runs or life lasts. Allow no let up in alert self-examination and mutual helping.

Verse 14, by means of two clauses, forges a complex sentence. "We have become partners of Christ" is the independent assertion. Perfect "have become" calls attention to the fact that what one "has become" he still is now. Of course the present standing as *partners* is conditioned: "if indeed we hold fast. . . ." This is 3rd class conditional with περ added to ἐάν to intensify the idea. βεβαίαν is an objective complement, "as a firm thing."

As the diagram shows it verse 15 is not a complete sentence. The author refers to the quote from Psalm 95 of verse 8 above and uses it as a means of introducing his series of rhetorical questions of verses 16-19. This connection with verse 16 is insured by the "for" which introduces the first of the questions, "for who got embittered?" Considering the structure of verse 15 the infinitive phrase "in the saying" introduces the quote. The quote divides into three clauses the first of which ("don't harden etc.") serves as direct object of the infinitive. The "if" clause presents a 3rd class condition. ὡς injects a comparative adverb clause. As suggested, the idea of the verse serves as preparatory to the questions which follow and should be read with them in mind.

Hebrews 3:16–19

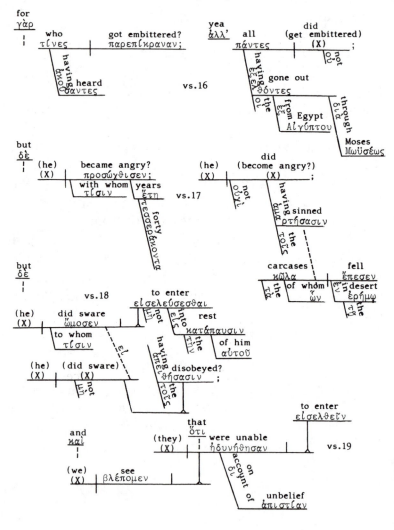

THE DIAGRAM OF HEBREWS 3:16-19

The sentences of 3:16-19 are six in number, in pattern three simple and three complex. The first four are rhetorical questions and are paired so as to have a question answer a question. Having launched in verse 15 a warning of Israel's historic wilderness rebellion the author proposes to enforce it by asking, "For who, having heard, got embittered?" This is a simple interrogative idea. "Having heard" represents a temporal circumstantial participle describing the "who" as exercising their bitter insurrection, not in ignorance, but with full knowledge for they "heard." And *after* they heard they revolted. παρεπίκραναν is aorist which, is conjunction with perfective use of preposition παρά, focuses the desert rebellion as a sharply defined experience even though the bitterness may have been quite extensive, as indeed it was. The second sentence of verse 16, also simple in structure, answers the first question with a question. "Yea, did not all . . . get embittered?" The negative οὐ in the question expects "yes" for an answer. The participle translated "ones having gone out" is attributive. ἐξ with ablative exhibits origin; διά with genitive declares the agent through which.

Verse seven displays a similar pair of sentences in which a second question answers a first. "But with whom did he become angry?" This raises the question of God's action in view of the people's mutiny. The "forty years" is accusative extent of time. This would suggest that the people's initial rebellion did not exhaust itself in their first uprising. It was repeated during the entire wilderness wanderings. So God's wrath extended that long.

Here again the answering question has in it the fatal negative οὐχὶ which expects the inevitable "yes" for answer.

"Did he not become angry with those who sinned whose carcases fell. . . .?" "Yes he did!" This second sentence of verse 17 is complex due to the adjective clause, "whose carcases fell. . . ." The death of a whole generation was the result of 40 years rebellion accompanied by 40 years of divine anger.

The sentence of verse 18 is also a rhetorical question but it does not depend on a paired second sentence for its answer. It has within it an "if" clause plus the direct object infinitive phrase that makes clear what the answer truly is. "To whom did he sware (that they were) not to enter into his rest, if he didn't sware to those who disobeyed?" The obvious answer is, "To no one!" In fact, the declarative sentence of verse 19 is a conclusion drawn not only in answer to this question of verse 18 but also in answer to the whole series of ideas proposed in 16 through 18 inclusive. In structure both 18 and 19 are complex sentences.

The καὶ with which verse 19 opens has the force of "and so." It introduces the conclusion of the argument. "We see" is present expressing continuous action. It may include the distributive idea. Each of his readers "sees." *They* were not yet and hopefully wouldn't be a part of those who were "unable to enter on account of disbelief." The sentence shows indirect discourse with ὅτι after verb of seeing.

A Translation
Hebrews 4:1-10

So then let us fear lest ever (a) promise being left to enter into his rest anyone of you think to have fallen short. For we have had good news announced to us as also they; but the word of hearing didn't profit them not having mixed itself with faith with the ones who heard. For we, the ones having believed, are entering into the rest, just as he has said,

As I swore in my wrath,

If they shall enter into my rest (I'm not God).
Even though the works became from the foundation of the world. For he has said somewhere concerning the seventh (day) thus:

And God rested on the seventh day from all his works,

And in this (place) again,

If they shall enter into my rest.

Since then that someone enter into it is left and that the ones having had good news announced did not enter on account of unbelief, he again designates (a) certain day, today, saying in David after such long time just as he has before said,

Today, if you shall hear his voice

Do not harden your hearts.
For if Joshua gave them rest he would not be speaking concerning another (day) after these days. Therefore, a Sabbath rest remains for the people of God. For he, the one who entered into his rest,

came to rest from his works, as indeed God did from his.

AN OUTLINE OF HEBREWS 4:1-10
A SABBATH REST FOR GOD'S PEOPLE

That men need rest is no marvel. But that God needs "rest" seems strange. The answer lies in the meaning of the term "rest."

I. THE UNREALIZED SABBATH REST
1. "They" heard good news but never entered Canaan. vs. 2
2. The 7th day Sabbath didn't fulfill the *meaning* of Sabbath.
3. In David's time the meaning of Sabbath still unrealized. vs. 7

II. GOD'S ONGOING REST REMAINS
1. God's rest been going on since creation. 3b-4
2. God intends for human beings to enter his rest. 6-7
3. "There remains a Sabbath rest for God's people" 9

III. ENTERING GOD'S REST
1. The good news to "us" is redemption from sin. vs. 2a
2. After starting "they" failed. Why? vs. 2b
3. Believers who don't yield up their faith enter. 3, 10

"Let us fear lest ever a promise being left we should fail to enter!

SOME EXPOSITORY THOUGHTS ON HEBREWS 4:1-10

When men get tired they rest. This is so normal that there seems nothing strange about it. Industry and labor recognize the need for vacations. To renew energy and to get fresh perspective each human being needs regular periods of refreshment. That men need rest is no marvel.

But that God needs rest is a paradox if not an outright contradiction. Is he who created the heavens and the earth so drained of energy, so haggard and bushed he needs time to recuperate? To ask the question is to answer it. The very idea of God leaves such a thing impossible! What then does "God rested" mean?

The meaning of the term "rest" is not to be determined by human nature, particularly that scarred by sin. It must be derived from the divine nature. God's "rest" is the prototype by which man's "rest" *ought* be measured. Cessation of labor for one to be rejuvenated rises from the fallen state of humanity. That wasn't at all the original concept of rest. After creation God didn't need to catch his breath. Yet after the six period process of creating God did enter into his "rest."

At the close of each day of creation a refrain appears in the Genesis account, "and there was evening and there was morning." But when the seventh day comes no such comment is made. The Sabbath "rest" into which God entered was timeless and ageless in its range. God's rest lasts through time and eternity. It's forever! Both for God and for any man who chooses to enter. After six days God ceased his creative activity, he "rested . . . from all his work" but not from laboring with his works. When Jesus was challenged for breaking the Sabbath He defended himself by referring to God's continuing labor in caring for his universe. "My father is working still, and I am working" (Jn. 5:17). So God's "rest" means more than just cessation from work. It means the entering into the joy and satisfaction of a job well done. It means the continuing pleasure derived from involvement in one's creation. It's like an author who, having finished his research, his relentless task of writing, its revision, polishing and refinement, sits down and reads his own book with *relaxed pleasure.* That is pure rest! The gratifying sense of accomplishment gives an inward warmth of satisfaction to anyone, God included, who is creative by nature. No outward threat or tumult, no inward discord ever scars such a peaceful "rest." For sinful man to enter God's "rest" means relief from the burden of guilt, pursuit of the purpose of life with the joy and peace of a right relationship to God. It means to be at peace with oneself and one's Creator! It begins at conversion and extends through time and eternity!

The unrealized Sabbath rest

God's promised rest was never attained under Old Testament conditions. When Israel left Egypt "they had good news announced to them." But those who began the journey to the promised land with such high hopes "fell short." Their "carcasses fell in the wilderness." They never entered Canaan and so never realized the fulfillment of even that limited promise of rest. But no such physical rest as a national homeland with political independence, material prosperity, and martial security could begin to give full meaning to the concept of "God's rest."

Lest someone should fall into the error of thinking that

an independent nation in Palestine could ever fulfill the promise of divine rest David, who lived so long time after Joshua, plainly declared in the 95th Psalm that "they (the Israelites under Joshua) shall not enter into my rest." There's simply no way that any outward political national unit be the "rest" of God. And that's true whether under Joshua, or David, or Ben Gurion or Menachin Begin. At best such caricatures are but signs and symbols of the idea involved in the "rest of God."

Nor does the seventh-day weekly Sabbath fulfill the *meaning* of "God rested from all his work." As a matter of fact God gave man the weekly seventh-day Sabbath as a *reminder* of his true Sabbath rest. The weekly Sabbath was a sign pointing to something far more meaningful than a cessation from vocational toil of the week. The seven-day Sabbath fulfilled a need in the physical life of man as he must live it in this world. But that's a far cry from the redemptive rest from sin that men find in Christ. Not to mention the fulfilling of the "image of God" for which they have been created. So the conclusion of the matter is, "There remains a Sabbath rest for the people of God."

God's ongoing rest remains

The creative works of God have been "completed from the foundation of the world." On the achievement of those works God "entered into his rest." And God's rest has been an ongoing reality ever since. From the beginning it has been his intent that humanity should enter into and enjoy his rest. In fact he placed our first parents right in the midst of his "rest," a perfect rest of peace with themselves and their God in an ideal environment. But Adam and Eve failed.

103

And the Israelites failed at the time of Joshua. And at the time of David! Nor does the seventh-day weekly Sabbath, or the jubilee Sabbath year, nor any other "festival, new moon or Sabbath" fulfill the meaning of God's rest. These things are "only a shadow . . . the substance is Christ" (Col. 2:17).

But God is insistent and persistent. He resolutely appoints another "Today" in which men will be invited into his rest. He is determined that "someone" shall enter into his rest. So it is that with the coming of Jesus as the Christ the offer of God's rest can now be fulfilled to its ultimate. Nothing is to be expected beyond that which Christ as man's redeemer offers. In him we may enter God's rest. That rest in which God himself lives and into which any man who chooses faith may enter. "Come unto me, all who labor and are heavy laden, and I will give you rest. Take my yoke upon you, and learn from me; for I am gentle and lowly in heart, and you will find rest for your souls" (Matt. 11:28f.). Such is the meaning of God's promised rest whether it be pictured under the figure of a weekly Sabbath, an earthly national heritage, or one's own personal "success" in a this-world earthy environment.

Experiencing the "rest" of God!

"We have had good news announced to us as also they; but the word of hearing did not profit them, not having mixed with faith with the ones who heard." Both "we" and "they" heard good news. "They" about redemption from humiliation and bondage of slavery of Pharaoh in a foreign land. "We" about redemption from the Egypt of our sin in an alien society. "They" looked to a land and life of their own in their own country. "We" to a freedom in the power of the promises of the gospel. "They" failed to enter into their hoped for land of promise. With them the issue has been settled. But with "us" the issue is still open. Will "we" fail or enter?

Why, after starting, did they fail? Is it possible that we learn our lesson from their failure? It's important to notice that "they" were not atheists, agnostics, rebels or renegades when they started. They had "heard" the good news. Being intensely human, some of them may have had some misgivings about their long journey through sandy wastes and rugged, trackless mountain land. But they heard the word and promise of God through Moses. They acknowledged enough of the word of Moses at least to begin the journey. But the text says, "the word of hearing did not get itself mixed with faith." That was the reason for their failure to enter. The faltering of their faith under the pressures of the desert life eroded their confidence in God and his promises. In the final analysis they preferred a stomach full of lentils and garlic in bondage than promises parched with sandy grit and only a fantasy of freedom. Belief broke under the responsibility of trust. They did not enter in "because of disbelief."

One must begin in order to enter. But to enter God's rest one must do more than begin. The text says that "the ones who get faith" are the "we" who "are entering into his rest." It is significant that the word translated "are entering" reflects the linear action describing a process going on, not just a past fixed point of faith. Those who actually enter after their promising beginning are those whose persistent faith does not falter under the disheartenments of the difficult journey. One enters God's rest when faith in

Christ takes over. But faith is also a process enabling a man to surmount all obstacles that hinder his final entrance.

Exhortation to enter

These things "were written for our admonition upon whom the end of the ages has come." The author of Hebrews enlightens the minds of his readers with true teaching. But he interrupts his doctrinal revelation to give practical exhortations. One must not only *know* the truth but he must be *persuaded to obey* it. Hence he pleads, "Let *us* be zealous to enter into that rest that no one should fall by the same pattern of disobedience." If faith fails, we fall; if we hold fast to faith we not only begin to enjoy the rest of God we shall share in it through all eternity.

Hebrews 4:1-3

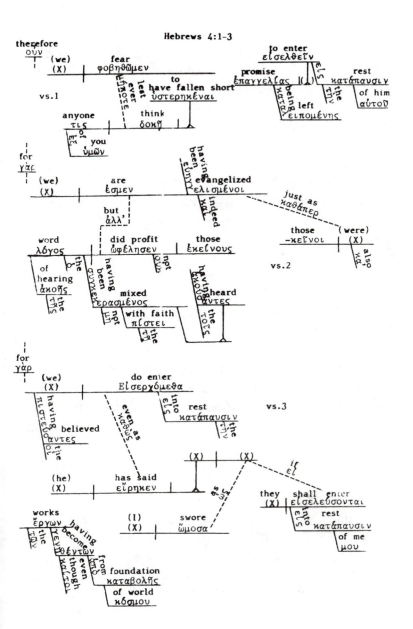

THE DIAGRAM OF HEBREWS 4:1-3

Verse one incorporates one independent clause, one dependent, and a genitive absolute. The term "absolute" indicates that the expression has no formal grammatical relationship to the rest of the sentence. However, the context makes clear a connection in thought. Here this one reads, ". . . promise being left to enter into his rest. . . ." The infinitive "to enter" is in apposition to the noun "promise" defining exactly *what* the promise is that is "being left."

φοβηθῶμεν is a first aorist passive volitive subjunctive, "Let us fear. . . ." It is an appeal to the will. The compound negative μήποτε is used with present subjunctive δοκῇ. "lest ever anyone of you should be thinking." This verb "think" stresses the subjective element in thinking. Why should anyone think (feel) that he had "fallen short" of the promise of rest? Because he had attached himself to the crucified Jesus and forsaken the panorama of Hebrew sacrificial ritual!!

The next sentence joins two independent clauses to assure the compound flavor. The first is supported by a comparative adverbial dependent introduced by καθάπερ (just as) which adds the complex aspect. The first independent is positive; the second negative. Adversative conjunction ἀλλ' connects them. ". . . we have indeed been evangelized . . . but the word . . . did not profit those. . . ." Note graphic contrast between the vivid periphrastic perfect indicative passive "we are having been evangelized" (ἐσμεν εὐηγγελισμένοι) of the first clause and historic aorist "didn't profit" (ὠφέλησεν) of the second. The periphrastic perfect gives extra stress to the continuance of the past fact. We still live under the responsibility of the announcement of good news. But though the Israelites carried their responsibility for forty years the fact they failed to profit is presented as a single past event. Tense has to do with what an author wants his readers to visualize regardless of how the action took place at the time.

Circumstantial perfect participle συγκεκερασμένος modifies the noun λόγος in the diagram rather than ἐκείνους as in some texts. "The word characterized by hearing (genitive ἀκοῆς) never did get itself mixed with faith." Whenever good news is heard it must infiltrate and get mixed with faith if it's to be effective.

Verse three admits of six clauses besides a genitive absolute. But only one is independent. "We are entering . . ." Εἰσερχόμεθα is present indicative active. It is descriptive of a process going on. It may also suggest a distributive idea. It is futuristic but not exclusively so. Aorist circumstantial participle πιστεύσαντες suggests antecedent action "(we), the ones having believed. . . ." The convert to Christ at the point when he believes enters into God's rest. That rest reaches its ultimate beyond death but the peace and satisfaction of God's redemptive rest begins at the moment of the obedience of faith, a restoration of the "rest" lost by our first parents in Eden. This is all "just as" (καθὼς) we should expect in view of what he "has said." The noun clause, object of "has said" is entirely eliptical. It must be supplied from context. The genitive absolute is concessive in force, ". . . even though the works having become. . . ."

Hebrews 4:4-7

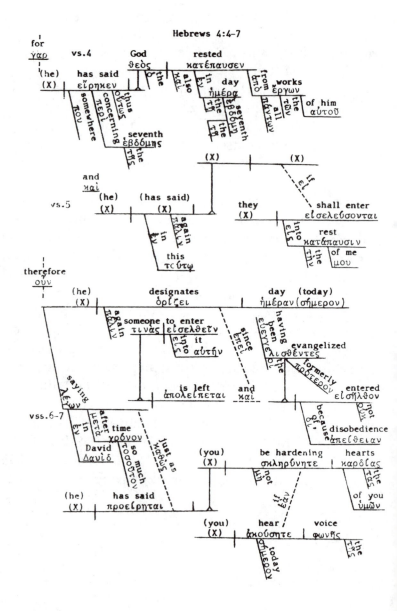

110

THE DIAGRAM OF 4:4-7

If verses four and five are viewed as separate sentences they shape up as complex. But if the conjunction "and" is meant to join them into one sentence then it is compound-complex. The diagram presents them as two sentences though quite closely related. In fact in verse five both the main clause, "he has said," and the dependent noun clause, object of "has said," are implied by and borrowed from the construction of verse four. The noun-object clause of verse five possibly should be, "I am not God" or some kindred idea. Such a supplied thought furnishes the apodosis to the adverbial "if" clause. εἰ introduces a first class conditional which assumes the condition to be true. The condition does not state a fact but the *assumption* of fact. Conditionals deal with presuppositions in order to draw logical conclusions. Such conclusions are not based on reality or unreality but on the *assumption* of reality or unreality. Conditionals are a device of logic.

The structure of the sentence of verses 6-7 is complex. The main clause states, "He again designates (a) day . . ." Off of that hangs a pair of subordinate adverbial clauses of cause prefaced by "since." Subject of one of these clauses is the infinitive phrase, "that someone enter . . ." τινὰς is accusative of general reference used as if subject of infinitive. ἀπολείπεται is present tense intimating that an open door for entering God's rest continues to remain open. The second of the causal clauses give added strength to the idea of the independent clause, ". . . since the ones formerly having been gospelized did not enter. . . ." The reason why they didn't enter is found in the διά with accusative, "because of disobedience." Subject of the clause is the attributive participle "the ones having been gospelized. . . ."

111

Further amplifying the main clause is the circumstantial participle λέγων with its modifiers. καθὼς announces an adverbial clause of comparison, "just as he has said. . . ." As direct object of "has said" (προείρηται) is the noun clause, "don't be hardening your hearts." And this in turn is the apodosis of the third class conditional, "today if you hear the voice . . ." 3rd class suggests "and you probably will hear the voice. . . ."

For one to approach any adequate meaning to this whole passage one must determine the meaning of the term κατάπαυσις. The root of the word means "to cause to cease" or intransitively, "to cease," "desist," "restrain." But the biblical idea must not be taken from the human experience of need for rebuilding or renewing because of physical exhaustion. The meaning must be derived from the nature of God, not man in his weakened fallen state. God's "rest" must install in man a "rest" which accords with that of the divine nature. God was not *physically* fatigued at the end of six days of creation when he entered his "rest." He rested from his "works" but not from continuing labor as John 5:17 indicates. His rest was a peace, joy, fulfillment and satisfaction of a task well done. He was at peace with himself with no discord, jar or disturbance within. Rest was a going on to enjoy his creative work as he sustained its performance.

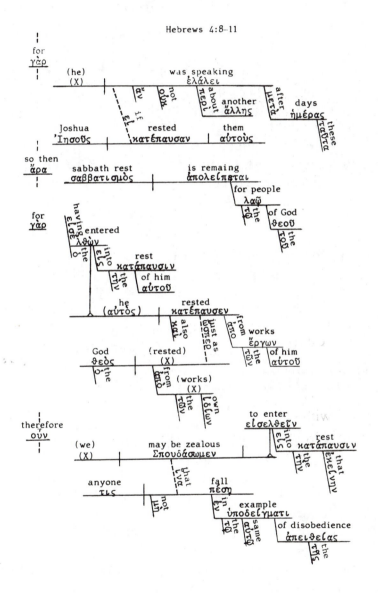

113

THE DIAGRAM OF 4:8-11

The two clauses of verse 8 merge into a conditional complex sentence. "If Joshua rested them" is dependent. "He would not have spoken concerning another after these days" is independent. The εἰ with aorist indicative offers a second class condition determined as fulfilled. "If Joshua rested them" but he didn't, the "he would not have spoken . . ." but he did. Though a whole generation of Israelites died in the wilderness and thus never entered Canaan, their children did enter. To guard against any idea that *that* entrance into the promised land was the true fulfillment of the meaning of the Sabbath rest idea our author plainly declares, "if Joshua gave them rest etc. . . ."

From the preceding it is obvious that Israel's entrance into Canaan under Joshua did not exhaust the idea of rest as implanted in Genesis 2:2. So that there will be no doubt, and to reinforce the logic of verse 8 the author inserts a straightforward declaration introduced by ἄρα (so then). "Sabbath (rest) is remaining for the people of God." This is a simple sentence. Its very brevity and simplicity gives it directness and force. Through history Sabbath in its deepest significance remained unfulfilled.

σαββατισμός defines κατάπαυσις. More than mere cessation from work is involved in "rest." As a benefit of redemption "rest" has been present from the moment that "God rested" from his works of creation. It was that which God intended man to enjoy when he placed him in Eden. And what God has held out to man ever since sin destroyed rest for man. After all, redemption is but the completion of the purpose of creation. For man's sin made redemption a necessary complement to creation. So, entrance into Canaan, the seventh day weekly Sabbath, the Sabbatical year, etc. were

114

but signs and symbols of God's rest into which he entered after creation and unto which God's people are still invited.

The sentence of verse 10 heralds a landmark statement. It is complex in structure with two clauses. But even the subordinate element is of paramount significance. The dependent is instigated by ὥσπερ, "just as." It sets up a touchstone by which "rest" may be measured. "Just as God rested from his own (peculiar) (works) . . ." In other words, God's rest is the standard by which the idea of "rest" is to be determined. Thus, this prepares for the statement of the independent clause, "the one having entered into his rest, he also rested from his works, as indeed God did from his own works." The reader has already been informed (verse 3) that "the ones having believed" are the ones who are entering into the rest." So, apparently redemption in Christ is the meaning of σαββατισμός, the "Sabbathing" for the people of God. We note that -μος is an action ending.

The final sentence (verse 11) on this page is a hinge sentence. It is a natural conclusion to what precedes while at the same time it is a preparation for that which immediately follows. In form it is complex with an independent idea and one subordinate. "Let us be zealous" is the main exhortation. Epexegetical to this main verb is infinitive phrase "to enter." It completes the idea in "be zealous." ἵνα clause indicates the purpose for getting zealous.

A Translation

Hebrews 4:12-13

For the word of God is living and energetic and sharper than every two-edged sword and piercing unto dividing of soul and spirit and of joint and marrow and skilled in discerning thoughts and intents of hearts. And every creature is not unmanifest before him but each (is) naked and laid open to the eyes of him with whom for us is the accounting.

AN OUTLINE OF HEBREWS 4:12-13
THE WORD OF GOD!

The Word is first and foremost *personal*; that is, God speaks in persons. Then it is spoken and written. It comes to us in all these media.

I. CHARACTERISTICS OF THE WORD. vs. 12
   1. It is living.
   2. It is energetic.
   3. It is sharper than a two-edged sword.
   4. It is piecing to body, soul and spirit.
   5. It discriminates thoughts and motives.

II. THE WORD'S UNIVERSAL RELATIONSHIP. vs. 13a
   1. Every creature manifest before him.
      (a) Creatures hide guilt, real or imagined.
   2. But before him there is no hiding.
      (a) We are naked: all shams removed.
      (b) All inherited coverings removed.

116

III. THE PERSONAL WORD. vs. 13b
1. Marks of the personal Word.
   (a) "eyes"
   (b) "him"
   (c) "with whom"
2. The accounting.
   (a) The Word in verse 12 is the spoken, written word. But in 14c it's an "accounting." An accounting to a *person* rather than a record.

"Be zealous not to fall . . ." (vs. 11). The word of God is an instrument of faith on the one hand; of judgment on the other. "Be zealous" to use the word. In it lies salvation or judgment.

SOME EXPOSITORY THOUGHTS ON HEBREWS 4:12-13

The "Word" is essentially personal. An idea first lives in the mind be it God's or man's. Then it is spoken or written. No word is ever born of a vacuum; it's conceived in mind, felt by emotions. Once conceived and felt it then comes to birth in some expression, spoken, written, or even a deed which communicates. This is the way God spoke "in Son" or "in the prophets" (Heb. 1:1-2).

Characteristics of the word

The word of God is "living" not just in the sense that it is indestructible but that it is in itself able to generate life. It takes impotent sinners and creates a "new heart" with dynamic motivations. It works within and pushes out into new, creative forms of behaviour. It is thus "energetic." It provides not only intellectual data but kindles moral action. It has power to expose the profound deeps of human nature. It is keenly cutting, piercing and severing the most secret parts of a man. The word wends its way through every crevice of our mortal make up. The point of verse 12 is that God's word effects distinctions that human beings of themselves cannot make. No area of man's being is beyond the stretch of God's penetrating word. Every aspect of human life lies within the compass of his investigative reach. Since he is the Creator he knows his creation inside and out. Body, soul and spirit are equally included in his divine vision. "O Lord, thou hast searched me and known me! . . . before a word is on my tongue . . . thou knowest it altogether" (Ps. 139:1, 4).

The Word's universal relationship

As men we have been born into a sea of sin. We have sopped up sin like a sponge. As such we hide the real ego from God, each other and ourselves. With innumerable devices we cover the shame of what we really are. After their sin our first parents "hid themselves from the presence of the Lord." We've been hiding, covering, dodging our true selves ever since. For our deviations we blame ancestry, environment in all possible forms. But before HIM whose word is divine there is no hiding. Like a wrestler's neck stretched back in a strangle hold we lie naked. Before the word of God, personal or written, all shams are removed, all fraud is torn away. "Whither shall I go from thy spirit? Whither shall I flee from thy presence" (Ps. 139:7)?

The personal word

At bottom we deal with the personal Word for the written word has its power because of its relationship to the λόγος of God. "The words I have spoken are spirit and life" (Jn. 6:63). We deal with a "him." Not an "it." A "him" who has "eyes" to look into our depths and call us unto an "accounting." When we come at the end to face the written word we shall find that it is he who "is clad in a robe dipped in blood, and his name . . . is the Word of God" (Rev. 19:13).

Let's be zealous to use aright the word of God for in it lies salvation or judgment!

Hebrews 4:12-13

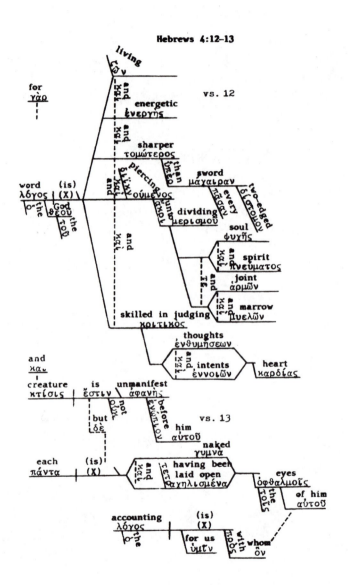

THE DIAGRAM OF 4:12-13

The "for" with which the sentence of verse 12 is launched relates this statement about the word of God to the appeal of verse 11, "Be zealous. . . ." Power to enter God's rest plus strength not to fall is provided by the use of the word of God.

A glance at the graphic picture of the diagram leaves an impression of a somewhat involved sentence. But it is really a simple sentence having just the one clause. "Word" is the subject. Genitive θεοῦ limits and characterizes the word as "of God." The compound predicate has five adjectival elements completing an understood "is." ζῶν is present active participle expressing one aspect of the word. It's "Living" from any point of view: it gives life; lives through fires of opposition and ignorance of friends; it might even refer to the living Personal Word as in John 1:1. At any rate it may be used in that Personal sense of "Word" without violence to its meaning as written or spoken. The Word lives in the Person before ever it is written on the page. ἐνεργὴς derives from ἐν (in) and ἔργον (work). The word "works in" and works from within. It energizes the heart that the heart in turn may give forth energy. τομώτερος is comparative adjective followed by ὑπὲρ, a normal way to express comparison, "sharper than. . . ." διϊκνούμενος is present middle participle, piercing through. The word has the ability to pierce through the whole person, inner and outer, physical and spiritual, body and soul as the text suggests, "soul, spirit, joint, marrow." The word is also κριτικὸς, a skilled critic. Expert in sifting, evaluating, judging, discriminating between concrete "thoughts" and hidden "intents," the outward word and the inward motive.

121

Verse 13 has two trunks and only one branch, two independent clauses from the second of which stems one dependent. The first quite literally says, "creature is not unmanifest before him. . . ." which, with its double negative idea, manifestly means that "every creature is manifest. . . ." The second independent clause brings to bear a compound predicate. The second member of that predicate has the perfect passive participle "having been laid open" forming a periphrastic verb "has been laid open." The perfect indicates the ever-present permanence of our nakedness to "the eyes of him with whom for us is the accounting." πρὸς ὄν introduces an adjective clause limiting αὐτοῦ.

λόγος is a word of manifold meanings. It has a long and varied history. It appears in these two verses with two distinct meanings, "word" and "account." But it is difficult not to think that the author saw some relationship between the two distinct definitions used so close here to each other. This finds some confirmation by the shift (if it really is a shift) from its use as the written or spoken "word" of God in verse 12 to such personal use in verse 13. The personal characteristics of "eyes" and "him" of verse 13 leave no doubt that the author thinks of the Person of God in Christ. Our "accounting" is personal to a person, not just an impersonal file of deed or misdeeds. We are to report our "account" (our word, record, deeds, thoughts, etc.) to a "him" rather than a thing.

A Translation
Hebrews 4:14-16

Having then a great highpriest who has passed through the heavens, Jesus, the son of God, let us be holding tight to the confession. For we are not having a highpriest not being able to sympathize with our weaknesses, but one having been tried according to (the measure of) every (trial) (as measured by its) likeness (to our trials) apart from sin. Therefore, we are to be approaching with bold confidence the throne of grace in order that we might get mercy and find grace for timely help.

AN OUTLINE OF HEBREWS 4:14-16
OUR GREAT HIGHPRIEST, A TIMELY HELPER!

Estrangement demands reconciliation. Weakness searches for power. Sin needs forgiveness! My sin against God requires priestly expiation. If I am to surmount weakness, find forgiveness, and be reconciled to God, I must find a qualified priest, adequate for the task. Is there such a person? One fit for my needs and God's holiness?

I. THE GREAT HIGHPRIEST. vs. 14

    1. He is *High*priest.
    2. He has "passed through the heavens."
    3. He is royalty - "Son of God."
    4. He merits *my* commitment - "hold fast!"

II. THE SYMPATHIZING HIGHPRIEST. vs. 15

1. Negatively.
   His greatness doesn't deny his service to *human* beings.
2. Positively.
   His trials qualify him to identify in my trials.
2. Yet "apart from sin."

III. A MERCIFUL, GRACIOUS HIGHPRIEST. vs. 16

1. Barriers to God's "throne of grace" completely removed.
2. Any and all may "approach with bold confidence."
3. Our needs are met:
   (a) for mercy.
   (b) for grace.

The timing of his help is perfect. He gives "timely help." At my cry he comes! When we fear he fails no one! When I hurt he helps. No one is so great or so little but that he may cry the cry of the publican. "Lord, be merciful to me the sinner."

SOME EXPOSITORY THOUGHTS ON HEBREWS 4:14-16

As weakness cries out for strength so sin cries for forgiveness. To supply strength for weakness and forgiveness for guilt is the work of a priest. In the realm of the spirit there's no greater work than that of the priest. He must clear my conscience!

The great highpriest

In Jesus we have a "great highpriest" because he is HIGH priest. In the Jewish sacrificial ritual the *high*priest alone had access to the Holy of Holies, the symbol of the sacred presence of God. Once a year he only passed through the veil between the Holy Place and the Holy of Holies. So Jesus alone is he who actually "passed through the heavens" to penetrate the real, not the emblematic, presence of God. As smoke of the burnt offering wafted its odor aloft so the crucified Jesus, God's offering for man's sin, ascended into the throne room of God to perform the priest's service for men. Who's greater than that?

Moreover, as "son of God" he was of royal quality. Kings of Israel were called "sons of God." Jesus presented himself as God's Son, accepted the acknowledgment of men as God's Son, and died under the accusation of being the "Son of God . . . coming on the clouds of heaven." Indeed, we do have a *great* highpriest!

So he merits all that I am and have. He's entitled to my total commitment. I must "hold fast" to my confession of him as priest-king, Son of God, anointed Saviour. In greatness none surpass him who turns my guilt into innocence, weakness to power!

A sympathizing highpriest

Is Jesus so lofty that he lies beyond me? How can he who is rich in righteousness feel with me in my moral poverty? But the text denies that his lofty position or divine nature are damaging to his ability to feel and serve my most human needs. Far more than a lesser being he suffers with me in total sympathy. Why? Because he "has been

125

tempted in all points" the same as I! There is no experience to which human beings are subjected by the forces of evil to which he hasn't been subjected. Torment of the physical senses or spiritual sensibilities he faced and successfully resisted. He said "No" to sin at any level or form. Even his sinlessness is proof of his ability to sympathize with us for we yield before the full impact. He endured *all* without yielding. His perfect sympathetic understanding is assured!

A merciful and gracious highpriest

We need not be rash or impertinent in the presence of God but neither should we lack confidence. Our highpriest enables us to be free in expressing every thought or feeling in God's presence. No awe or fear should intimidate us. The work of our great highpriest has removed all barriers to that "throne of grace." Hence we come "with boldness," and with a double purpose conforming to two basic needs in every man's life. I need mercy for former failures. I need grace for present struggles and future labors. Both are granted through the person and work of our "great highpriest."

He is present in the hour of my need. His help comes at the time of my need but not until then. His is a "timely help."

Hebrews 4:14-16

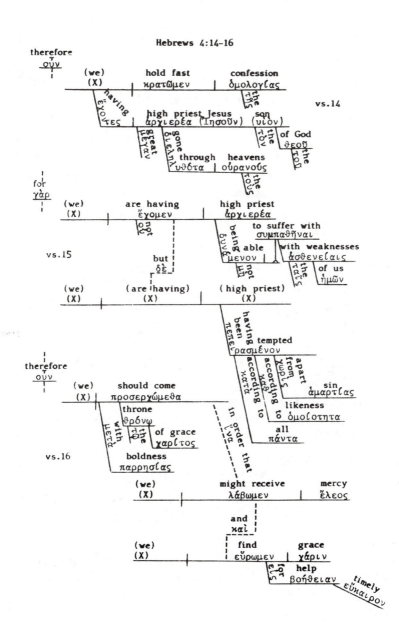

127

THE DIAGRAM OF HEBREWS 4:14-16

The sentence contained in verse 14 admits of only one full clause hence is simple in form. "We are to be clasping tight the confession." Present tense underlines the constant necessity of never letting up on our hold. We have an ongoing trust to concentrate on clinging tight. Direct object ὁμολογίας is genitive rather than accusative. More than anything else that might grab our attention we must "hold tight" to our *confession*. We assumed the confession in the first place. "Let's hold tight to *that* and nothing other." ἔχοντες is circumstantial present participle giving a reason why we should hold fast. In apposition to "highpriest" are two terms: (1) "Jesus" is the name of the human, reminding of the highpriest's humanity, (2) "son of God" directs attention to his deity. μέγαν is attributive adjective pointing out a characteristic without making an affirmation. In addition to the appositionals mentioned above, *how great* the highpriest is finds expression in the perfect circumstantial participle διεληλυθότα, "having passed through. . . ." Perfect tense propounds the permanency of the highpriest's present position in the heavens. He's in the real presence of God. "He passed through" and still is there.

Verse 15 comprises a compound sentence of two independent members. The first is negative; the second positive. "We are not having highpriest but (we are having highpriest . . .)" Except for its modifying participle phrase the second clause is entirely understood, implied in the context by the first. The very negation (οὐ with indicative) intimates that the author anticipated his readers' awe of the "greatness" of the highpriest. He might be *so* great he couldn't understand their pressures and problems, "not being able to sympathize with weaknesses." The first clause negates such a thought. But the second, by its circumstantial participle πεπειρασμένον, "having been tempted," declares that he's in a position to understand. Perfect tense says that the effects of his trials equipped him permanently to sympathize. What he gained by his temptations "in the days of his flesh" he hasn't lost at God's right hand. The κατά phrases present the standard of measurement, "according to *all*" trials, and "according to similar" trials as those which we faced. χωρὶς ἁμαρτίας "apart from sin," that is, no temptation of his arose due to any previous sin of his as is so often the case with us.

Verse 16 proposes a complex sentence. The main clause is, "Let's be (continuously) coming. . . ." Off of this two ἵνα subordinate adverbial purpose clauses stem. (1) "That we might get mercy" and (2) "that we might find grace. . . ." The verb in the main clause is present tense, "let's keep on coming. . . ." But the verbs in the dependent clauses are both point action aorists. We must ever come but whenever we come each is its own experience of getting or finding. The ideas in the verbs match the two human needs of "mercy" and "grace." Man "receives" mercy; he "finds" grace. The attributive adjective εὔκαιρον adds the idea of seasonable," "propitious," "timely." It's like the "nick of time" idea. The timing of God's help is always opportune!

Translation

Hebrews 5:1-10

For every highpriest, being taken from among men, is appointed in behalf of men in the matters pertaining to God in order that he might be offering both gifts and sacrifices in behalf of sins, being able to suffer gently with the ignorant and erring since he himself is surrounded with weakness and on account of which he is obligated, just as concerning the people, thus also concerning himself, to be offering concerning sins. And not to himself does anyone take the honor, but being called by God as indeed also (was) Aaron. Thus also the Christ did not glorify himself to become highpriest, but the one who spoke to him,

"My son are you, I today have begotten you."

Just as also in another (place) he says,

"You (are) priest unto the age according
to the order of Melchizedek."

Who in the days of his flesh, with strong crying and tears, having offered both prayers and petitions to the one able to save him out of death, and having been heard from his godly reverence, even though being son, he learned the obedience from which things he suffered, and having been perfected he became to all those hearing him responsible author of eternal salvation, having been addressed by God "highpriest" as of the order of Melchizedek.

AN OUTLINE OF HEBREWS 5:1-10
TOOLS OF THE TRADE!

Skills without tools generate frustration and defeat. Skills plus proper tools assure success in any endeavor. Whoever serves as priest must be properly equipped!

I. THE BADGE OF PRIESTHOOD. 5:1-4
1. The purpose of priesthood. vs. 1
   (a) He deals with "matters relating to God."
   (b) He bears "gifts and sacrifices in behalf of sins."
2. Qualifications for priesthood. vss. 2-4
   (a) Capacity for calm and carefully gentle judgment toward "the ignorant and erring."
   (b) Must face any sin in his *own* self. vs. 3
   (c) Not self appointed but called by God. vs. 4

II. CHRIST, THE PERFECT PRIEST. 5:5-10
1. Appointed by God as priest-king. vss. 5-6
   (a) Not self-appointed.
   (b) Psalm 2 designates him "son" therefore *king.*
   (c) Psalm 110 designates him priest as of Melchizedek.
2. His discipline of suffering. vss. 7-10
   (a) Learned "obedience" from his suffering. vss. 7-8
   (b) Was "made perfect" to perform priestly service for mankind. vss. 9-10

God "addresses" him as priest-king and shares his throne during the days of regeneration of man. As priest he's my Saviour!

SOME EXPOSITORY THOUGHTS ON HEBREWS 5:1-10

A sculptor without stone or chisel is as fruitless as a sailor without a ship. Or a carpenter without saw and hammer! Or a farmer without land and plow. To have the finest skills but to lack the proper tools with which to exploit those skills is an invitation to madness. Life is defeated because it cannot accomplish its manifest purpose. This is as true in "matters pertaining to God" as in any other field of service. To be "priest of the Most High God" without proper tools leaves man floundering in the slough of sin without hope in the face of the doom of death.

The badge of priesthood

What is the purpose of a priest? Does he serve any vital need? Couldn't we live just as well without priestly service? The text claims that he deals in "the things relating to God." That is, he has a place in God's redemptive hope for man. But that appointed place has special meaning to man's present condition of guilt. The priest "offers sacrifices in behalf of sins." That is, he deals with a man's conscience. Man's sense of righteousness has been violated. It's the priest's function to deal with that.

The materialistic sophistication of this modern age has ridiculed God off the stage and has relegated sin to the rubbish heap of primitive man. Yet the priestly function is so important that we have substituted the psychiatrists's couch and the medicine man's drug. We dignify the modern "priest" with the term "Doctor" and give the sign of his priesthood by conferring on him the degree of M.D. Medical fees are the sacrifices, the waiting room is the Holy Place. His inner office where Dr. and nurse offer up their incense to the idol of scientific gobbledegook is the Holy of Holies. Yes! The priest is an essential ingredient to human life. Abandon the highpriest of religion and of necessity he comes back in the mitre of the Doctor's drugs. We can change the name but we cannot change the need for dealing with sin and conscience. Sin is still the underlying sickness of our society. It's the task of a priest to deal with this sickness.

And what are the qualifications of a priest? What are the tools of his trade without which he can only fail in his vital task? One fundamental requirement is that he first face and deal with his own sin. "Physician, heal thyself" is no more needed than here. A medical Doctor with a communicable disease will have a hard time not spreading the disease. A teacher must remove his own ignorance before he can enlighten his students. The Old Testament priest could not offer any acceptable sacrifice for the sins of the people until he had first offered up the sacrifice for his own wrongs. To give to others moral health a priest must himself be morally healthy. To make one well one must be well!

But that's not all. Having dealt with himself he must now be able to perceive sympathetically the desperate need of those whom he is to serve. He is to "bear gently" with those whose transgressions spring from ignorance rather than willful rebellion and from waywardness rather than determined wickedness. He must be able to feel the gnawing agony of the adulterer without being an adulterer, the crush of conscience on the murderer without having murdered. He must know the depravity of the drunkard, the greed of the thief, the shame of scandal, the discredit of defeat, the angry pride of the jealous, and a thousand other sins, near-sins, and frustrations to which men are heir during their pilgrimage through life. He must know them all, yet, in so far as possible, partake in none. God's priest who serves man's need shares the hurting heart of the sinner while keeping himself from the sin.

But how? Can the fully clothed know the harshness of the totally naked? Or the man with shoes know the pain of the barefooted? Can the sinless feel with the sinful? Strange to say, the answer is "Yes!" The gymnast who lifts with *apparent* ease a thousand pound weight resists more pressure than he who is quashed by five hundred. It's not the sin, but the strength of temptation that gives the ability to sympathize. He who struggles with anger, murder, robbery and rape but does not yield gains more understanding of the conflict than he who crumples before the temptation spends its full force. Holy men are more sensitive to the horror of evil than the wicked. The law provides no sacrifice for the willful wicked. But for the "ignorant and erring" God sends his priest with gentle patience to save from sin.

That God does the sending is important. "One does not take the honor unto himself, but he is called by God, just as Aaron." God's servants are not self-appointed; they are called of God to their tasks. A tenant farmer doesn't begin farming a field until the landowner agrees. Nor does a factory assembly-line worker join the plant work force just because *he* decides to do so. It's the employer who "calls" him to his task. Just so God is the one who appoints the priest to his sacrificial service.

Christ, the perfect highpriest

In keeping with the general practice Jesus did not decide on his priestly function without being sent of God. In his final great prayer Jesus said, "I glorified you upon the earth, having brought to its intended end that which you gave me that I should do" (John 17:4). Furthermore, in our present text the author plainly declares, "Christ did not exalt himself to be made high priest, but was appointed by him who said, . . ." And at this point the author quotes from two Old Testament Psalms to verify that Jesus was not self-appointed. The quotation from the second Psalm sets forth the royal sonship of the Christ, his kingly deity: "Thou art my Son, today I have begotten thee." In the Old Testament the kings of Israel bore the title of "son of God." They represented God's sovereign leadership over the people. Messiah (Christ) was to be revealed on earth as Son of God. The quotation from Psalm 110 designates just how God expects the Christ to exert that kingly role; "Thou art priest forever after the order of Melchizedek." God appointed him to be king-priest. And he was to rule through his priestly function. He lives by dying; he gives life by losing it! He dissolves sin in others by assuming its consequences in himself. He rules by doing a highpriest's work. All this by God's appointment!

Jesus also gained that which enabled him to "deal gently" with those he came to serve. The suffering he bore during the "days of his flesh made him the perfect priest." "The days of his flesh" denotes his human adventure from in-carnation to crucifixion, from birth to death. These were days when he experienced the confinements of mortal weakness; its restrictions, impediments, liabilities and anguish. So dependent was he as a human that throughout his whole life he offered daily the olive branch of prayer. And that with "strong crying and tears!" He was so vulnerable during those "days of his flesh." Yet it was the frank recognition of his human weakness that led him to pray to "the one able to save him out of death." And thereby he gained strength as the mighty Son of God. Thus recognizing his weakness he was able to be strong. For he was heard because of his "godly fear." It was his constant sense of dependence, his willingness to subject himself to the will of the Father, this reverent submissiveness that kept the channel to God open. It kept him strong amidst his human limitations.

This habit of prayer with "strong crying and tears" finds its supreme example in the garden of Gethsemane. Compressed within a few hours was this whole agony of "fleshly" (human) experience. The shrinking from a terribly humiliating painful task, his inward struggle to keep in clear focus the will of God, the "grief unto death," the sleep of disciples when he needed their alert comfort, the disappointment of a friend's betrayal, the loneliness of his agony capsules not only *his* life but every man's who aspires to lofty living in an evil world. All these things equipped Jesus to be the perfect highpriest. They enable him to enter into the feelings of any human being who seeks his service as priest. He's our "great highpriest" because he's suffered all that we must.

There's yet more about his suffering! "Though being Son, he learned the obedience from which things he suffered, and having been made perfect he became to all those obeying him author of eternal salvation." This says, "he learned the obedience." That is not to say that Jesus had to learn to obey. That he always did! But he did learn what were the consequences of obeying God in a godless world. Goodness in a wicked world invites pain and hurt. Jesus always did the right! Therefore he learned the meaning of obedience—tribulation, anguish, pain.

But by such suffering he was "made perfect"! Did he who was "without sin" have to be "*made* perfect"? Yes! Perfection as priest. It was his suffering as man that gave him that which he didn't have before, the ability to enter into the suffering of other men. It's his suffering that fully furnished him for saving the worst of men. It made him capable of bringing man unto his divine destiny for which he had been created.

For this God recognized and "addressed" him as priest-king. Moreover, God shares his throne of grace during the days of man's regeneration. "Sit on my right hand . . . you are priest forever. . . ." There is no need for anyone not finding salvation. We have a great highpriest who can reach to any man's need.

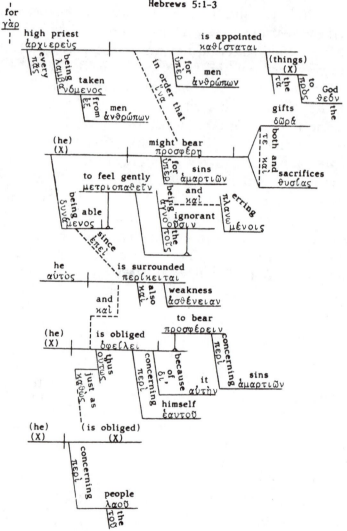

138

THE DIAGRAM OF HEBREWS 5:1-3

The γὰρ is illative and closely relates 5:1-10 to the preceding paragraph, particularly 4:15. By his trials and temptations Jesus is equipped to be a sympathizing highpriest. "For" all priests must measure up to certain criteria else, in the nature of the case, they can't perform the necessary service. These qualities the author proceeds to present in 5:1-10.

The three verses of 5:1-3 embrace one sentence, complex in structure. When all modifying factors are removed the bare independent thought is, "highpriest is appointed."

The priest has certain relationships to men. The present circumstantial participle λαμβανόμενος . . , "being taken from among men" brings in the important idea that all priests are human. That is, they come from the ranks of the mundane people they serve, not from supernatural sources. Those who serve humans are taken from among humans! A second relationship to men finds expression in the ὑπὲρ phrase, "in behalf of men." In other words, he is "from men for men."

But the priest also has relationship to God as set forth in the adverbial accusative phrase governed by neuter article τὰ, "the matters pertaining to God." These would include "gifts and sacrifices," temple services, and various responsibilities within the sacred precincts. He represents God as well as man!

The immediate purpose of a priest's function comes out in the adverbial dependent ἵνα clause, "in order that he might bear both gifts and sacrifices." He is to mediate between man and God. One basic qualification which prepares a person to serve as priest is instigated by present

139

circumstantial participle δυνάμενος "being able to feel gently. . . ." Those for whom he feels this "gentle modera-ation" are announced by the attributive participles "the ones being ignorant and erring." Furthermore, the reason why he can feel such sympathy appears in the adverb clause of cause (ἐπεὶ). "Since *he* also is surrounded by weakness. ἀσθένειαν is an adverbial accusative. Parallel to this "since" clause is another which sets forth the fact that the priest, having weakness, must face and deal with it before he can deal with other peoples' sins. ὀφείλει is present tense of linear action. In view of weakness repeating itself in his life the priest is under a continual obligation to be dealing with his own sin. Infinitive προσφέρειν is also present tense complementing the action in the "being obliged." The priest is under a recurring debt to be bearing sacrifices for his own recurring weakness which ever expresses itself in overt sin.

A final subordinate adverb clause enters the picture with καθὼς, "just as." It injects a clause of comparison. It sets a standard by which he may measure how much he is "being obliged." He must be bearing offerings etc. for himself; ". . . just as he is being obliged to be offering sacrifices for the people thus (οὕτως) by this much he is obliged to. . . ."

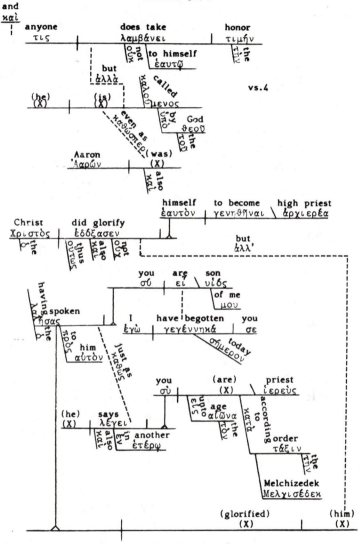

141

THE DIAGRAM OF HEBREWS 5:4-6

Two sentences decorate this page. Both classify as compound-complex. The sentence of verse four embraces two independent clauses, the first negative, the second positive. "Anyone does not take the honor to himself." The indefinite pronoun "anyone" is subject. That, in conjunction with the strong negative οὐ, in effect says, "No one does take. . . ." λαμβάνει is present tense the linear action of which pictures habitual action of "any" one particular person. It also might contain the distributive idea of each separate possible individual priest "not taking." It's kindred to the gnomic idea. That a man "take for himself" such an honored position just isn't to be done. τιμήν is direct object. The term first came into use among the Greeks with primary reference to the material economic value belonging to someone. Then it developed the more aptly ethical sense of "honor." Here its usage reflects the meaning of "position" or "dignity of office." Adversative "but" joins the two independent parts together while at the same time setting the positive idea over against the negative, ". . . but (he is) being called by God . . ." καλούμενος, "being called" is supplementary predicate participle. It conjoins with an understood "is" to form a periphrastic present, thus giving added performance to the linear idea of the present tense. ὑπό with the ablative tells who the direct agent is who does the calling. To this second independent element is attached the sole dependent addendum, "even as (was) Aaron." The call of Aaron to the priestly office by God was the measure by which all successive priests were to enter the duties of that office.

Again two independent sections form the basic frame of the sentence contained in verses 5-6. The sentence carries

142

within it two quotations from two separate Psalms but, as punctuated in Nestle's text, they mesh into the one compound-complex passage. And once again the initial negative clause is followed by a positive with another "but" connecting them. "Christ did not glorify himself . . ." is the first basic idea. Object of the verb is first aorist passive infinitive γενηϑῆναι with accusative of general reference "himself" acting as so-called subject. The accusative case of "highpriest" is predicate agreeing with "himself."

Except for its subject the second of the independent clauses is elliptical. Its substance must be borrowed from the context, suggested by the first clause. "The one who spoke . . . (glorified him)." The subject of this clause is quite elaborate. Sheared of all additions the subject is the attributive aorist participle translated, "the one who spoke. . . ." But from that bare subject sprouts four subordinate clauses. Quoted from the second Psalm are two clauses each of which serves as a direct object of the subject-participle. "You are my son" and "Today, I have begotten you." A third dependent segment is brought in by καϑὼς, "just as he says. . . ." It's an adverbial idea of comparison. Direct object of λέγει is the noun clause, a quote from Psalm 110, "you are priest forever after the order of Melchizedek."

Hebrews 5:7-10

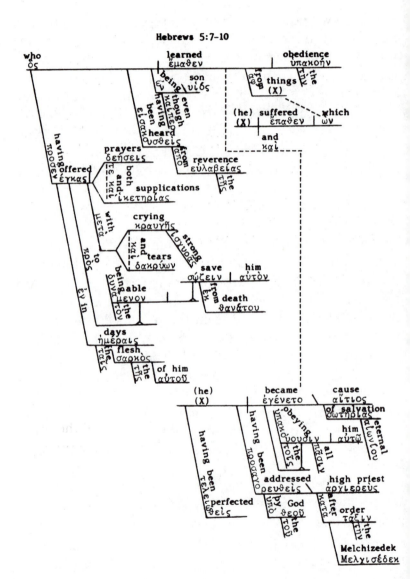

144

THE DIAGRAM OF HEBREWS 5:7-10

At first glance the diagram of this sentence leaves the impression of a very complicated arrangement of a number of tangled clauses. But as a matter of fact only three clauses are involved, two independents and one dependent. The other expansions are largely confined to participial and prepositional expressions. So the sentence classifies as compound-complex. The two chief elements say, "who learned obedience" and "he became cause."

In the first main clause the relative pronoun ὅς serves as subject. Antecedent to the pronoun is "Christ" found back in verse five. So the thought, though not the words, is "Christ learned obedience." The verb translated "learned" is a constative aorist. The aktionsart (action native to the root of a word) of "learn" is linear. Jesus' earthly experience of learning was a long drawn out process taking almost a third of a century. But by use of this aorist the author of Hebrews brings the whole long experience into a single focused act. It's the fact that Jesus "learned" not the unfolding course of action that the author wants the reader to visualize.

Every phrase may be classed as one of three of the basic parts of speech; noun, adjective, or adverb. The prepositional phrase "from (ἀφ') things" is adverb answering the question *where* or *from whence* Jesus learned obedience. Describing the understood "things" is the adjectival dependent clause, "which (he) suffered."

Three circumstantial participles add their descriptions to the subject "who." ὤν, "though being son . . ." is clearly a concessive use of the participle. The other two, "having offered" and "having been heard" may be either time or

145

occasion or a combination of both. No doubt Jesus suffered throughout his life and so "learned" throughout his life. But this passage refers to his suffering in Gethsemane when he offered "prayers and petitions with strong crying and tears." And it was also there where he was heard "for his reverence." From these in particular he "learned" what was involved in "obedience" in this kind of a world.

The prepositional expression "in the days of his flesh" is adverbial answering the question "when" he offered his prayers, etc. ἐν with the locative presents a point "within which." Genitive σαρκὸς specifies the *kind* of days in which he did his praying. The phrase is a most expressive description of the humanity and mortality of Jesus. He was thoroughly endowed with "human nature" and hence well suited to be a priest.

The infinitive phrase, "to save . . . from death" brings into play ἐκ with ablative the basic idea of which is "separation" or "origin." God saved Jesus, not from dying; that's why he sent him here. But God saved him "out of." That is, he took him clear through death and brought him successfully out of it.

The final independent expression reads, "(he) became cause of eternal salvation. . . ." The attributive participle translated "the ones obeying him" is in dative, the case of personal interest. Eternal salvation is not for all but *for* all who obey him." The two other participles in this part of the sentence are circumstantial.

146

A Translation

Hebrews 5:11—6:20

Concerning whom our message is immense and difficult to divulge, since you have become stagnant in your hearing. For indeed, though, on account of the time, you ought to be teachers, you are having need again that someone be teaching you the ABC's of the primal (teaching) of the oracles of God and you have become having need of milk, not of solid food. For everyone partaking of milk (is) without trial in (the) message of righteousness, for he is (such as a tiny) babe. But the solid food is for mature ones, the ones who, on account of use, are having their organs of perception exercised for differentiating both good and bad.

Wherefore, having left the word of the basic (teaching) of the Christ, let us be borne along to maturity, not again laying foundation of repentance from dead works and trust upon God, teaching of lustrations and putting on of hands, of resurrection of dead (bodies) and eternal judgment. And this we will do if God permit. For, that the ones enlightened once and having tasted the heavenly gift and having become partners of the Holy Spirit and having tasted God's word and powers of the coming age, and having fallen away,—(that they) freshen up again unto repentance (is) impossible, (seeing that they are) crucifying to themselves the son of God and (are) displaying (him) to public mockery. For land, the one drinking often the rain coming upon it and bearing herbage useful to those on account of whom it is cultivated, receives blessing from God. But if (it be) bearing thorns and thistles (it is) rejected, the destiny of which is burning.

But we have been persuaded the better concerning you, beloved, indeed (the things) having salvation, though indeed thus we are speaking. For God is not unjust to forget your work and your love which you demonstrated in his name, when you served the saints and (still) are serving. But we desire each of you to show the same zeal toward the fullness of the hope unto the end, that you become not stagnant, but through faith and patience, imitators of the ones inheriting the promises. For God, having promised to the Abraham, since he was having no one greater by whom to sware, swore by himself, saying. Truly if blessing I will bless you and multiplying I will multiply you. And thus having gotten patience he obtained the promise. For men are swearing according to the greater and with them the oath is the end of every dispute: in which (fact) God, wishing to show more abundantly to the heirs of the promise the immuntability of his counsel interposed with an oath: that by two immutable things, in which impossible that God lie, we may have strong comfort, (we) the ones having fled to lay hold the hope lying before us, which we have as anchor of the soul both sure and firm and going into the inmost of the veil, where Jesus as forerunner entered, having become high-priest forever according to the order of Melchizedek.

AN OUTLINE OF HEBREWS 5:11—6:20
PERILS OF APOSTASY!

Dullness delays growth; limits teaching. Victory is the fruit of unremitting effort!

I. FAITH, UNRIPENED, PRODUCES NO FRUIT. 5:11-14

1. Use or lose. In Christian growth one uses what he has or loses what he wants. 5:11-12
2. A baby's lack prevents his adult growth. 5:13-14 Reject pablum and you'll never get steak!
3. Experience gives maturity; past exercise is present power!

II. POWER THROUGH PROGRESS. 6:1-8

1. Move from elemental; foundation not repeatedly laid. 6:1-2
2. Move forward in spite of childish condition. 6:3
3. Peril of apostisizing. 6:4-8
   (a) Impossibility of repeating the past. 4-6
   (b) Illustrated from natural creation. 7-8

III. THE HAZARDS DO NOT EXCLUDE HOPE. 6:9-12

    1. Active love evidences that divine life is still present. 9-10

    2. Hope arouses zeal, offsets sloth, fires faith. 11-12

IV. CERTAINTY OF GOD'S PROMISE. 6:13-20

    1. The example of Abraham. 13-18

       (a) Hope rests on God's promise. This demands patience.

       (b) Hope rests on God's oath. This offers certainty.

    2. The sure anchor of our hope! 19-20

Apostasy avoided by the power of hope! "Let's be borne along. . . ."

SOME EXPOSITORY THOUGHTS ON HEBREWS 5:11—6:20

Dullness delays growth. In fact if one persists in being lazy, sluggish, stagnant it will destroy growth on the part of a learner. And as for the teacher the dullard's lethargic attitude limits the teacher's prospects of teaching anything of substance. As in other endeavors victory to the Christian is the fruit of dedicated effort. God's grace gives power for triumphant work!

Faith, unripened, produces no fruit!

To say that faith produces no fruit is false. But faith, untended, uncultivated, neglected, taken for granted will certainly produce no fruit worthy of the name. In life we lose what we do not use. Money buried in the ground or hidden in a mattress is useless. But when spent or invested it brings in goods or interest. In the Christian life one uses what he has or loses what he wants. Grow or die is the law of life, physical, spiritual, secular and sacred! The Hebrews had fallen into the trap of stagnation for the author chides that the difficulty of this theme was due to their dull lack of effort. ". . . you have become stagnant . . . though you ought to be teachers, you have need that someone again be teaching you the ABC's . . . of the oracles of God."

A baby needs milk if he is to grow into sturdy manhood. But if he fails to take the milk or, having taken, fails to absorb it he will never develop the sound body and strong muscles of maturity. If one rejects pablum he'll never get steak. Milk is for babes; solid food for the mature. Failure to grow as a babe leaves one too weak for growth as an adult. Exercise strengthens a baby's tissues so as to increase him for harder tasks. It's not abuse but non-use that destroys. That's true whether it be muscle or the fibers of the soul. The text says that "on account of the time you ought be teachers." Failure to use time at the beginning keeps us from having time at the end. If we don't grow in the first grade we can't advance to the second.

Maturity comes from the exercise of experience. If one learns the ABC's but never uses them in reading he will lose even the knowledge of the ABC's. Using what one has at each stage of growth leads to mature power. The mature is he who has let God draw out of him his full potential of latent powers. Past exercise gives present power. We come to "know" Christ by using what we know of Christ. *Use* brings maturity!

Power through progress

Laying foundations over and over is not only childish, it is dangerous. We must move on to build the superstructure. If we don't the peril of apostasy is always present. He who has "tasted the good word of God" and then with determined malice repudiates faith in the Christ, has nothing left but the curse of judgment like a field of thorns and thistles is burned. Remember! He who apostasizes cannot repeat the past. He may be entered in the race again but he can't go back and start at the beginning. That has been done once and for all. To repudiate the only Christ leaves NO Christ! And if one does come back, he must come to the *same* Christ for there is no "second." If one rejects the ABC's how can he ever read again? He's rejected the only thing that enabled him to read in the first place. The "impossibility" of return lies in the nature of the sin, not in the willingness of God to receive. The point of no return lies within the individual sinner committing that particular sin of repudiation. The moral quality of rejecting Christ, having once accepted him, is such that to "repent" lies beyond his *human* possibility. Though God may "renew" him, it's "impossible" for *him* to renew!

Danger does not exclude hope

"We are persuaded better things of you. . . ." Specific work done and love shown give abundant evidence that the divine spark is still present. Where love is God can't be wholly absent. Unnamed by the author and hence unknown to us the Hebrews had done an outstanding "work" and thereby had demonstrated active "love." Furthermore they had done it "in the name" of Christ. If a lazy sluggard is fired up to lay his life on the altar of a sacrificial service to a brother that proves that the life and love of God lies dormant deep within him. Then if that sacrifice is repeated that reinforces and kindles the divine life in him. God doesn't "forget" that service. And God will help fan into flame the smouldering coals of divine love. Nor does the author forget their service to the saints for he exhorts, that "each of you show the same zeal toward the fullness of hope unto the end." Such fullness of hope in God's promise stimulates zeal, overcomes sluggishness and motivates to "faith and patience" after the example of the ancients whose hope rested in the promise of God. God's oath gave incontestable certainty.

The certainty of God's promise reinforced

Using Abraham as a pattern we learn two things. God keeps his word. No matter the delays, the defeats, the frustrations, God honors his promise. If the word of a gentleman is enough then the word of God is more than enough. God doesn't say "Yes" today and "No" tomorrow so as to welsh on his word. "God is faithful" and that means that he keeps his pledge.

This demands patience on the part of men. If God keeps his word then men must keep their trust through all the dark ways of life. Certainly they are not to abandon hope in the Christ.

But more than this, God reinforced his word to Abraham with an incredible oath. What more should a man need than the pledged word of the living God? Yet the validity of Abraham's hope was sealed by God's oath. By his sworn oath God vowed even above his promised word. It added certainty for the patriarch. Thus for all time men may be assured of Jesus as the "anchor of the soul, sure and steadfast, and entering into the innermost place beyond the veil." How certain is the Christ? As certain as the fact that it's "impossible for God to lie." God's word and God's oath are directed toward his Christ, man's Saviour. "All the promises of God find their Yes in him" (II Cor. 1:20). God's oath piled on top of his promise is like a storm door placed over a front entrance to a house. It seals the home from the storms that beat against it. The oath added certainty!

With Jesus acting as the sure anchor for our faith there's no need for apostasy. He has penetrated the unseen to the very throne of God. And he has his hand on our unsteady hearts to hold us firm through all storms.

Hebrews 5:11-14

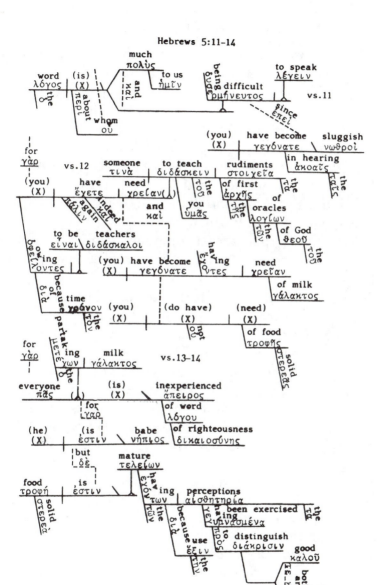

THE DIAGRAM OF HEBREWS 5:11-14

Two clauses combine to form the sentence of verse eleven. One is independent, the other dependent. So it is classed as complex. The phrase "of whom" relates back to Melchizedek at the close of the previous verse. However, it is to Christ, "Son," "designated" as "highpriest after the order of Melchizedek. . . ." The independent clause has a compound predicate; it affirms two things about the subject, ". . . the word is much" and ". . . is being difficult. . . ." The ἐπεὶ clause is a subordinate adverbial clause telling the reason why it is "difficult."

Verse twelve packages a compound-complex combination. It has three independent elements the first of which entertains a noun clause in apposition to "need" (χρείαν). The first independent declares, "you indeed have need. . . ." There follows the appositional, "that someone be teaching you the rudiments. . . ." τινὰ is accusative of general reference with an infinitive. This infinitive "to teach" takes two accusatives after it, one the accusative of the thing, "rudiments" (στοιχεία) and the other, accusative of the person, "you" (ὑμᾶς). The diagram places the accusative of the person as an adverbial instead of a second object. In this first of the independent clauses the subject "you" has a present circumstantial participle ὀφείλοντες "owing to be teachers. . . ." modifying it. It seems to suggest a causal idea. That is to say, *why* they "have need again that someone be teaching" them. This causal idea seems to be sustained by the accompanying διὰ with accusative "on account of the time" modifying it.

The second independent clause includes a periphrastic perfect "you have become having. . . ." Certainly ἔχοντες is predicate participle supplementing the idea in perfect γεγόνατε, you have become. The word "need" is object of the participle and is modified by genitive "of milk" specifying the *kind* of "need" which the Hebrews have. A third independent idea is implied by a negative and the rest of the context; ". . . you do not have need of solid food."

Three independent clauses frame the sentence embodied in verses 13-14. While a number of phrases amplify the ideas, strictly speaking, no other clauses appear. So it's classified as compound. The first main idea states, "Everyone is inexperienced. . . ." The subject is πᾶς (everyone). To clarify that subject the author inserts an attributive participle "the one partaking." Object is the genitive of the word rendered "milk." Verbs of sharing take genitive. Such an "inexperienced" one is described by a second independent clause, 'he is (a) babe. . . ." But in contrast to such a "babe" the third independent states, "solid food is of mature. . . ." τελείων is predicate genitive. Just how mature those who partake of solid food are is developed in a present attributive participial phrase "the ones having perceptions. . . ." Another participle, this time a perfect circumstantial, is added to αἰσθητηρία to describe these organs of "perception." The perfect tense suggests that through regular use their perceptions have an abiding result. The purpose of this "exercising" of perceptions is expressed by πρὸς and accusative of "distinguish."

Hebrews 6:1-6

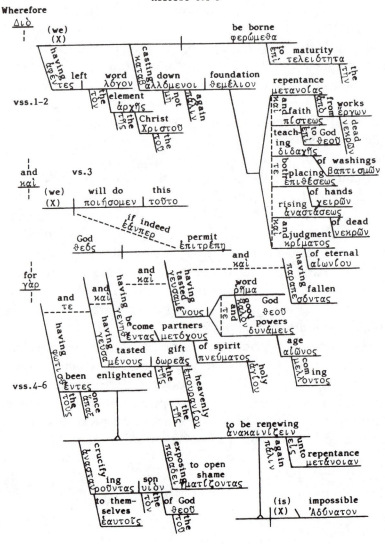

THE DIAGRAM OF 6:1-6

The conjunction Διὸ bases the exhortation of verses 1-2 on the point just made about the difficulty of the subject and the dullness of the readers. Having just one complete clause it proves to be a simple sentence. The volitive subjunctive φερώμεθα urges, "let us be borne. . . ." The point to which (where) we must be borne comes out in the prepositional adverb phrase "to the maturity." Two circumstantial participles add descriptions to the subject "we." The first is aorist ἀφέντες, "having left the elemental message of the Christ. . . ." The tense marks a decisiveness that's absolute. The second one is present tense with negative, ". . . not again casting down foundation. . . ." That presents a ludicrous picture of a constant repetition of doing nothing but laying and relaying a foundation, at least the negative of it. Direct object of the participle is the term translated "foundation" to which is affixed a series of six genitives amply specifying the *kind* of foundation.

Verse three inserts a brief complex sentence of two clauses. The conditional clause introduced by ἐάνπερ is third class, the condition left undetermined as to whether God will permit or not, but with some likelihood that he will. On the basis of such a condition the author makes a strong affirmation of intent by volitive future indicative, "This we will do."

In spite of what looks like a long complicated sentence that of 6:4-6 has but one independent clause. It must needs be classified as a simple sentence. The plain unadorned subject is present *active* infinitive ἀνακαινίζειν, to be renewing. It does not say, "to be renewed" (passive). The so-called "subject" of the infinitive in the Greek is placed in

159

the accusative case. In this instance the subject is set forth in five attributive, aorist participles joined together by one τε and three καί's. This combination of conjunctions indicates a very close connection between the things connected. This so-called "subject" is more accurately defined as a series of accusatives of general reference. In other words, those who perform the action in the infinitive are placed in the accusative case and discharge the *function* of subject. Thus it is that the "ones enlightened, . . . who tasted, . . . became partners, . . . tasted the word, etc., . . ." are the very ones who are to do whatever the action in the infinitive calls for. That is to say, *they* are to "*be renewing* unto repentance.*" They are to renew is active voice. In effect the clause is saying that for "them to be renewing is impossible." The sentence does *not* affirm it's impossible for them to be renewed. It only states that it is impossible that *they* renew. The predicate of the single independent clause is the adjective ἀδύνατον with the connecting verb "is" understood. The impossibility or inability lies in the "ones having been enlightened, . . . having tasted, . . . etc."

The nature of the sin that causes them to have such impotence is clearly announced in the two present circumstantial participles (ἀνασταυροῦντας) "crucifying" and παραδειγματίζοντας) "putting to open shame." The nature of their sin instills its deadening effects within the one sinning that particular sin. Hence they become impotent to have any ability to "freshen up again."

Hebrews 6:7-10

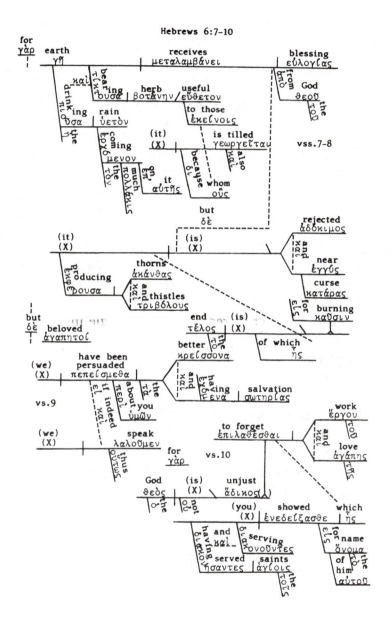

161

THE DIAGRAM OF HEBREWS 6:7-10

Verses 7-8 house four clauses, two independent and two subordinate. Hence the sentence is classed as compound-complex. The first clause, denuded of all modifiers, declares that the "earth receives blessing. . . ." Whence the blessing comes is validated by the prepositional phrase "from God." Two attributive participles, describe the subject "earth." They are both descriptive presents, "the one drinking rain . . . and bearing herb. . . ." Direct object ὑετὸν has a present attributive participle modifying it, "the one coming." The direct object βοτάνην has a predicate adjective εὔθετον completing "herb." εὔθετον carries the main point of the phrase. δι' οὓς ushers in an adjective clause describing the demonstrative pronoun ἐκείνοις.

The subject and verb in the second independent clause are elliptical and must be supplied from the context. But the predicate really comes out in adjective constructions, "rejected" and "near a curse." ἀδόκιμος is a true adjective. The other adjective part of this predicate is a preposition "near" (ἐγγύς) with genitive "curse" (κατάρας'). This is predicate nominative referring back to subject "it." Another expansion of the subject is circumstantial participle "producing" followed by its direct objects "thorns" and "thistles." This participle might be classed as *cause* or possibly *condition*. This clause too has one adjectival subordinate modifying the subject "it" (earth); ". . . of which the end is for burning." The word τέλος contains more than termination; it carries the idea of "goal" or "destination." Unproductive land, like a reprobate life, has a well-calculated final act, that is, a "burning," a self-destroying, self-consuming destiny!

The sentence of verse nine is complex. The dependent idea is a concessive conditional "if indeed." It's a first class

162

with condition determined as true. "If indeed we are speaking thus (and we are). . . ." Stated in the independent clause, the conclusion follows, ". . . we have been persuaded. . . ." πεπείσμεθα is perfect tense giving emphasis to the permanency of the "persuasion." Paul is established in his persuasion that "better things" than sluggish behaviour shall come from his readers. The participle ἐχόμενα is predicate. It could be viewed as supplementary to the main verb "persuade." It may be circumstantial modifying implied "things." "We have been persuaded . . . and (things) having salvation."

Verse 10 also entails a complex arrangement. The main clause states, "God is not unjust. . . ." But in order to specify more particularly the way that justice manifests itself the author adds the appositional infinitive phrase, "to forget work and love." Words of remembering and forgetting take genitive case as object. The infinitive is further augmented by the dependent clause advanced by relative ἧς, "which you showed. . . ." The manner in which they showed "love and works" appears in two circumstantial participles modifying subject "you." One is aorist and the other present giving a sharp contrast in action. All former action is concentrated into a single focused point. But the "serving" still goes on. God doesn't forget such service!

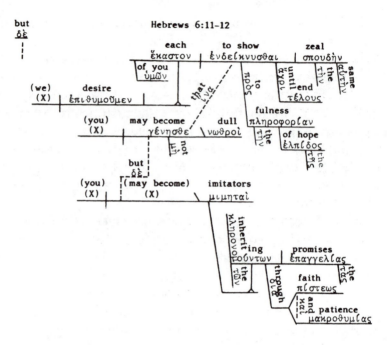

THE DIAGRAM OF HEBREWS 6:11-12

Hebrews 6:11-12 embraces a complex sentence. The independent clause states, "we are desiring." The infinitive "to show" express that which "we desire." It is the direct object of the main verb "desire." Appearing with the infinitive is the accusative of general reference "each" (ἕκαστον). This present infinitive takes as its direct object "zeal" (σπουδὴν). Two prepositional phrases, adverbial in usage, modify the infinitive: "until (the) end" is temporal telling when or how long; "toward the fulness of hope" introduces the idea of how much. Two purpose clauses, inaugurated by ἵνα, give the reason why the author "desires" his readers "to show zeal etc. . . ." First, "that (you may) not (become) dull," and second, "but that (you may become) imitators of the ones inheriting the promises through faith and patience."

ἐπιθυμοῦμεν is present tense expressing its linear idea by describing the author's ongoing, unbroken desire. The infinitive ἐνδείχνυσθαι is also linear present and also descriptive of the continuing action he wants his readers to "keep on showing." They are to be unremitting in "showing the same zeal. . . ." The attributive participle χληρονομούντων is a present linear too. But this present is distributive in force. Each single person who inherits is another in a long list of "imitators."

διὰ with genitives of "faith and patience" is the normal way of expressing *agent* through which.

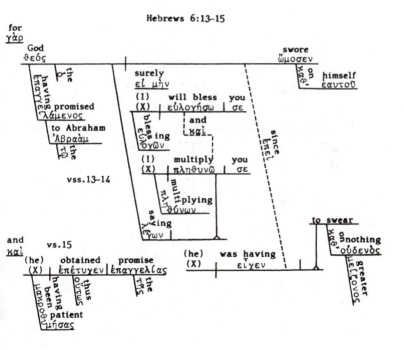

Hebrews 6:13-15

THE DIAGRAM OF HEBREWS 6:13-15

If the καὶ introducing verse 15 were joined directly to the sentence of verses 13-14 then the whole arrangement would be a compound-complex. But it seems best to treat verses 13-14 as complex and the sentence of verse 15 as a separate simple sentence. The sentence of 15 says, "He obtained the promise." The aorist of the verb presents the fact as fact without any embellishment as to the struggle through baffling trials of doubt. The circumstantial participle is also aorist ("having been patient") which does imply a long period of travail. But the tense gathers together the long toil as a single focused effort.

When we remove the bark and branches from 13-14 the trunk that's left is "God swore." The occasion which brought forth God's oath taking is displayed in the aorist circumstantial participle ἐπαγγειλάμενος "having promised." The action of the participle is coincident with that of the main verb "swore." λέγων is another circumstantial participle attached to the subject "God." It has for its object a brace of noun clauses both of which are quotes from Genesis 22:16f. The ἐπεὶ clause brings in a dependent adverbial idea. "Since he was having to swear according to no one greater. . . " εἶχεν is descriptive imperfect.

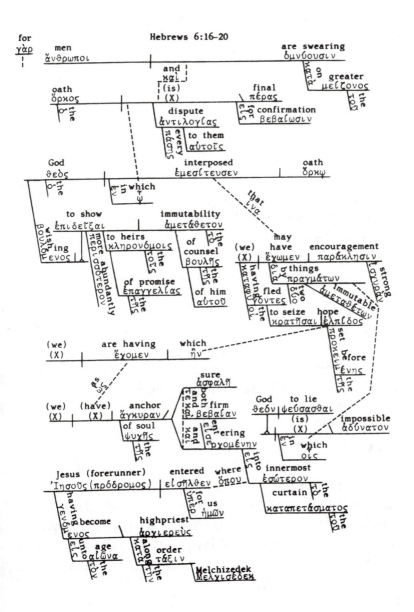

Hebrews 6:16–20

167

THE DIAGRAM OF HEBREWS 6:16-20

This is a lengthy sentence of 84 words expressed in eight clauses, the first two of which are independent. The six dependents stem from the second of the major clauses. The two basic ideas lay a foundation on which the rest is built. "Men swear . . ." and "the oath is final. . . ." The present tense of ὀμνύουσιν is gnomic in force for this is universally true among men. The second clause establishes by adverbial phrases two final results accomplished by an oath. (1) It settles disputes. (2) It certifies that which the oath pledges; it is "for confirmation."

The initial dependent clause is ushered in by prepositional phrase "in which." At bottom it is an adjectival idea referring back to the general idea set forth in the two basic clauses about man's custom of oath-taking and its use in finalizing disputes, "in which (fact) God interposed (mediated) an oath." The object ὅρκῳ is instrumental case, "with an oath." Two purpose ideas spring off of this ἐν ᾧ clause. The circumstantial participle βουλόμενος gives God's inner purpose, his divine secret counsel which looks to someone or something beyond himself; ". . . wishing to show more abundantly. . . ." The comparative "more abundantly" alludes to God's wishing to go beyond the simple promise which normally would be adequate. But by adding to a promise an oath he could fulfill his desire to reassure man "more abundantly" than a word. The ἵνα clause is an adverbial of purpose, "in order that we may have encouragement. . . ." The present ἔχωμεν emphasizes continuous action, "that we may go on having. . . ." In the infinitive phrase "to seize hope" the genitive of "hope" is normal after words of sense such as "touch," "grasp," "hold."

The clause inaugurated by ἐν οἷς is adjectival amplifying πραγμάτων. Subject of the clause is the aorist infinitive ψεύσασθαι "to lie" used with accusative of general reference θεόν. Yet another adjective clause is that advanced by ἥν, "which we are having. . . ." It describes "hope." And here again the present of continuing action ἔχομεν suggests that our "hope" is an unbroken constant to which we "grasp." ὡς inserts an adverb clause telling how we hold to our hope, that is, "as we hold to an anchor." Three adjective ideas help fill out to completion the idea of anchor, "sure," "firm" and "entering into. . . ." The adjective aspect of participles is prominant in εἰσερχομένην. It is descriptive of "anchor." Yet it is still a verbal with present tense and passive voice; it is circumstantial, ". . . an anchor . . . entering into the innermost of the curtain. . . ." ἔρχομαι is a defective verb, that is, passive in form with an apparently active meaning.

ὅπου submits the final dependent clause, "where Jesus (as) forerunner entered. . . ." The purpose of his entering comes out in the prepositional expression "for us." ὑπέρ literally means "over" but adopts a variety of resultant meanings determined by context such as "in behalf of . . .," "because of . . ," "concerning. . . ." In this instance when Jesus entered, in his person, we entered; as indeed the "people of God" did in the person of the Old Testament priest when he entered the Holy of Holies. By the priestly work of Jesus the way is open for us into the personal presence of God!

A Translation

Hebrews 7:1-28

For this Melchizedek, king of Salem, priest of God Most High, who met Abraham returning from the slaughter of the kings and who blessed him, to whom also Abraham divided a tithe from all, first indeed being translated, king of righteousness, and then also king of Salem, which is king of peace, without father, without mother, without ancestral lineage, having neither beginning of days nor end of life, being likened to the son of God: (he) abides as priest evermore. But behold how great this one is to whom Abraham the patriarch gave tithe from the top of the spoils. On the one hand they of the sons of Levi receiving the priesthood possess command to tithe the people according to the law, that is, their brothers, even though they have come out of the loins of Abraham; but on the other hand the one not having ancestral lineage has tithed Abraham and he blessed the one having the promises. And without any dispute the lesser is blessed by the greater. And here dying men receive tithes but there one being attested that he lives (receives tithes). And, so to speak, Levi, the one receiving tithes has been tithed through Abraham; for he was as yet in the loins of his father when Melchizedek met him. If, then, perfecting was through the Levitical priesthood (for they have been given law upon it) what yet were the need for another priest to arise according to Melchizedek and not be called according to Aaron? For the priesthood being changed of necessity a change of law becomes. For he upon whom these things are spoken has partaken of a different tribe from which no one has served the altar. For that our Lord has arisen from Judah is evident, about which tribe Moses spoke nothing concerning priests. And it is yet more abundantly clear if according to the likeness of Melchizedek another priest arises who comes not according to law of fleshen commands but according to the power of an indissoluble life. For he is attested to that you are a priest into the age according to the order of Melchizedek. For on the one hand a disannulling becomes of a foregoing command because of its weakness and uselessness—for the law perfected nothing—but on the other hand a bringing in of a better hope (becomes) through which we are drawing near to God. And by as much as not without oath-swearing—for they indeed without oath-swearing have become priests, but that one with an oath-swearing through the one saying to him, The Lord swore and will not repent, You are priest into the age—by this much Jesus has become surety of a better covenant. And the priests have become many because by death (they) are hindered from remaining but that one, because he abides into the age, holds priesthood without change. Because of this he is able to save unto the uttermost the ones coming to God through him since he is always living to intercede in their behalf. For such a high-priest was appropriate for us; holy, without bad-ness, unstained, having been separated from sin-ners and having become higher than the heavens; who does not daily have necessity first to offer sacrifices for his own sins, then for the people even as those priests (do). For he, having offered him-self, did this (for the people) once for all. For the law appoints men having weakness as highpriests but the word of the oath, the one after the law, (appoints) Son perfected forever.

AN OUTLINE OF HEBREWS 7:1-28
PERFECT PATTERN; PERFECT PRIEST

The value of a priest lies in the performance, not in his office, dress, or religious rites. Does the priest deal with sin or is he merely perfunctorily performing a pantomime!

I. THE PERFECT PATTERN OF A PRIEST. 7:1-12

    1. Priesthood essential to fallen *humanity.*

    2. The best pattern of priesthood seen, not in Hebrew history but in the Canaanite Priest-King, Mel-chizedek. 1-3

    3. But even Melchizedek furnishes the background pattern, not the ultimate absolute priestly service. 4-12

II. CHRIST, THE PERFECT PRIEST. 7:13-28

1. All others, including other priests, pay tithes to him.
2. All others receive blessing from him.
3. Death doesn't limit his tenure as it does the others.
4. Change in Law and Priesthood implies they were temporary expedients of which Jesus the fulfillment.
5. The priesthood of Jesus is everlasting. vss. 11, 23-25
6. His priesthood rests on a divine oath, not natural birth.
7. His intercession for his people is superior.
8. The nature of his Person qualifies him as superior.
9. The nature of his sacrificial offering is superior! He gave "himself."

But the bottom line for man is the elimination of sin and its consequences. Man's problem is neither lack of authority or knowledge. It is moral! It is here that Jesus rises to his highest service. He is the ultimate, the absolute priest. He is able to deliver from the curse of the law, the darkness of ignorance, but most of all the moral depravity of sin and its aftermath, death.

SOME EXPOSITORY THOUGHTS ON HEBREWS 7:1-28

The little acorn holds the promise of the mighty oak! But it's the tree, not the acorn, that provides shade, lumber, and fruit. The purpose of the acorn is not buried within itself. It points to the mature tree beyond itself through sunshine, storm, and years. The value of a shadow lies, not in the shadow, but in that which it foreshadows. The worth of a prophecy, is not in the prophecy, but in that which is prophesied. The profit in a promise does not consist in the promise but in the fulfillment. The value in a car is not in the showroom but on the highway. Performance, not price, determines the value!

So it is with priest and priesthood. His value does not lie in his office, dress, temple, ritual, family or politics. It's in his power and performance in dealing with sin in the sinner. A doctor may be ever so knowledgeable, skillful and famous but if his medicine doesn't dissolve *disease,* he might as well be ignorant, stupid and unknown. He might as well be a butcher as a surgeon if his scalpel can't cut out my cancer! The function of a priest is to eliminate sin, restore fellowship with God, and abolish the moral madness that issues in death! A priest is not to pantomine a play or to dramatize death. On the contrary he must dissolve sin, introduce the sinner into the presence of the living God and thereby restore life and eliminate death. Is there such a priest or priesthood that does this?

The perfect pattern!

Priests and priesthood are not matters on the fringe of human concern. They are at the core of all that affects humanity. Even to the irreligious the priest's function is vital. Though he rejects the very idea of priesthood and denies the existence of God, still he, being a moral moron, must deal with the priestly function. Call him Psychiatrist or Mental Therapist, but the fact remains that he needs the priestly service. From the aborigine witch-doctor to the most sophisticated physician the problem of sin, moral, mental, and physical sickness, demands the skill of a priest. We are out of kelter with the universe (religion calls it *God*). But regardless of name, it's the work of the priest to put man back into harmony with his moral and spiritual environment. Priesthood is essential to fallen humanity. It's not a cultural lapse or a national deviation. Wherever sin rises to the conscious level there will be a priest by whatever name he be called.

And the quality of the priesthood will be determined by the sensitivity to the moral depravity of sin as perceived by the sinner. If sin is conceived as only a physical defect the priest may be nothing more than a masseur of muscle and bone. But if it be moral rebellion against a holy God then the priest must offer a reconciling atonement. The fact remains that a priest is essential for fallen humanity.

Various forms of natural priesthoods appear in Old Testament history. The father of the clan, the king of the people, the sorcerer are samples. But that which dominates the Old Testament is associated with the people of Israel. Particularly the tribe of Levi from whom was consecrated Aaron and his sons. They taught Law, pronounced blessings, staged temple worship, administered rituals. Furthermore, in his own person, the Highpriest represented the people in the Holy of Holies before the Mercy Seat. If space in the Old Testament about the Hebrew priests is a measure then the Aaronic priesthood is the model. But no! The perfect pattern of priesthood is Melchizedek, priest-king of a mountain city-state of the Canaanite city of Salem (Gen. 14:18-20). In his only historic appearance he is set forth as "priest of God Most High." Abraham, patriarchal forefather of all Israel, paid tithes to and received blessings from this venerable priest of the living God. The Psalmist pointed to this Melchizedek as the model for King-Messiah to whom he looked for redemption. "You are priest forever after the pattern of Melchizedek" (Ps. 110:4). And the burden of the Hebrew letter is that this Melchizedek, not Aaron, was the perfect pattern of the ideal, absolute priest. At any level, natural, pagan, Hebrew or Christian, Melchizedek offers the one perfect etching of what priest and priesthood must be.

But observe that even this Melchizedek provides only the background model, not the ultimate absolute priesthood itself. He's the perfect pattern, not the perfect priest!

Christ the perfect priest!

A model is not the real thing even as an acorn is not the tree, nor a shadow the substance. But a model does sketch the lines along which the real picture is painted. Melchizedek is the rough sketch of which Jesus Christ is the full portrait. That which Melchizedek was and what happened between him and Abraham is but a miniature compared to the Person of Christ and that which exists between sinner and Saviour. One is acorn; the other is tree. One is promise, the other fulfillment. One is prophecy, the other performance. One is shadow, the other real. So that which appears in Melchizedek in original figure finds fulfillment in Jesus as absolute redeemer. Melchizedek was representative priest; Christ is actual, absolute priest!

One idea threading its way through all Hebrew thought is that the act of the progenitor has consequences on the posterity. "In Adam all die" is the first of a long series. Thus what Abraham did, good or bad, his progeny did.

When Abraham offered tithes to Melchizedek and received a blessing he was recognizing in worship the superior greatness of the priest-king of God. Yea! Even more! He was worshipping the Most High God of this priest-king. And with Abraham's worship went that of all his descendents, including Aaron and his sons.

Yet it wasn't to Melchizedek, the shadow, that Abraham really submitted his worship. It was to the Christ for whom Melchizedek was only a symbol. Giving tithes to the prophetic figure Abraham was in fact giving worship to the absolute Christ. Had not God said of the Christ, "You are priest forever after the pattern of Melchizedek"? It is Jesus the Christ who is the perfect object of devotion, not the king of Salem! Melchizedek is the acorn; Christ the full grown oak!

As perfect pattern Melchizedek is presented without ancestral lineage. And so far as the biblical story goes he had no "end of life." The Bible presents him as a *living* man and nothing else. On the pages of the Bible he lives evermore! In contrast Aaronic priests are "mortal men." Each dies, succeeded by another. And by each priest's death those who depended on his service had to turn to someone else. Not so with Christ! He retains the power of priestly service "without change." He abides in God's presence forever. He's *always* available as intermediary and intercessor. Death could not destroy him nor mortality hinder his service. He lives forever as priest "after the order of Melchizedek." Because his person and priesthood are permanent he's the perfect priest.

But there's more to Christ's priesthood than the negative fact that he doesn't die. He performs his function of redeeming by the "power of an indissoluble life." He not only tramples over death and thus removes my guilt but he instills into me the sustaining power of *his indissoluble* life. He wipes out my past record but he also dissolves the stain of what I *am*. He introduces into *me* the "power of an indestructible life."

Childhood is a temporary stage in the growing of a man. The Aaronic priesthood was but a temporary stage. It obtained at the childhood level of redemption. It was the high school adolescent period of preparation. It was designed to teach lessons about sin and salvation. It revealed the need for the perfect priest who transcends external laws of ritual pantomine. The perfect priest came with the energy of an inner law of life. In symbolic service Melchizedek appeared as priest before the law in which Aaron was established as priest. Christ, the antitype of Melchizedek, appeared after the Mosaic system had served its temporary purpose. So God inserted the Aaronic system as a parenthesis in history, an accommodation to the immature needs of immature people. But from the planting of the seed to the plucking of the fruit God anticipated the unchanging, absolute, priest. "If perfection had been attainable" or expected under "the Levitical priesthood . . , what further need for another . . . after the order of Melchizedek?" If one has doubts about God's plan for his perfect priest consider that Jesus, humanly speaking, did not come from the priestly family of Levi but from Judah.

The sons of Aaron became priests by natural birth. Whether good or bad they were born priests. Not so him who is priest after the pattern of Melchizedek. He was personally appointed and not without a divine oath. God's spoken word is normally enough to verify a fact. When God adds an oath he is underscoring the importance of that to which he swears. Of Messiah the Psalmist said, "The Lord sware and will not repent himself, You are priest forever." On this basis the author of Hebrews claims that "by so much also has Jesus become the surety for a better covenant." Surety means more than mediator. For the insuror guarantees the fulfillment of that which he mediates. The Levitical system had a mediator but no surety. But Jesus, priest after the mold of Melchizedek, guarantees the continuing fulfillment of the new covenant of which he is the mediator. He guarantees to nullify the guilt of my soul and the consequences of my sin. "Because I live you also shall live!" That's the word of the insuror.

To identify with suffering, to make propitiation, are roles which a priest performs. He also does duty as intercessor. Thus because Christ is permanent priest he "is able for all time to save those who draw near to God through him, since he always lives to make intercession for them" (vs. 25). This conjoins with the prophetic word, ". . . he bore the sin of many, and made intercession for the transgressors" (Is. 53:12). Nor was this intercessory work of the priest absent from Paul's thought. Of Christ he said, "who is at God's right hand, who also makes intercession for us" (Rom. 8:34). Even in "the days of his flesh" he performed the part of intercessor. At the last supper Jesus said to Peter, "I have prayed for you that your faith may not fail; and when you have turned again, strengthen your brethren" (Luke 22:32). And the great intercessory prayer of John 17 is an excellent example of just how he intercedes in behalf of his people. What was spoken by prophet, confirmed by apostle and practiced on the earth by Jesus is no less true of his ministry in heaven. His service as priest on man's behalf is never-ending. His continuing ability to save is absolute. His intercession is effective and efficient.

By his nature Jesus is perfect priest! Though the "law appoints men . . . having weakness, but the word of the oath . . . appoints a Son, perfected forever." In Jesus no weakness appeared. He endured the worst that evil could offer and never yielded. He shared with sinners but not in their sin. Though he had no need to offer sacrifice for himself he offered himself for the people. His sacrifice of self is befitting for us since he's "holy, guileless, undefiled, separated from sinners, and higher than the heavens." Because of the person that he is, he's a superior priest. He alone is the perfect priest.

At the outset of the letter the Son was pictured as one who "made purification for sins . . ." but here in the present text the nature of his sacrificial offering is plainly declared. "He has no need, like those priests, to offer sacrifices daily, first for his own sins, then for the people. For he, having offered *himself* did this (for the people) once for all." The sacrifice was not that of a reluctant, unwilling, bellowing, dumb animal. On the contrary, he freely, willingly, and with loving devotion gave "himself" as a qualified, acceptable, efficacious sacrifice for sin.

Man needs a king to point out the path, a prophet to declare God's message. God needs representatives to rule and reveal. But in man's moral marshland the need of all needs, both for God and man, is that of a priest to dissolve the differences propelled by sin. Sedative for sin cannot be coerced by king. Nor can sin be expelled by prophet. In fact king must punish and prophet must prick the conscience. So the bottom line is the elimination of sin and its consequences. And without question *that* is the work of the priest. Man's is a moral problem, not just one of authority and knowledge. It is just here that Jesus rises to the ultimate, the absolute priest. He is able to deliver from the curse of the king (Law), from the darkness of ignorance, and most of all from the depravity of sin and its aftermath, death! One hardly improves on perfection!

Hebrews 7:1-3

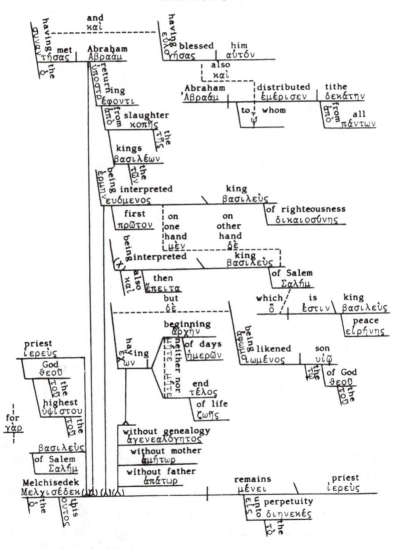

182

THE DIAGRAM OF HEBREWS 7:1-3

Of the numerous expressions which make up the building blocks of 7:1-3 only three are classed as clauses. The bare independent clause reads, "Melchizedek remains priest." Prepositional phrase "unto the perpetuity" (forever) answers the question *how long* he remains priest. The subject, Melchizedek, is expanded by four rather extensive appositional expressions. In fact they constitute the rest of the sentence.

First comes two nouns with modifiers. They identify this enigmatic figure as being "king" and then "priest." As king he's characterized as "of Salem"; as priest he's "of the God of the highest." These genitives specify the *kind* of priest and king he was.

A second apposition consists of a couplet of attributive participles with their modifiers, "the one having met" (συναντήσας) and "having blessed" (εὐλογήσας). Abraham is object of συναντήσας) and, though a fixed case form, is instrumental with a verb that uses that case. Modifying "Abraham" is present circumstantial participle ὑποστρέφοντι. It is descriptive present; the context suggests *time,* ". . . as he was returning. . . ." To continue his appositional description of "this Melchizedek" the author changes from the attributive participle to a full subordinate clause; "to whom Abraham also contributed tithe. . . ." The aorist of the two participles as well as of "distributed" concentrates attention on the facts, not any description of those facts. "He met . . . he blessed . . . Abraham distributed. . . ." In the present argument the facts were the important items more than colorful circumstances surrounding the facts.

Why was this puzzling man called Melchizedek? The answer is found in a third apposition, this time circumstantial present "being interpreted" (ἑρμηνευόμενος), which seems to suggest cause. He was called Melchizedek because the name signified his character and function among the Jebusites. It also points to his place in redemptive history. The "of righteousness" and "of Salem" are genitives which characterize the *kind* of king he was. "Salem" is more particularly described by the adjectival relative dependent clause "which is king of peace."

The fourth appositional identifying Melchizedek consists of five elements, two substantives, one verbal adjective and two participles. "Fatherless" and "motherless" are the substantives, not at all meaning that he appeared in history as an apparition with no roots in flesh and blood. But so far as recorded history goes none are chronicled. That is to say, he has no recorded pedigree as indeed the verbal "with genealogy" makes clear.

The present participle ἔχων with its compound objects "the beginning of days nor end of days" has been wrongly taken to mean that he appeared in the world as a specter without natural birth or death. But what is involved is really an idea that the author is trying to communicate. So far as the historical story is concerned Melchizedek has no lineage nor do we know anything about him after Genesis 14. He stands isolated in history. In that respect he stands as perfect pattern for Jesus as perpetual priest, "like unto the Son of God."

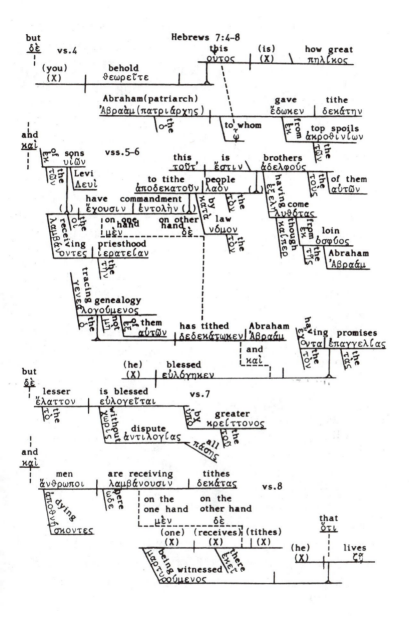

Hebrews 7:4-8

185

THE DIAGRAM OF HEBREWS 7:4-8

Verse four enfolds a complex sentence. It has two dependent clauses stemming from the one independent. θεωρεῖτε is present imperative exhorting the readers to "keep on beholding." In other words, don't let your attention be diverted; be concentrating. The first of the dependent elements is a noun clause object of θεωρεῖτε. The second is an adjectival idea introduced by "to whom" (ᾧ) further identifying οὗτος, subject of the noun clause. The prepositional phrase "from the top of the spoils" is adverbial in function telling what the source (ablative) of the tithe was. ἀκροθινίων is a compound word built from ἄκρος top and θίς heap. Abraham gave his tithe "from the top of the heap." He gave from the first and the best of the booty.

The sentence stretching over verses five and six accommodates three independent clauses and thus gives the compound flavor. The sentence also includes a dependent noun clauses. So it is to be classed as a compound-complex. The initial independent idea states, "they have commandment. . . ." The subject "they" is represented by definite article οἱ as it identifies who "they" are. That is, "the (ones) of the sons of Levi." This subject "they" is further pinpointed by the present circumstantial participial phrase "receiving the priesthood." The "commandment" is direct object of the main verb. It is expanded by the present infinitive ἀποδεκατοῦν "to tithe the people." This infinitive phrase is appositional to "commandment." In turn λαὸν, object of the infinitive, is itself augmented by an appositional clause, "that is their brothers" (τοῦτ᾽ etc.). Perfect participle ἐξεληλυθότας is circumstantial, concessive in force, describing "brothers."

186

The second independent idea is set in sharp contrast to the first by μὲν . . . δὲ. Those "of the sons of Levi" tithed their own brothers even though they were of the "loins of Abraham." But "on the other hand" that one not tracing genealogy "has tithed Abraham." The perfect tense δεδεκάτωκεν insists on the fixed quality of that act of tithing. That Melchizedek tithed Abraham is a fact of history and its significance stands as a permanent consequence.

The third of the independent clauses states, ". . . and he blessed the one having the promises." The verb of the clause is aorist εὐλόγηκεν which, though not denying the permanent significance, does not call attention to that feature. It merely presents the fact as an event. In the aorist the fact as fact is emphasized; the perfect stresses the ongoing effect of the action.

Verse seven is a simple sentence. "Without any dispute the lesser is being blessed by the greater." The present εὐλογεῖται is gnomic in force; it represents what is universally true.

Verse eight frames a compound-complex ordering of the clauses. It has two independent clauses and one dependent. Once again μὲν . . . δὲ indicate a pointed contrast. And this time the contrast is sharpened by the two adverbs "here" and "there." The "here" refers to the Levitical priesthood; the "there" alludes to Melchizedek. The distinction is further magnified by contrasting the circumstantial participle "dying men" with the subordinate object-noun clause, "that he lives." The second of the independent clauses is largely elliptical, its subject, verb, and object being implied by and borrowed from the first.

Hebrews 7:9–12

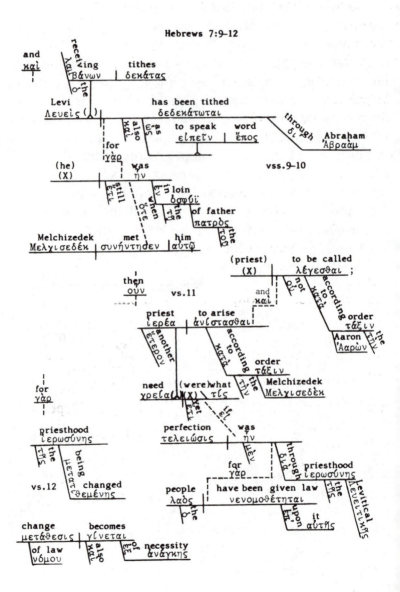

188

THE DIAGRAM OF HEBREWS 7:9-12

Two independent clauses, the second of which is supported by a dependent, makes of verses 9-10 a compound-complex sentence. "Levi has been tithed" is the initial independent notion. Again to be observed is the perfective action highlighting continuing result of past action as set forth in perfect tense δεδεκάτωται. "Levi has not only been tithed but he remains a tithed one." How that is conceived to have been done gets added clarity by means of διά with genitive expressing indirect agent, "through Abraham." ὡς with infinitive εἰπεῖν is an idiom used in older Greek meaning "so to speak." It is used in the New Testament only here. That Levi had been tithed was certainly true "in a manner of speaking."

An extended explanation of this fact of Levi having paid a tithe "through Abraham" is presented in the second independent observation, "for he was still in the loins of his father." An adverbial temporal clause signifies *when* the tithing took place, ". . . when Melchizedek met him. . . ." The third personal pronoun αὐτῷ is direct object in the instrumental case following a verb of association.

Four full clauses in verse eleven make the sentence look terribly entangled. But only one of them is independent, ". . . need (were) what. . . ." A lengthy appositional expression having two infinitive phrases makes clear the "need" which the author has in mind; ". . . that a different priest arise according to the order of Melchizedek and that he not be called according to the order of Aaron." ἱερέα is accusative of general reference with infinitive. And yet another accusative of general reference ("he" or "priest") is implied with infinitive λέγεσθαι. Preposition κατά with accusative presents a standard of measurement, "according to. . . ."

189

The "if" clause is the protasis of a second class conditional sentence determined as unfulfilled. It assumes that the condition is not true. "If perfecting were possible (but it isn't), then what would be the need (but there is such a need). . . ." τελείωσις is an action noun picturing a process more than a state or quality of being. "Perfection" is more than a static condition at which one arrives. It is a maturity toward which one is constantly moving. Christ is an irreplacable priest. His sacrifice takes care not only of past guilt of sin but current sinning. He "makes perfect" the sinner.

The final clause in the sentence of verse eleven is introduced by γὰρ and the diagram attaches it to the "if" clause. It almost seems a parenthetical expression, ". . . for the people have been given law upon it," that is, on the Levitical priesthood. The validity of the law rests on the validity of the priesthood.

Though it displays a genitive absolute the sentence encompassed in verse twelve is simple in structure. The absolute hangs there without grammatical relationship although the thought is quite clearly related. After the absolute, "the priesthood being changed," there follows the main postulate, "of necessity a change of law becomes."

The verb γίνεται is present passive of the defective verb γίνομαι. The "defective" aspect indicates that it is passive in form but apparently active in meaning. The verb does not mean "be" or "come" but "become." It expresses the idea of an unfolding of something inherent within that must, in the nature of things, spring into being.

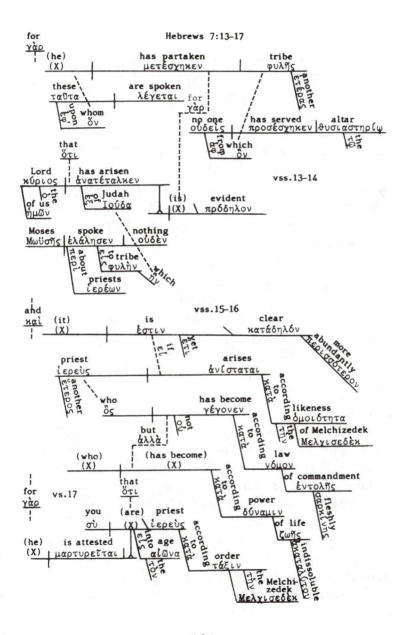

Hebrews 7:13–17

191

THE DIAGRAM OF HEBREWS 7:13-17

The sentence embraced by 7:13-14 is a neatly packaged collection of six clauses. Two independent and four dependent classify it as compound-complex. "He has shared (in a) tribe" is the first independent. φυλῆς is genitive direct object after a verb of sharing. The subject "he" is further identified by an adjective clause, "upon whom these things are spoken." Indeed the object "tribe" also is described by another subordinate adjectival clause, "from whom no one has served the altar." The perfect tenses μετέσχηκεν and προσέσχηκεν both call attention to the prolonged continuance of past action. "He . . . has occupied a permanent place in a different clan than Levi's" *and* "from which no one ever got or held a permanent function at the great altar at which all Aaronic sacrifices were offered."

Subject of the second independent thought takes the form of a noun clause, ". . . that our Lord has arisen out of Judah. . . ." This, claims the author, "is evident." Another subordinate clause, this time adjectival, identifies "Judah." ". . . to which tribe Moses spoke nothing concerning priests. . . ."

The four clauses of verses 15-16 frame a complex sentence. The one main clause states, "It is more abundantly clear. . . ." Just how very clear is brought forward by the comparative "more abundantly" used as an adverbial accusative. And the ἔτι adds to the "more abundantly clear" idea. The comparison suggested by this combination of adverbs points toward everything presented in the preceding sentence of verses 13-14. That is, that Moses spoke nothing about Judah out of which it is quite evident that the Lord arose, and that he shared in that tribe from which no one ever served at the great altar.

The εἰ thrusts forward a supporting conditional dependent. It is a first class with the "if" idea assumed to be true. ". . . if another priest arises (and he does), it is more abundantly clear (and it is). . . ." Two dependent clauses, one negative and the other positive, are advanced by the relative ὅς. They are adjectival describing the "another priest." The second of these two borrows its subject and verb from the first, ". . . who has not become (arisen) according to law of fleshen command but who has become (arisen) according to power of indissoluble life. . . ." The perfect γέγονεν should not be ignored. Both negative and positive action are permanently fixed circumstances. Note that ἕτερος modifying the subject of the "if" clause is another of a "different" kind and not another of the same kind of priest. Also observe that the -ινος ending of the adjective σαρκίνης indicates that the commandment is "fleshen," that is, in its essential constitution the command is "made of" not just "like" flesh. That is to say, it deals with what is essentially external and not of the inner spirit. Its meaning is contrasted to ἀκαταλύτου which describes the "life" inherent in "our Lord." Because it could not, death did not "dissolve" the life in Jesus. And that fact determined the indissoluble nature of his priesthood.

Verse 17 shapes a complex combination of two clauses. ". . . is testified" is the main idea. "You are priest . . ." serves as noun clause, object of the main verb "testified." ὅτι introduces indirect discourse after the verb "testify."

Hebrews 7:18–22

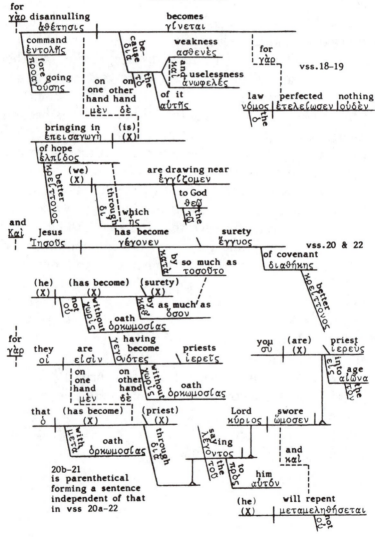

194

THE DIAGRAM OF HEBREWS 7:18-22

In joining together two parts of a sentence the μὲν and δὲ act as mortar to bricks. Mortar keeps bricks separate from one another yet is the cohesive force that holds them together. These particles keep the two clauses apart in contrast and yet tie them together as two elements in this compound-complex sentence. "On the one hand a disannulling becomes . . . but on the other hand a bringing in (becomes). . . ." Contrast extends also to the modifying genitives "command" (ἐντολῆς) and "hope" (ἐλπίδος). The genitive is the specifying case; it indicates *this* and not *that*. It's none other than the "command" kind of disannulling; it's none other than the hope" kind of bringing in. Even the modifiers of these two genitives continue the contrast, the circumstantial participle "foregoing" and the comparative adjective "better." Contrast survives in the two διά expressions. διὰ with accusatives is a prepositional phrase used as an adverb to tell why the disannulling became; "because of its weakness and uselessness." The δι' ἧς inserts a dependent adjective clause further describing "hope." A third independent clause appears as a sustaining explanation as to why a disannulling might have been expected to "become." " . . . for the law perfected nothing. . . ." ἐτελείωσεν is aorist of the word that signifies "to bring to its intended goal." In other words, to bring to maturity, to fulfillment, to complete realization! By its very nature, law didn't, wasn't expected to, and doesn't bring anyone or anything to its final goal. It is inherently weak.

Verses 20a and 22 reflect one sentence. But verses 20b-21 display a parenthetical interruption. In the diagram these verses appear as a separate compound-complex sentence.

195

The sentence of 20a-22 is complex having one independent and one dependent clause. "Jesus has become surety" is the basic idea. The degree to which he has become a "better" surety is presented by κατά with the quantitative demonstrative pronoun which corresponds to the relative καθ' ὅσον phrase; "by so much by as much as. . . ."

The parenthetical sentence of verse 20b-21 has as subjects for both of its independent clauses the demonstrative use of the article οἱ and ὁ = "they" and "that one." The verb of the first independent clause is a periphrastic perfect formed by present εἰσὶν plus perfect participle γεγονότες which supplements the εἰσὶν. Literally, "they are having become . . ." though we translate, "they have become. . . ." The same construction is implied for the second independent concept with proper adjustment to singular.

Two noun clauses appear as objects of the verbal aspect in the present attributive participle λέγοντος. "Lord swore and will not repent. . . ." As direct object of "swore" another noun clause emerges in the statement "you are priest unto the age. . . ." We note the similar mortar, conjunctive-adversative effect of μὲν . . . δὲ in this sentence as that which obtained in verses 18-19. It aids in keeping the contrast "without oath" versus "with oath" before the readers. It's another link in the chain which the author is forging setting forth superiority of the new over the old!

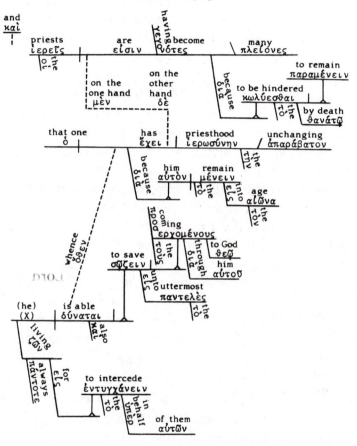

197

THE DIAGRAM OF HEBREWS 7:23-25

This sentence is compound-complex in form with two independent ideas contrasted and joined by μὲν . . . δὲ. The periphrastic perfect "have become" in the first clause displays extra insistence on the continuing extension of the multiplicity of the "many" priests as experienced by the old Aaronic regime. That which "has become" still is becoming. The very fact there are the "many" is itself a built in weakness to the essential work of that priesthood.

The Greek definite article was originally a demonstrative pronoun. Even after it became a distinct particle with a function and history all its own, it occasionally retained the old demonstative use and persisted on into koine times. The article is basically a pointer. It points out individuals from other individuals, classes from classes and qualities from qualities. The article with subject "priests" is an instance of the article designating a "class." They were "the" class of functionaries known under the Mosaic system as "the priests." Note too the old demonstrative use of the article ὁ used as subject of the second independent clause. It is to be translated "that one."

The verb of the second independent clause is linear action present ἔχει. The tense stresses the unbroken, continuing *possession* of priesthood on the part of "that one." ἀπαράβατον is predicate adjective (complement). It brings to completion the idea about the object "priesthood." A predicate adjective carries the main idea on which the writer wants the reader to focus. That is, "that one has the priesthood; and as an *unchanging* thing."

διά with an infinitive occurs twice in the sentence. Once with each of the main clauses. The first: "because the to be hindered by death to remain. . . ." The second: "because him to remain unto the age. . . ." These are extremely literal translations. In somewhat more readable English: ". . . because they, by death, were being hindered from remaining . . ." and " . . . because he remains forever . . ." διά with accusative is a normal expression for cause.

ὅθεν inserts a dependent clause of cause. Since his priesthood is unchangeable so is his ability to "be saving." σῴζειν is present tense expressing a continuing process. As each trial or opportunity arises "he is able to save. . . ." The infinitive has a direct object in the form of attributive present participle translated "the ones coming." Present tense here seems to suggest a distributive idea. That is, as each separate one "comes to him."

ζῶν is a circumstantial participle modifying the subject "he" of this dependent clause. The adverb πάντοτε "always" indicates how long he is "living." And the εἰς with infinitive ἐντυγχάνειν, "to intercede" expresses purpose. The infinitive is present tense which would suggest a continuing, repeated, ever available intercession as occasion demands.

A summary outline of this sentence:

1. Aaronic priests are "many" because they die.
2. Christ is priest, unchanging, abiding forever!
3. Therefore he is able:

   (a) To "save to the uttermost"
   (b) To intercede as needs arise.

Hebrews 7:26-28

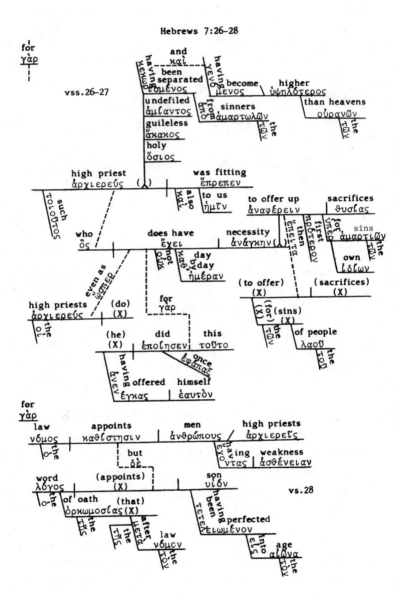

200

THE DIAGRAM OF HEBREWS 7:26-28

In keeping with the notion that words grouped about an infinitive form a phrase rather than a clause the sentence of 7:26-27 has four clauses. Only one is independent so the sentence is complex. Disrobed of its modifiers the chief clause says, "highpriest was fitting. . . ." In apposition to the subject, highpriest, are three adjectives coupled with two verbal adjectives (participles). This highpriest was "holy, without badness, without stain, having been separated from the sinners, having become higher than the heavens. . . ." οὐρανῶν is ablative after comparative. ἔπρεπεν is an imperfect tense expressing linear action in past time. The fitness, of *such* a highpriest has been present from the very beginning of the need of priestly function. The seemliness of it continues "for us."

Beginning with ὅς three subordinate clauses appear not to mention two infinitive phrases. The relative ὅς not only relates an adjective clause to "highpriest" but is also used as subject of its clause, "who does not have daily necessity. . . ." There follow the infinitive phrases both of which are in apposition to ἀνάγκην. But the second also sustains an adverbial relationship to the first as indicated by ἔπειτα = then. The present tense of ἔχει matches the linear "was fitting" of the preceding clause. Our highpriest *repeatedly* "does not have" necessity . . ." and therefore he "was" and is constantly appropriate for us. The γάρ clause parallels the ὅς clause with an explanation as to *why* he "doesn't have necessity. . . ." That reason is: ". . . for he did this once for all when he offered himself." The clause advanced by ὥσπερ is adverbial of comparison, ". . . even as those highpriests do (have necessity to offer . . .)." The definite article οἱ is anaphoric in that it points back to "the" well known Aaronic priests who were always offering sacrifices "first for their own sins" and "then for the sins of the people."

It should be noted that the γὰρ clause, when it says "he did this . . ." does not mean to claim that the "this" refers to Jesus having to "offer sacrifices first for himself etc. . . ." That is perfectly clear from the circumstantial participle ἀνενέγκας "having offered himself." No man offers himself for his own sins. Jesus offered "himself" for the sin of the people. Furthermore, he did it "once." ἐφάπαζ is stronger than just ἅπαζ. By his being sinless and by having done "this" sacrifice "once for all" there was no necessity for his offering any repeated sacrifice for the people, much less for himself.

Verse 28 is a two-pronged compound sentence. The two independent ideas are set in adversative relation. "The law appoints men having weakness *but* the word of the oath . . . appoints son having been perfected. . . ." The present ἔχοντας contrasts with perfect τετελειωμένον. The "men having weakness" not only as individuals were having repeated weaknesses but distributively they, each separate one, were having weaknesses. But the "son" as priest is permanently perfect for time and eternity. The article τῆς makes the whole μετὰ phrase definite and it ties it to ὁρχωμοσίας as adjective.

A Translation

Hebrews 8:1-13

But the chief point on the things being said (is this): we have such a highpriest who sat at the right of the throne of the majesty in the heavens—as minister of the Holy of Holies and the real sanctuary which the Lord pitched and not man. For every highpriest is appointed for the offering of both gifts and sacrifices whence it is necessary that this one have something which he may offer. If indeed, then, he were upon the earth he would not even have been priest, there being those who bear gifts according to law who serve copy and shadow of the heavenly things, even as Moses, when he was about to complete the tent, has been warned; for, he says, (You) see (that you) make all things according to the type, the one having been shown you on the mount. But now he has obtained a more excellent ministry by howsoever much he is also mediator of a better covenant which has been enacted on better promises. For if that first were faultless a place for a second would never have been sought. For, blaming them, he says, "Behold! the Lord says, Days are coming and I will fulfill upon the house of Israel and upon the house of Judah a new covenant, not according to the covenant which I made with their fathers in the day of my taking their hand so as to lead them from the land of Egypt—all this because they did not abide in my covenant and I disregarded them, says the Lord. Because this is the covenant, the Lord says, which I will covenant with the house of Israel after those days. I will give my laws into their mind and I will write them upon their hearts, And I will be to them for God and they shall be to me for people, And each shall not teach his fellow-citizen and each shall not teach his brother, saying, Know the Lord, because all, from the little unto the great of them, shall know me. Because I will be merciful with their iniquities and I will not any-more remember their sins. In the saying "new" he has made the first (covenant) old; but the one grow-ing old and aging (is) near (for) vanishing away.

AN OUTLINE OF HEBREWS 8:1-13
CHRIST'S PRIESTLY WORK: IT'S PLACE AND PERFORMANCE!

An imitation can never be an adequate substitute for the *real*.

I. CHRIST'S PRIESTLY WORK: ITS SANCTUARY. 8:1-6
   1. At the "right hand of the Majesty." vs. 1
   2. In the *real* "Holy of Holies," not a copy. vs. 2
   3. Because in the *real* his is a "more excellent ministry."

II. CHRIST'S PRIESTLY WORK: ITS COVENANT. 8:7-13
   1. The necessity for a new covenant. vss. 7-9

(a) The first "wasn't faultless." It lacked. vs. 7
(b) A new was promised by the prophet. vs. 8
2. The nature of the new covenant. vss. 10-12
   (a) God's word on inner heart, not outer stone. vs. 10
   (b) Based on knowing God, not natural birth. vs. 11
   (c) Based on God's forgiveness, not man's performance. vs. 12

Second best, not the worst, is enemy to the best. Don't choose any lesser when the best is available!

SOME EXPOSITORY THOUGHTS ON HEBREWS 8:1-13

An imitation is not the equivalent of the real thing. An impersonation is "like" but not the "same." Make-believe mimics but can never be the genuine. An artificial flower, even if it fooled a bee, would never fill the comb with honey. And so far as the human need for priestly work is concerned imitations won't do. For his redemption man needs what's real! Even the divine pattern can't clothe with real garments of righteousness; it takes the finished suit, not just the pattern.

The real sanctuary

While here in the flesh Christ was the *real* priest. He performed priestly functions while living among men. Certainly death on the cross was his adequate sacrifice for sin. But neither synagogue, temple or wayside pulpit could furnish the place where his saving priestly work could be perfected. That must be in the personal presence of God. And we have just "such a highpriest." He "took his seat at the right hand of the Majesty." Thereby he's in a position to exercise any authority he might need for priestly functions. He serves man's needs in and from the "Holy of Holies," the *real* sanctuary. It is not pattern, make-believe, or shadow; it is the real thing. It is that tabernacle "which the Lord pitched, not man." It is not of human origin, conception or construction. It wasn't begun by political party or created by human wealth or wisdom. It is *for* man but not *of* man. It is the real thing!

And because it's real Christ can offer a "more excellent" ministry. He's a better mediator of a better covenant based on better promises (vs. 6). Moses cut the pattern but Christ wore the cloth. And even though every religious philosopher after Moses cast some light, Jesus was (and is) the source and substance of that light. In fact, he is the full-orbed sun that ever filters through any human bulb. He's *real*, working in the one *real* sanctuary, the presence of the living God beyond the veil.

The real covenant

Anything short of full health leaves a man less than well. Negotiation in human contracts is always open when the existing one embodies a flaw. How much more then does a non-negotiable divine covenant need change if it falls short of dissolving sin? The very fact that God provided for a new covenant implied some lack in the old. And he confirmed that fault by sending the prophet to announce a new (Jer. 31:31-34).

The nature of the new is radically different from the old in three particulars. First, "I will give my laws into their mind and I will write them on their hearts." The new finds its power from the moral persuasion of the heart within rather than coerced conformity from police power without. In the old, God's laws were etched by God on stones. And they weren't enforced by a sense of right and wrong springing from the conscience. They were imposed by society without, policed by threats, curses, punishments by external forces. If the outside force failed one could, and often did, evade obeying the standards.

Consider a sample. In a certain city it takes 200 policemen to maintain "law and order." Yet in spite of the police, murder, robbery, rape and other forms of violent crime break out. In emergency session the city fathers decide to raise taxes and employ a thousand policemen. Now everyone feels safe. With a policeman literally on every corner crime is reduced to zero. Robbers refuse to rob, rapists reject raping, murderers resist killing. As long as a policeman stands nearby with drawn pistol the number of actual violent crimes falls to absolutely nothing. There is now a situation in which there is NO crime. Yet here is a point overlooked. The criminal population has not been reduced by one single individual!

The city fathers meet again. They conclude, "We've solved the problem of crime. Why have a police force at all? We can now do away with the police and get relief from these heavy taxes." But when such a naive decision is made what happens? Murder, robbery and rape shoot up to heights far beyond what they were before. And added to the violence come looting, arson, vandalism and unrestrained evil in unimaginable forms. So as long as law is enforced by a thousand policemen we eliminate crime but we don't eliminate criminals. One thousand policemen can reduce stealing but they can't reduce the number of thieves. Thieves are thieves even when they aren't stealing. A man is a liar even when he isn't lying. An adulterer is an adulterer even when he isn't committing adultery. As long as righteousness must be enforced by the pressure of outside muscle it leaves the disease of sin on the inside untouched. If some super technology could cap the cone of an active volcano so that all the ash, lava, and heat could be forced back into the bowels of the fiery mountain, it would not insure safety. All the bubbling, boiling, churning fury imprisoned would smolder, simmer and sizzle until it blew off any capping placed there by man. If the fires within aren't quenched no outside power can restrain forever the blow-off.

God said, "they continued not in my covenant." The people would not, could not, certainly did not, live up to the laws of the covenant. So God made judgment, "Since they regarded not my covenant, I regarded not them." But then God said something about a new covenant. "I will put my laws into their minds, and on their hearts I will write them." No longer is law to be imposed by outside force. It is to be written by God on the heart springing up with the energizing power of the Spirit of God. Fruit in a painting of still life is imposed on the canvass by the artist. But the fruit on a living tree is impelled forth by the life within the tree. The demands of the New Covenant are the same moral, ethical and spiritual fruit as the Old. But instead of being forced by threat of punishment and the curse of death the new springs from the power of life generated by the Spirit of God.

A second difference of the new is its demand of a spiritual rather than natural birth. And this particularly as it hinges on one's knowledge of God. That God works from "within" stems from the fact that "all shall know me from the little to the great."

In the Old one was born by natural birth into the people of God, the nation of the Jews. After birth one had to be taught, "Know the Lord." No so under the New. One must "know the Lord" before he is begotten into God's kingdom. We are "begotten again, not of corruptible seed, but of incorruptible through the word of God . . ." (I Pet. 1:23). There's no way to become a child of God under the New Covenant apart from first "knowing the Lord."

Knowledge of God belongs to the least little citizen as well as the oldest grey-beard. Moreover, it's experiential knowledge, not intellectual perception that initiates one into the kingdom. It's the inner awareness of a sensitized perception of right versus wrong. In a small eastern city of the U.S. there lived a forty-year-old moron whose intellectual perception was that of a twelve-year-old child. But his "knowledge" of God was 100% pure. His was a highly sensitized conscience. With his sensitive fingers he had the peculiar talent of being able to open any and all kinds of locks. On one occasion a local bank's vault became jammed. The authorities were faced with dynamiting it open. But then they thought of the town moron. He who was an intellectual dwarf but a spiritual giant. The fact that his moral life was determined by his sense of God's holiness governed the use of his "talent." He could have been a thieving destructive element. Yet it was his "knowledge" of God that gave him a spiritual advantage over moral "idiots" with an intellectual I.Q. of 150. It's this kind of "knowledge" of God that makes the "least" in the kingdom of God superior to any who by self-effort or police power strive to "live up to" the impossible heights of holiness required by divine law.

The third distinctive element of the New Covenant over the Old springs of the mercy and grace of God. "I will be merciful to their iniquities, and their sins will I remember no more." That is to say, this new covenant rests on God's forgiveness, not on man's performance. This covenant is founded on what God did at calvary, not what a man does during his lifetime.

If the people of the old covenant weren't able to live up to the law which said, "Thou shall not murder" then we can't live up to Jesus' "Thou shalt not be angry. . . ." Just here is the point of this new kind of covenant—we don't have to "live up to" anything! We don't strive, struggle and strain! It's Christ who did the struggling; it's Gethsemane and Calvary where the striving took place. Our covenant with God doesn't depend on my righteous acts but on his redeeming work. The old depended on man; the new depends on God. My standing with God hangs on his loving disposition, his willingness—not to overlook, but to forgive my rebellious sin. And above all what he has done at a specific point and place in human history on the cross. And this confirmed by raising Jesus from the dead! Our redemption has been accomplished; it is a thing finished, completed, done, perfected by God in Christ.

The Old Covenant is "old and worn out" "nigh unto vanishing away." If a drowning man cannot swim from the mid-ocean storm then someone must come from the shore to rescue him. If man is ever to be saved it is God who must lift him to safety. Man cannot struggle and strain his way out of his moral mess. God declared, "their sins I will remember no more."

When a shirt gets frayed at the collar it's "nigh unto vanishing." It's time for a new!

Hebrews 8:1-3

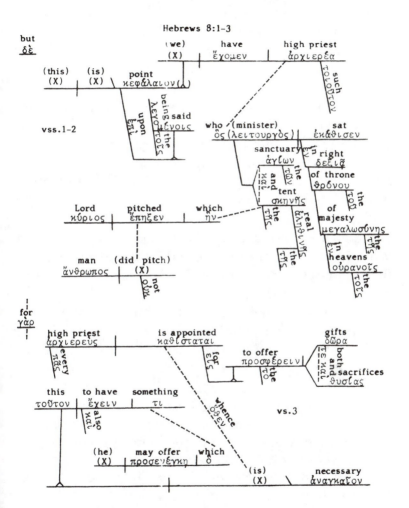

211

THE DIAGRAM OF 8:1-3

The bare independent clause of the complex sentence of 8:1-2 is, "This is the point. . . ." And the word "point" includes the idea of "head point." Modifying "point" is the prepositional ἐπὶ phrase declaring the basis "upon" which the point is being made. That is, "the point upon which the things being said."

Four dependent clauses stem off the main clause. First is a noun clause in apposition to κεφάλαιον, "we have such a highpriest." The qualitative demonstrative pronoun is used as an adjective describing *highpriest* and it refers back to the "superior" priest of 7:1-28 as well as forward to what he is to say in his resume of 8:1-6. This is "such kind of highpriest we have." The relative ὃς clause describes the priest as one "who sat at the right hand etc. . . ." λειτουργὸς is in apposition to the relative and further identifies where this highpriest "sat." He is one who not only "sat at the right hand of the throne of the majesty in the heavens" but also a "minister of the Holy of Holies and the real tent. . . ." This tent is further described by adjective clause, "which the Lord pitched." The adjective idea is doubly enforced by adding a negative adjectival clause, ". . . and not man."

An explanatory word about the adjective ἀληθινῆς is in order. All adjectives ending in -ινος indicate the idea of *made of*. Such adjectives suggest that the thing described in its essence is constituted of the element involved in the root of the word. So σάρκινος in I Cor. 3:1 is "fleshen" (made of flesh) rather than "fleshly" (like flesh). Thus the "ἀληθινῆς tent" here is the "true and real tent" and not just a pattern like the real.

The second sentence appearing on this page is also complex in structure. It has one independent and two dependent

212

clauses. The statement of the independent element consists of, "Every highpriest is appointed. . . ." The purpose for which he is appointed is set forth by εἰς and the present infinitive, "for to be offering. . . ." Both the main verb as well as the infinitive are present tenses. They portray the constant and continuous activity in both the appointing and the work of the highpriests. προσφέρειν is both repetitious as well as distributive. The offering of "gifts and sacrifices" is something the priests are continually repeating.

The fact stated in the main clause furnishes the basis for the necessity expressed in the ὅθεν subordinate clause. Because "every highpriest is appointed to offer . . ." is the reason why it is necessary "this one also have something which he may offer." The relative ὅ clause is adjectival in function describing τι. ὅ προσενέγκῃ is an indirect deliberative question = "What may he offer?" As far as time is concerned all subjunctives are future from the standpoint of the speaker or writer. But the aorist tense of προσενέγκῃ is quite significant, especially in contrast to the present infinitive of the preceding independent clause. Punctiliar "may offer" suits the single act of Jesus in offering himself *once*. The iterative present "to be offering" fits the idea of every Aaronic highpriest bringing annual offerings in never ending succession as the years rolled on. Note also contrast between their plural "gifts and offerings" and "this one's" single "somewhat."

213

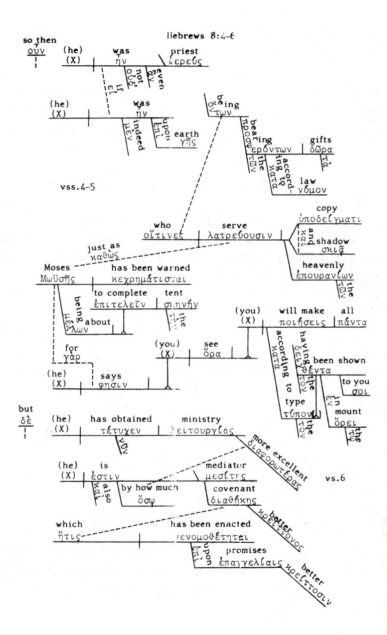

Hebrews 8:4-6

vss.4-5

vs.6

214

THE DIAGRAM OF HEBREWS 8:4-6

Verses four and five incorporate one complex sentence of seven clauses. The apodosis (conclusion) of a second class condition is the only independent idea: "So then he would not even be priest. . . ." The supporting "if" (protasis) clause predetermines that the condition is not true. ". . . if he were upon earth (but he's not . . .)" then he wouldn't even be a priest (but he is . . .)." Strictly speaking the rest of the sentence hangs grammatically unrelated because it begins with a genitive absolute. Present participle ὄντων modifies an understood "they" referring back in thought (though not in grammar) to the priestly tribe of Levi. The context calls for a causal idea, ". . . seeing (they are) the ones bearing gifts according to law. . . ." The "they" is carried forward by use of the relative pronoun οἵτινες subject of the adjective clause, "who serve a copy and shadow of the heavenly (things). . . ." The verb λατρεύω both in classical as well as koine Greek is used in reference to official service to deities. It is used with the dative of person or thing.

The next dependent is thrust forward by καθὼς = just as. It introduces an adverbial idea modifying the verb "serve." The clause indicates the standard of comparison upon which "they serve the copy etc." That is, "just as Moses has been warned. . . ." μέλλων is circumstantial participle of time, ". . . as he was about to complete." The last three dependent clauses are closely related to each other. The clause "(You) see" is object of "says" and "(you) will make all . . ." is object of "see." All are tied back to the comparative "just as" clause by the coordinating conjunction "for" (γὰρ).

215

The core of the argument of 8:1-6 rests in the different *places* in which the Aaronic priests served and the one in which Christ serves. Different sanctuaries call for different types of priests. And he who serves in the superior sanctuary would be of a superior rank of priesthood. Consequently verse six unfolds three ways in which his priestly ministry is better than that of the Levitical system.

The sentence of six is complex. It has three clauses. The independent idea conveys, "He has obtained a ministry." Of course the comparative adjective διαφορωτέρας indicates that this ministry which he has obtained is "more excellent" than that which the old system ever obtained. τέτυχεν is perfect tense emphasizing the fact that he holds this more excellent ministry on a permanent basis. That verb takes genitive as its direct object.

The degree to which Christ's ministry is "more excellent" is set forth in the adverbial clause introduced by the relative ὅσῳ in the instrumental case = "by how much." This is a quantitative relative expressing the idea of "as much as." The full clause reads ". . . by how so ever much as (he) also is mediator of a better covenant. . . ." Substantives ending in -της are *agent* words. That is, the one who does an action. μέσος mean "middle." A μεσίτης is one who performs the act of getting in the middle. What he does when he gets there is determined by the context. ἥτις is a qualitative relative = which by its very nature. The very quality of the "new" covenant makes it "better" than the older.

216

Hebrews 8:7-9

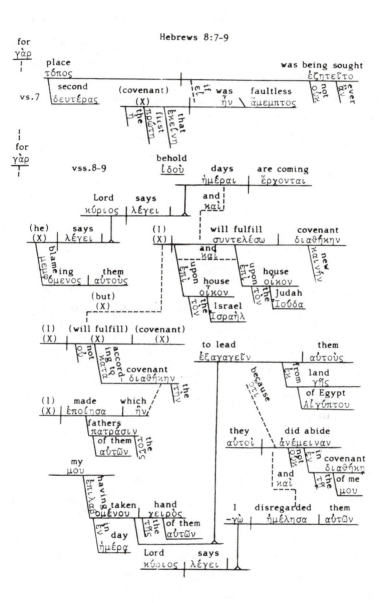

217

THE DIAGRAM OF HEBREWS 8:7-9

"For if that first (covenant) were faultless (and it's not), a place for a second would not ever be sought (as indeed it is)." That is a complex sentence of two clauses. It represents a second class conditional determined as unfulfilled. δευτέρας is objective genitive. The verbs in both clauses are imperfects, linear in force. They mark a repetition of action. All during the time during which the first covenant was in force there was a sense of lack, an ongoing desire for something better. It wasn't God searching but men. ἄμεμπτος is an old compound adjective meaning "without blame," "free from fault." Used here as predicate adjective.

As punctuated in Nestle's text verses 8-9 comprise one sentence. Except for the first four words it is a quotation from a part of Jeremiah 31. Taking the introductory four words as an independent clause that leaves the rest as dependents attached in one way or another to the λέγει of this main clause. The participle μεμφόμενος is circumstantial, possibly causal, describing the circumstances surrounding "he says. . . ."

The first dependent clause, "Lord says," is object of λέγει. As compound object of this second "says" three more noun clauses appear: "days are coming," "I will fulfill new covenant," and "(I will) not (fulfill . . .)." Two prepositional phrases used adverbially and introduced by ἐπὶ modify the verb "will fulfill." They indicate where the new covenant is to be instituted. And the fact that both sections are separately designated ("Israel" and "Judah") would suggest that the new covenant is to be for the *whole* of the people of God. The third noun-object clause follows.

It is almost entirely elliptical: "(I will) not (fulfill). . . ." the standard of measurement by which he "will not fulfill" is told by the κατὰ phrase, "according to the covenant. . . ." That "covenant" is described by the adjectival relative clause, ". . . which I made with their fathers. . . ." At this point the sentence as quoted from Jeremiah has a break in the grammar. A genitive absolute carries the thought forward: ". . . in the day my having taken (hold) of their hand. . . ." Grammatically this is not directly connected with the sentence. But in thought it is clearly referring to that point in time when the earlier covenant was inaugurated. An infinitive expressing purpose (ἐξαγαγεῖν) stems off of the genitive participle. He took them in hand "in order to lead them from the land of Egypt. . . ."

As the diagram shows the ὅτι clause is an adverbial clause of cause. But it is not to be attached to the infinitive. In thought it really goes all the way back to the three noun-object clauses, ". . . days are coming and I will fulfill, not according to . . . etc. . . ." The reason why the new covenant is brought in is "because they did not abide in my covenant. . . ." But the diagram is not able to show any mechanical connection to those clauses so the ὅτι on the slanting dotted line isn't attached to any particular point. The presence of another κύριος λέγει almost makes this a separate sentence. But if so it would leave the ὅτι hanging without any grammatical reference at all. So in thought we connect it to those noun clauses serving as objects of the earlier "Lord says." As the sentence stands it is complex.

Hebrews 8:10–11

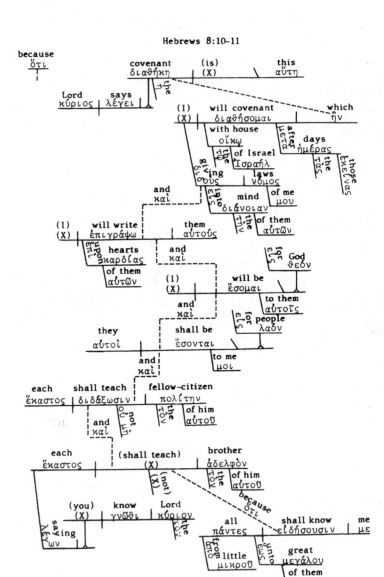

220

THE DIAGRAM OF HEBREWS 8:10-11

As punctuated in Nestle's text verses 10-11 fashion one complete sentence. It is still a part of the quotation from Jeremiah. As it stands the sentence is complex, the main clause being "Lord says." Note that this expression, "Lord says," is from Jeremiah and is the prophet's claim that he was the mouthpiece of God. After this independent clause nine dependents follow stating *what* the "Lord says."

First is a noun clause, object of λέγει, "says." "The covenant (is) this. . . ." To identify better the covenant of which he speaks the adjective dependent clause injected by ἦν is added. It's the "covenant which (1) will covenant. . . ." The time when it is to be given is pictured in prepositional phrase "after those days. . . ." The question where or with whom it will be made is displayed in the phrase, "with house of Israel. . . ." Participle διδούς suggests both purpose and time as the circumstances which surround the giving of the new covenant, "giving my laws into their mind. . . ."

Instead of paralleling the participle διδούς with another participle the author changes the construction to the finite verb ἐπιγράψω, "I will write. . . ." The adverbial idea of *where* he will write is reported in the ἐπί phrase, "upon their hearts. . . ."

Following the clause, "I will write them upon their hearts," and coordinate with it are four clauses joined by the coordinating conjunction καί. "I shall be to them for God" is the first of the four. Note that the predicate idea is the Hebraistic εἰς with accusative "for God" rather than a normal predicate nominative after copula verb. The same construction appears in the next of these four clauses, "and they shall be to me for a people. . . ." The third clause says, "and each shall not teach his fellow-citizen. . . ." The verb διδάξωσιν is aorist subjunctive used with strong double negative οὐ μὴ. Both verb and negative, though not stated, are implied in the next clause. ". . . each shall not teach his brother. . . ." Under the new covenant the essential knowledge of God comes *before* entrance into the kingdom. It's real, immediate and personal. In the Old one was born and then he learned. Under the new one learns and then he's born. Certainly one grows in knowledge and experience with God after his new birth. But essential personal knowledge by its nature must precede.

Of the final two dependent clauses one is noun and the other adverbial. Indicating the manner in which "each" is "not" to be teaching his brother the circumstantial participle λέγων appears. The noun clause "(You) know the Lord" is object of participle "saying."

The ὅτι clause is adverbial of cause. It presents the reason *why* there's no need that "each shall teach his brother." It is "because all shall know me from the least unto the greatest of them." εἰδήσουσιν is future perfect active of οἶδα. Note that γνῶθι from γινώσκω to know by experience is used in the previous clause. In other words, under the new covenant one starts with intuitive knowledge before he "learns" God.

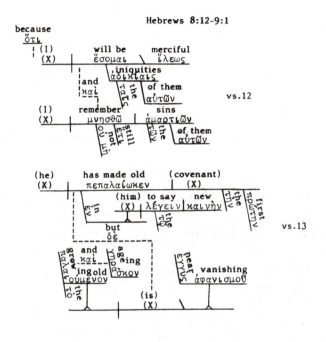

vs.12

vs.13

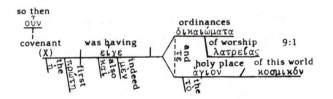

9:1

223

THE DIAGRAM OF HEBREWS 8:12—9:1

The ὅτι with which verse 12 begins frequently introduces a subordinate clause of cause. Here, however, it serves to inaugurate the sentence while at the same time it gives a logical reference to the preceding idea. The fact that "each shall know the Lord" before and when he becomes a part of God's people is based on God's mercy, not man's attainment. Here it is ushering in a compound sentence of two independent clauses rather than a dependent idea.

When all modifiers are removed from the two clauses the bare sentence reads, "I will be merciful" and "I will remember sins. . . ." The predicate adjective ἵλεως is an old Attic word which appears only here in the New Testament. God's mercy extends "to their iniquities" (ἀδικίαις). This is dative case personifying "iniquities" as though it were iniquities to whom he would be merciful when in fact it was "them" (people) to whom he's actually merciful.

οὐ μὴ is the very strongest kind of negative. "I will *not at all ever* remember their sins." ἁμαρτιῶν is direct object in genitive case after verb of remembering. It is because of the expiating effect of Jesus' priestly work that God is able to erase from his mind the sins of his people.

If infinitive λέγειν be treated only as a phrase then verse 13 structures a compound sentence. There are two independent clauses. The first says, "He has made old the first (covenant)." Perfect tense πεπαλαίωκεν calls attention to the fact that the covenant's old age is a fixed fact. It will never be anything but an old one. The infinitive phrase literally says, "in the to say 'new'" but may be more smoothly rendered, "in his saying 'new'—. . . ." English grammars designate the pronoun "him" as "subject" of the infinitive. But by virtue of its being "infinite" an infinitive is not limited by a subject. The so-called "subject" is really an adverbial accusative identifying who does the action in the infinitive. To call the "him" a subject is an accommodation to the limitations of English.

Subject of the second independent clause of verse 13 consists of a compounding of two attributive participles: ". . . the growing old (thing) and the aging (is). . . ." The predicate is a prepositional phrase, "near vanishing."

The sentence embodied in 9:1 is simple in form. It has a compound object of imperfect εἶχε. The imperfect tense describes that which the first covenant "was having" all through its entire duration. κοσμικόν is a late adjective from κόσμος and means "relating to this world." Here it is predicate, not attributive. It is objective complement carrying forward the idea involved in "holy place."

ANOTHER SAMPLE

Included here is another sample of an expository sermon. It too is abridged but it was delivered to a worshipping audience.

Again, studious research must precede all else. Consult the translation, outline, diagrams and SOME EXPOSITORY THOUGHTS on pages 203-210. From the outline on pages 204-205, it is obvious that expository sermons other than the one below might be prepared. In fact this sermon concentrates on verses 10-12 under point 2. "The nature of the new covenant."

The basic proposition is the *superiority of the new kind of covenant over the old*. The topic is drawn from the basic proposition. Eighteen paragraphs make up the sermon. The introduction consists of two brief paragraphs. The first uses an experience common to any audience, a ragged collar etc. Most anyone can visualize and identify with that image. It is designed to stir the imagination. The second paragraph alerts the audience to three specific points that will unfold as the sermon develops.

The *body* consists of fifteen paragraphs (3-17). The third of the three major points is presented first. It seems logical to develop the idea of God's gracious mercy as a foundation on which to develop the other ideas. What God did at Calvary is the basic thought. The fourth paragraph confirms the thought of three by pointing out that redemption is a finished fact not a subjective feeling. Paragraph five pictures the weakness of the old due to the weakness of the people of the old. This prepares for the idea in paragraph six which explicitly says that the new covenant is a new *kind* of agreement. A covenant springing out of the necessity created by man's weaknesses.

Paragraph seven introduces the second major point, *Power from within.* The eighth reminds that the old laws were outward, "on stone." They must be enforced by external power. Paragraphs nine and ten give illustrative material. One from a human problem and one from nature. They are designed to reveal the weakness of trying to force moral law on sin's deeply embedded power. Paragraph eleven calls attention to the fact that God resolved the weakness of the old by instilling his will inside the human heart. And it includes an illustration from art and nature to enforce the logic of such a procedure. Paragraph twelve reviews the two basic points thus far made. Paragraph thirteen restates with a slightly different approach the basic points.

226

The third major point is introduced in paragraph fourteen. It contrasts the natural birth into the old with the knowledge preceding the spiritual birth into the new. Paragraph fifteen details the kind of knowledge meant by "know the Lord." It's the knowledge of experience; an inner awareness of a sensitive conscience. This kind of knowledge finds concrete illustration in paragraph sixteen. Finally paragraph seventeen reviews in more detail the knowledge of experience that comes in the new covenant.

The conclusion makes several appeals. It reminds of the clarity of the logic of the sermon. Sentences 3, 4, and 5, suggest that good, not evil, hinders from choosing the best. So "choose the best." The idea about a "frayed shirt" looks back to the opening sentence in the introduction. The image appeals to one's pride. The final three sentences are a review of the major points.

A NEW KIND OF COVENANT
Hebrews 8:6-13

When a shirt gets ragged at the collar it is "nigh unto vanishing away." Whether it be clothes, cars or people when it "waxes aged" it is replaced with a new. It ought not be startling that God replaced an old covenant with a new. 1

The author of Hebrews points out from Jeremiah three items which make the new covenant significantly different from the old. (1) "I will put my laws on their heart." 2
(2) "All shall know me . . . from the least unto the greatest." (3) "Their sins will I remember no more."

God's grace

Verse 12 declares, "I will be merciful to their iniquities, and their sins will I remember no more." In other words, this new covenant rests on God's forgiveness, not on man's performance. This new kind of covenant is founded on the rock of what God did at Calvary, not what we do during our lifetime. My standing with God hangs on his loving disposition, his willingness—no, not to ignore, but to forgive my rebellion. And above all, that which he has done at a specific point in human history on the cross. And this he confirmed by raising Jesus from the dead.

My redemption has already been accomplished. It's a thing done, finished, completed, perfected beyond fault. Done by God in Christ! Human redemption lies on the firm underpinning of the death of Jesus Christ. "This is my blood of covenant poured out for many unto remission of sins."

The Old covenant was weak, inefficient, temporary. Yet it was not the program announced in ten commandments that made it weak. It was puny, feeble, fragile and faulty because of the weakness of people. The text reads, ". . . they continued not in my covenant, and I regarded them not, says the Lord." Which is to say that the covenant failed because the people faltered and failed. By refusing to keep their part of the bargain they made shipwreck of it. The weakness of the law was not in the requirements of law but in the fallible, frail, decrepit corruption of the people of Israel. God's law is adapted to man as God created him, suited to human needs. But man is rebellious, strong-willed and selfish. Man broke his part of the covenant contract.

So God through Jeremiah announced, "This covenant is old and worn out." In the 6th century B.C. the prophet proclaimed that there would be a new *kind* of covenant. An agreement dependent, not on man's weakness, but on God's power. Such a new covenant must be saturated with divine qualities strong enough to circumvent human corruption. If man is to be saved it must be God who lifts him out of the mire; not man who by his own slipping, splashing, scrambling in the muck of sin finally struggles his way out of it. If a man cannot swim from the storm in mid-ocean, 6 then someone must come from the shore to rescue him. Jeremiah described this new covenant, "I will be merciful to their iniquities, and their sins I will remember no more." So the new is based on God's gift, not man's merit.

Power from within

The new covenant provides strength from moral persuasion of the heart within rather than from coerced conformity from outward law enforced by police power. "I 7 will put my laws into their mind, and on their heart also will I write them."

In the old covenant the laws were literally written on stone. The laws didn't rise from a sense of right rising from within. They were imposed by society from without. They were policed by a series of curses, punishments and threats 8 prescribed by outside forces. Apart from this outside power enforcing the covenant demands a man would slip aside to evade the restrictions.

Consider a modern effort at "law and order." In a city of a given population 200 policemen attempt to curb crime. Yet violence breaks out. A store is robbed, a woman raped, a murder committed. The city fathers, in emergency session, decide to employ 1000 policemen. With a policeman on 9 every corner crime is reduced to zero. Robbers won't rob; rapists refuse to rape; murderers resist killing as long as an officer stands with drawn gun. Violent crimes fall to absolutely nothing. Now we have a situation in which there is NO crime! But the vital question is: Has the criminal element been reduced?

The city fathers meet again. They conclude, "We have no crime! Why have any police? We'll fire the force and save taxes." What happens? Not only robbery, rape and murder get worse than before but every other imaginable crime in or out of the books erupts. So we note as long as law is enforced by 1000 policemen we eliminate crime but we do not reduce criminals by one. Policemen can reduce stealing but they cannot diminish by a single digit the number of thieves. Thieves are still thieves even when they aren't stealing. If a man doesn't steal only because a holstered policeman stands before him, then he's still a thief. A liar is a liar even when he doesn't lie. As long as righteousness must be enforced by pressure of outside muscle, it leaves the disease of sin on the inside untouched. If the power of government could cap the cone of Mount St. Helen's so that ash and lava could be restrained in the bowels of the volcano, it would not solve the problem. All the fiery fury, the boiling, bubbling, seething power of imprisoned steam would simmer and sizzle and smoulder until it blew off any concrete capping man could devise. If the fire isn't quenched no outside power can forever restain the eventual blow-off.

The text says, ". . . they continued not in my covenant." The people would not, could not, certainly did not, live by the laws of the covenant. Thus God said, "Since they regard not my covenant, I regarded them not." But of the new God revealed, "I will put my laws into their mind, and on their heart will I write them." Now no longer is the law to be imposed from the outside by force. It is to be written by God on the inside springing up with the energizing power of the Spirit of God. Fruit in a painting

of still life is imposed on the canvass by the artist. But 11
the fruit on a tree in the back yard springs from the necessity of life pulsating with the tree. The law of the new
covenant demands the same moral, ethical and spiritual
fruit as the old. But instead of being enforced by threat
of punishment and the curse of death the new springs
from the power of life within generated by God. "Whoever drinks of the water I shall give him shall never thirst
. . . shall become in him a well of water springing up unto
eternal life."

The text has taught two facts. (1) God remembers our
sins no more. At Calvary the life of Jesus, offered in his
blood, removes the guilt. (2) God invades us with the 12
energy of his redeeming Spirit. And that Spirit pushes
obedience to the moral laws of the covenant up from
within the heart and conscience.

It is obvious that if people of the old covenant weren't
able to "live up to" the law, "Thou shalt not murder" then we
surely can't accomplish Jesus' "Thou shalt not be angry...."
But just here is the point of the new kind of covenant— 13
we don't have to live up to anything! We don't strive,
struggle and strain. It's Christ who did the struggling; it's
Gethsemane and Calvary where the striving took place. It's
not my work but God's work that redeems me. It is his
work that I must respond to and honor. This is the new *kind*
of covenant. The old rested on man; the new hinges on
God; what he has done and does do. Even the inner power
to rise to obedience springs from God within. "It is God
who works in you, both to will and to work" (Phil. 2:13).

The knowledge of God

That God, in the new covenant, works from within

stems from the fact that "all shall know me, from the little to the great." In the old one was born by natural birth into the people of God, the national entity of the Jews. After his birth he had to be taught "Know the Lord." Not so under the new. He must "know the Lord" before he is begotten of God's people. Peter refers to this by saying, ". . . having been begotten again, not of corruptible seed, but of incorruptible through the word of God. . . . And this is the word of good tidings which was preached unto you." No way can one become a child of God under the new covenant apart from first "knowing the Lord."

Knowledge of God belongs to the least little citizen in the kingdom as well as the oldest grey-beard. And that because it is the knowledge of experience, not the intellectual perception of factual information. It's not the knowledge in a dictionary but that gained in personal experience with God. It's not even knowing facts about God from the Bible. It's knowing the Lord in the conflicts and experiences of daily walk through life. It's an inner awareness of sensitized knowledge of right versus wrong!

Some years ago in a small eastern city of the U.S. there was a forty-year-old moron with the intellectual perception of a twelve-year-old child. But he was an active member of a local church and was involved in an adult men's Bible class. His "knowledge" of God was simple but pure. A body of 40; a mind of 12; yet a soul of unalloyed purity of character. His "talent" was an ability to unlock all kinds of locks with his sensitive fingers. When a local bank vault became jammed, the authorities were faced with the possibility of using dynamite to open it. Then someone thought of our moronic saint. Within minutes he had the vault open. The fact that his moral life was surrounded by and determined by his perception of the holiness of God governed how he used his "talent." The fact that he "knew the Lord" gave him an advantage over that of a genius with an I.Q. of 150.

Knowledge of God comes from a walk with the Lord in the conflicts of life. Knowledge of one's wife or husband is not gained by the information of address, phone number, name and ancestry. It's determined by the day-by-day, hour-by-hour joys or sorrows, tensions and conflicts of married experience. When one discovers in daily trials that life has a moral, ethical, spiritual quality and one em- 17 braces that quality *that* is to find God—to "know God." Nor is it learned in formal school. Of course, the initial "knowing the Lord" comes in the confrontation with God in Christ involved in what is termed conversion. To accept what God has done in Christ at Calvary and to respond to it favorably is to "know the Lord." That is the beginning of the knowledge of the Lord!

Conclusion

It is quite clear that God's new covenant is better than the old. It accomplishes in fact what the old held out in promise. The good is the enemy of the best. Choose the 18 best! The old way of life might be good but it isn't the best as indeed for the Hebrew the old was good but not the best. Don't wear a shirt with a frayed collar; put on a new. The new which the Lord provides. Find security in what God has done for you. Let the power of God flow out into a life of obedience. "Know the Lord" and thus enter the family of God's people!

A Translation
Hebrews 9:1-28

So then the first (covenant) indeed was also having ordinances of worship and the Holy Place pertaining to this world. For the first tent, which is called Holy (Place), was prepared in which was both the lampstand and the table and the putting forth of the loaves. But after the second curtain (was) the tent, the one being called Holy of Holies, having the golden incense altar and the ark of the covenant having been overlaid with gold on all sides in which was a golden urn having the manna, and Aaron's rod, the one budding, and the tablets of the covenant. And the ark had above it the cherubs of glory shadowing the mercy seat about which it is not (practical) that we now speak.

But these things having been thus prepared, on the one hand the priests do always enter executing the services but on the other hand the highpriest (enters) alone once a year into the second (tent), not without blood which he offers for himself and the errors of the people. The Holy Spirit declaring this, The way of the Holy of Holies not yet to have been manifested (while) the first tent (is) yet having a standing (which thing is a parable for the present time) by which both gifts and sacrifices are offered though not able to perfect the conscience of the one worshiping. (But they are offered) only upon (basis of) meats and drinks and various (ritual) washings, ordinances of flesh being imposed until (the) time of making (all) straight.

But Christ having become highpriest of the coming good things through the greater and more perfect tent, not hand made, that is, not of this creation, neither through blood of goats and bulls, but through his own blood entered once into the Holy of Holies, having found eternal redemption. For if the blood of goats and bulls and ashes of heifer sprinkling the ones having become unclean sanctify to the cleansing of the flesh, how much more shall the blood of the Christ, who through eternal Spirit offered himself faultless, cleanse our conscience from dead works so as to serve the living God? And because of this he is mediator of a new covenant that the ones having been called may receive the promise of the eternal inheritance, death having occurred for redemption from the transgressions uopn the first covenant. For where a covenant (exists) it's a necessity that the death of the one making it be borne. For a covenant (is) firm upon dead (people) since it never prevails when the one making it is living—whence not even the first has been dedicated without blood. For every commandment having been spoken to all the people by Moses according to the law, he, having taken the blood of the heifers and the goats with water and scarlet wool and hyssop, sprinkled both the book itself and all the people, saying, This is the blood of the covenant which God commanded you. And likewise he sprinkled with the blood both the tent and all the vessels of the ministry. And almost everything is being cleansed in blood according to the law, and without shedding of blood forgiveness does not come. So then, on the one hand that the copies of the (things) in the heavens be cleansed with these is a necessity, but on the other hand that the heavenly (things) themselves (be cleansed) with better sacrifices than these. For Christ did not enter into handmade Holy of Holies, copies of the real, but (he entered) into the heaven itself now to appear in the presence of God for us. Neither (did he enter) that he might offer himself many times, as the highpriest enters yearly into the Holy of Holies in blood not his own, but now once upon the end of the ages he has been manifested for putting off of the sin through the sacrifice of himself. And by howeversomuch once to die is appointed to men and after this judgment, thus the Christ once having been offered for the bearing sins of many, will appear a second (time) unto salvation apart from sin to those expecting him.

AN OUTLINE OF HEBREWS 9:1-28

ATONEMENT: THE OLD AND THE NEW!

To make amends for injury done is to atone! The verb "atone" is short for the phrase "to set at one." Atonement dissolves differences and brings peace. In Judeo-Christian tradition the Old set the stage for atonement; the new fulfilled the actual atonement.

236

I. ATONEMENT UNDER THE OLD. 9:1-10
  1. Furniture of the sanctuary, the background stage. vss. 1-5
  2. The tabernacle service testifies to:
     (a) Repeated annual offering; thereby admitting to failure to accomplish real atonement. vss. 6-7
     (b) Free access to Holy of Holies not yet manifested. vs. 8
     (c) The "gifts and sacrifices" are temporary offerings pointing forward to the *real* atonement. vss. 9-10

II. ATONEMENT UNDER THE NEW. 9:11-28
  1. The necessity of *life's* blood in atonement. vss. 16-22
  2. The New offers atonement:
     (a) Of intelligent life. vs. 14a
     (b) Freely offered. vs. 14b
     (c) Without fault. vs. 14c
     (d) Resulting in living service to the living God. vs. 14d
  3. The New gives the real:
     (a) Sanctuary. vs. 11
     (b) Sacrifice. vs. 12
     (c) Mediator conveying the ultimate promise. vs. 15
  4. Atonement under the New is *final*! "Once for all." vss. 25-26
  5. It's in presence of God, a living atonement. vs. 24

The atonement in Christ is "unto salvation." It eliminates the "one" death for which every man appears destined as having any abiding force. Christ our atonement, our life, our saviour, will appear a "second time apart from sin."

We need not fall back upon "copies" of the real when we have the real at the heart of our faith!

SOME EXPOSITORY THOUGHTS ON HEBREWS 9:1-28

God controls all power; sin disturbs that power! God governs man. Sin disconcerts God's governing of man. Creator and creature, designed for each other, have become enemies. Sin is the disrupting force. Man has offended against God. Man has usurped the will of God and placed himself on the throne of God. Man and God are at war!

To atone means to make amends for injury done. Expiation is to remove the barrier between enemies. Propitiation, expiation atonement are at the heart of man's dilemma. They are elements in any religion that makes claim to the reality of a living, personal relationship with God. Propitiation removes the wrath of offended holiness; expiation removes the stain of sin; atonement dissolves differences and brings peace between God and man. It "sets at one" the two enemies.

Atonement under the Old

Before Christ and apart from Christ no religion surpassed the Mosaic system in its lofty concept of atonement. Pagan religion, ancient or modern, places on man the responsibility and initiative of making expiation for his own sin. No physician is to be had, or used even if available. Unaided, the sick must heal himself. This leaves man in the impossible situation of salvation in terms of self improvement. That means putting a band-aid over a terminal, corrupting cancer and calling it cured.

The Old Testament covenant was an advance over that self-deceiving compromise with the deadliness of sin. It did place on God's priest and his appointed blood (life) sacrifices the means, symbolic though they be, of expiation of man's guilt. Even though it was temporary ritualistic, shadowy and symbolic it at least looked to life beyond itself for redemption. It had in it the symbols of truth if not the realities. It deposited in human thought the essential needs of man and pointed him to the ultimate perfect, final, real reconciliation to God. In its earthly sanctuary and its ritual of blood sacrifice it provided the platform and set the stage for final real religious fellowship with the living God.

Yet the very presence of the repeated sacrifices was impressive testimony that free unhindered access to the genuine Holy of Holies was not yet come. The annual repetition on the day of atonement was confession of failure to accomplish real atonement. The way to God was open for a day but then was shut again. It stirred the conscience without touching the conscience. It reminded of guilt without cleansing from guilt. There was nothing "perfect," final or finished with the "gifts and sacrifices" any more than a sign that points *to* a city is that city. The Old pointed the right way but it was never able to bring anyone to "perfection." To attain God's goal for sinful man was still left in God's hands to work out the expiation and reconciliation. The offended must himself redeem the offender. If atonement is to be made God must provide the atoning sacrifice. If divine and human fellowship is to be restored God must take the initiative. Then man must make his response!

Atonement under the New

One fact the older covenant established: ". . . everything is purified with blood, and without the shedding of blood there is no forgiveness." And it wasn't so much blood as physical molecules of matter as that "life was in the blood." Blood shed must be redeemed by blood shed; life taken must be bought back by life given. Life can only be redeemed by life; someone's life other than that of the guilty.

Guilt can only be felt by a rational, intelligent, responsible, moral person. One whose sense of right and wrong has been violated is the only one who feels estrangement. Guilt is a matter of the conscience. He who is not morally responsible can't experience the sense of sin. For this reason *things* are not able to "perfect the conscience." "Gifts and sacrifices" are "things," not morally responsible people. Likewise, "the blood of bulls and goats" are things taken from, not given by, irrational, dumb brutes who, if they could, would protest the shedding of their life's blood. But not so the offering of Christ's blood, the atonement of the new covenant. His was the free gift of an intelligent moral person. And he gave it as an act of obedience to the will of God who would expiate man's moral rebellion. Christ did not die on an impulse; he wasn't off on a youthful irresponsible lark. He didn't think it up himself; it was in obedience to the will of God that he died. It was a choice to obey God who thereby could make it possible for sinful men to have fellowship with Him.

Because Christ's death is an intelligent, freely given sacrifice and is offered by one who is "faultless," it reaches the area of guilt, that is, the conscience. It's not a formal ritual of religion. It's a living force that transforms a dying producer of dead works into a living servant of the living God. Christ's death does two things: (1) It nullifies the wrath of God while it expiates the sin that induced the wrath. And (2) by placing us in a state of redemption it relieves the conscience and sets it free from its guilt. Though "gifts and sacrifices" are not able to cleanse the conscience of the one worshiping, . . . the blood of the Christ does "cleanse our conscience from dead works to serve the living God."

Furthermore, the new covenant presents our priest performing his priestly service in the real presence of God in heaven itself, "the greater and more perfect tent." It's no longer an acted out pantomime of fellowship with God. He serves our redemptive needs in the very presence of God in heaven. And that, not by the blood of dumb animals, but by his own blood's life. He thus secures for us "eternal redemption" through the "eternal spirit." That is, Christ offering himself to God in death is absolute, final, ideal beyond which nothing superior is left to offer for sin. His sacrifice is final, complete, perfect, real, eternal. The death of Christ is the one efficient force by which sin is annulled as a barrier to man's fellowship with God.

Christ's atonement is "unto salvation." It eliminates death for which each man seems destined, as having any real force. Christ will appear a second time "apart from sin" to receive those who await his salvation. Why, then, should we fall back to any copy of the real thing?

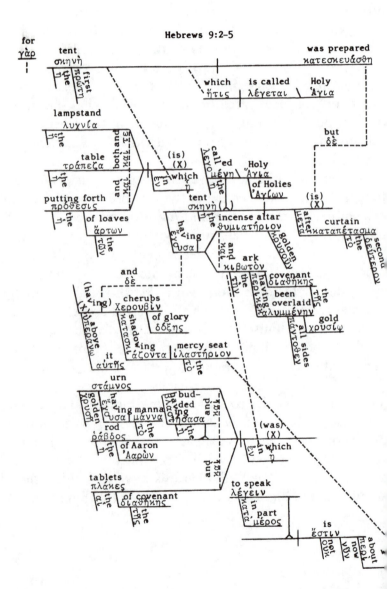

242

THE DIAGRAM OF HEBREWS 9:2-5

The verses of 9:2-5 involve a lengthy sentence of 77 words, two independent clauses, four subordinate clauses besides two participial expressions that have the practical force of clauses. It should be classified as compound-complex. The two chief clauses identify the two "tents" which really refer to the two rooms of the tabernacle. "The first tent was prepared . . . but the tent, the one being called Holy of Holies, (was) after the second curtain. . . ." The first "tent" is described by two adjective clauses. The clause thrust forward by the locative relative phrase "in which" identifies the "tent" by its furniture. It contained "both the lampstand and the table and the putting forth of the loaves. . . ." when conjunction τε is used along with καί the relationship between the items which are thus connected have some vital union. But the context must determine what that inner union is. A second dependent clause gives the name of this "first tent," that is, "which is called Holy."

The subject of the second independent clause is also "tent" but is further identified by an attributive participle in apposition, "the one called Holy of Holies." The prepositional expression "after the second curtain" might have been placed on a pedestal and treated as predicate nominative referring back to subject "tent." However, the diagram places it in an adverbial position telling *where* the Holy of Holies is located.

The remainder of the sentence expands and describes this "tent" that lies "after the second curtain." Two circumstantial participles and two subordinate clauses are the methods used to describe the "tent." As compound objects of the first participle ἔχουσα are θυμιατήριον (incense altar) and κιβωτὸν (ark). Though the second participle is not stated it is clearly implied, ". . . having cherubs. . . ." The

243

prepositional expression "above it" is adverbial in function telling *where* the cherubs were holding forth. The participle κατασκιάζοντα is circumstantial explaining what they're doing there, that is, "shadowing the mercy seat." Note the -τηριον ending of both ἱλαστήριον (vs. 5) and θυμιατήριον (vs. 4). Such suffixes for substantives derived from verbs indicate *place*. That is to say, ἱλαστήριον is the place where mercy is extended. And θυμιατήριον is the place where incense is offered.

The ark (κιβωτὸν) has describing it the adjective clause prefaced by another locative relative "in which." And in that clause are three items of furniture mentioned, "the golden urn," "the rod of Aaron" and "the tablets of covenant." The urn is further described by the circumstantial participle ". . . having the manna. . . ." The "rod of Aaron" is further specified by an attributive participle in apposition, ". . . the one having budded. . . ."

The final clause of the sentence is adjectival describing "mercy seat." It is inaugurated by περὶ and the genitive relative ὧν = about which. Subject of the clause is the infinitive λέγειν, *to speak*. κατὰ with neuter accusative μέρος is used distributively, "to speak about each several part now is not (practical)."

Hebrews 9:6-10

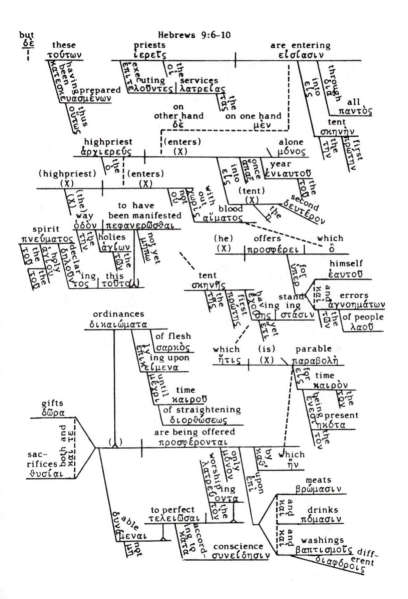

245

THE DIAGRAM OF HEBREWS 9:6-10

In Nestle's text 9:6-10 is one compound-complex sentence. It has three independent clauses which declare, ". . . priests enter . . ." ". . . highpriest enters . . ." and ". . . (highpriest enters) not without blood. . . ." The third is negative and borrows its subject and verb from the context.

A genitive absolute initiates the sentence with the information, "these having been prepared thus. . . ." This is the first of three genitive absolutes appearing in this sentence. Both the next two show up in verse eight: ". . . the Holy Spirit declaring this . . ." and ". . . the first tent having a standing. . . ." Genitive absolutes, especially coming so close together, tend to give a sentence a feeling of looseness. They have no grammatical link to the sentence though the connection in thought is usually quite clear. Though without grammatical yoke they do have logical and psychological connection with the rest of the sentence. The reader's mind must be flexible enough to bridge grammatical gaps to make the logical bindings.

In the second of the genitive absolutes the participle has for its direct object the demonstrative pronoun τοῦτο. Appended to this pronoun by apposition is the infinitive phrase, "the way of the holies not yet to have been manifested. . . ." Between the first and second absolutes the diagram shows a short broken line yet it does not join either. This line is intended to suggest that though they fail to relate grammatically they are closely related in thought. In fact an element of *time* between the two is suggested: ". . . way not yet manifested (while) the first tent has a standing. . . ."

Three dependent clauses also appear in this sentence. The first (vs. 7) ὁ προσφέρει = "which offers" is adjectival in function describing αἵματος. The second (vs. 9a) is probably best taken to be adjective describing the entire thought of the third of the genitive absolutes. The third dependent clause is introduced by καθ'ἥν = "by which." As it unfolds, this clause completes the sentence. Subject of the clause is compound: "both gifts and sacrifices." It is amplified by appositional "ordinances" modified by present circumstantial participle ἐπικείμενα = "lying upon." Yet another present circumstantial particple δυνάμεναι with μή "not being able" modifies the subject "gifts and sacrifices." And that verbal-noun itself has a direct object, the attributive participle translated "the one worshiping."

In the prepositional phrase introduced by ἐπὶ the three nouns are locatives, "upon the matter of meats and drinks and different washings." It may be noted that the word for "washings" is βαπτισμός and not βάπτισμα. The root of both words contains the idea of immerse. But the word ending in -μος is an "*action*" word whereas the one ending in -μα designates "*result*" of the action in the verb. In the New Testament βάπτισμα is confined to the religious commitment involved in baptism. βαπτισμός is descriptive of the processes involved in immersing whether ritual or otherwise.

Hebrews 9:11-14

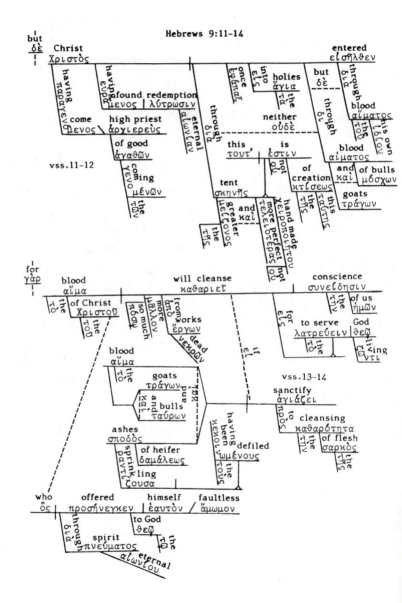

vss.11-12

vss.13-14

248

A first glance at 9:11-12 seems to signal an intricate sentence yet it has but one clause. In form it's classed as simple. Without its modifiers it states, "Christ . . . entered."

Two participles recount circumstances that surrounded Christ before he "entered." One, "having become high-priest. . . ." And two, "having found eternal redemption. . . ." Both participles and the main verb "entered" are aorists representing coincident action. They took place at the same point or in close relation to one another. Adverb ἐφάπαξ denotes *when* (how often) he entered. And the prepositional phrase "into the holies" serves an adverbial sense marking *where* he entered. διά with genitive appears three times introducing adverbial ideas signifying the *means by which.* διά with genitive is normal construction for expressing agency "through which" something is done. He entered "through the greater and more perfect, tent. . . ." In apposition to σκηνῆς is the idiomatic expression τουτ' ἐστιν, "this is (to say) not of this creation. . . ." A second non-agent declares, "neither through blood of goats and bulls. . . ." The final διά phrase says, "but through his own blood. . . ." This expresses the positive means through which Christ entered.

This offers a fine example of how the frame of a diagram may supply an effective outline.

Proposition: Christ entered the real Holy of Holies.

    Two experiences are the basis for his entrance:

        (1) Having become highpriest.

        (2) Having found eternal redemption.

    Two negative and one positive agencies:

        (1) Not through handmade sanctuary.

        (2) Not through non-rational, non-ethical sacrifices.

   (3) Through his own ethically determined, freely given life's blood.

Futhermore, he did it "once for all." It was final!

9:13-14 contains a complex sentence involving three clauses. The independent element states, "Blood will cleanse conscience. . . ." Genitive "of Christ" specifies whose blood and the genitive "of us" identifies whose conscience. The dependent clause ushered in by relative ὅς is adjectival describing Χριστοῦ: "who offered himself faultless." ἄμωμον is objective complement filling out the object ἑαυτόν. διά with genitive "eternal spirit" makes clear the agent "through whom" he was able to offer himself. A second dependent clause is announced by εἰ. It is a first class condition assumed to be true: "if the blood . . . and ashes . . . sanctify (and they do . . .)." As a matter of fact, they can't and didn't sanctify. But the condition doesn't have to do with the fact but with the determination of the condition. For the sake of argument it is *assumed* to be true though in fact it's not. Describing "ashes" is circumstantial participle ῥαντίζουσα. Direct object of the verbal element in that participle is the perfect attributive participle translated "the ones having been defiled." Modifying the main verb "will cleanse" is an expression of purpose. It is to be noted in the εἰς phrase "for to serve the living God." It is adverbial.

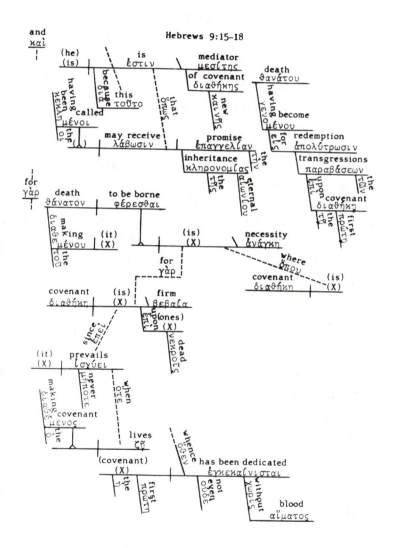

Hebrews 9:15–18

251

THE DIAGRAM OF HEBREWS 9:15-18

Verse 15 constitutes one complex sentence. It includes one genitive absolute besides the independent and one dependent clause. The independent affirms, "he is mediator." The kind of mediator is specified by genitive translated "of new covenant." The διὰ τοῦτο expression ("because of this") refers back to what has been stated in the preceding sentence.

ὅπως advances a purpose clause, "in order that. . . ." Subject of this purpose clause is the attributive perfect passive participle translated "the ones having been called." The verb λάβωσιν is aorist. It looks to the fact and point of "getting" not to the process. As mediator "he" sees that they really "get" the promise in experience and not just enjoy it as a hope. The genitive absolute suggests *cause*. Because "a death having taken place for redemption . . ." therefore he is mediator etc.

Five clauses comprise the structural frame of the compound-complex sentence in verses 16-17. The two independent clauses say, ". . . death to be borne (is) necessary" and "covenant (is) firm. . . ." The subject of the first clause is the present infinitive δέρεσθαι. θάνατον is an adverbial accusative (acc. of general reference) indicating who did the action of the infinitive. English grammars inaptly call it "subject." Modifying that "death" is an aorist attributive participle "the one making (it—covenant)." Adverbial conjunction ὅπου introduces a dependent adverbial clause telling *why* it's necessary that a death be borne.

The second of the main clauses declares that a "covenant (is) firm" and then adds a prepositional phrase to point out *when* it is firm, that is, "upon (the basis of) dead (ones)." νεκρὸς is an adjective, not a noun, and when used alone always implies some noun which it modifies. In the present instance conjunction -επεί ushers in a dependent clause of cause, "since (it) never prevails. . . ." Tacked on to that clause is another dependent stating a limitation to the "never prevails." ὅτε is a temporal particle meaning "when." Here the "when" conspiring with present tense ζῇ might suggest "while" as a satisfactory translation. Subject of ζῇ is the aorist attributive participle translated "the one making."

Nestle's text punctuates verse 18 as a separate sentence. As such it is to be classed as simple in form. The ὅθεν with which the sentence begins is causal. The diagram presents it on a solid-broken slanting line. Although distinct, the preceding sentence furnishes a solid reason why "even the first covenant has not been dedicated without blood" that is, without death.

The verb ἐγκεκαίνισται is perfect = "has been dedicated." At the heart of this infrequently used word is καινός = new. At bottom it means to inaugurate, renew, dedicate. "The first covenant stands dedicated not without blood." Dedication by means of blood stands as a permanently determined factor in the covenant relationship.

Three thoughts suggested by 9:15-17
1. Christ, mediator of a new covenant.
2. He validates the promise of eternal inheritance.
3. The necessity of death; his death.

253

Hebrews 9:19-21

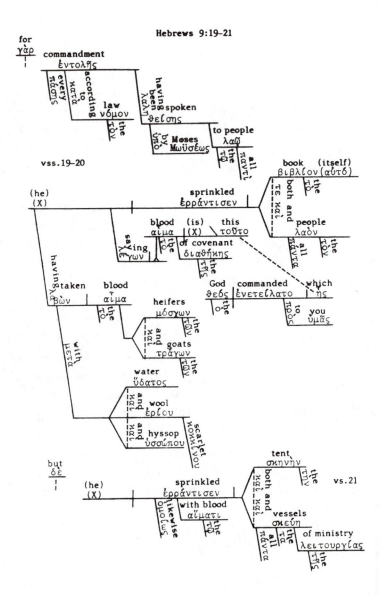

254

THE DIAGRAM OF HEBREWS 9:19-21

The conjunction γάρ serves to tie the sentence of 19-20 to that of verse 18. To sustain the idea that "not even the first covenant has been inaugurated without blood" the author cites historical proof.

The sentence begins with a genitive absolute, ". . . every command having been spoken according to the law by Moses to the ͳ ople. . . ." κατά with accusative presents a standard of measurement. ὑπό with ablative expresses agent by which, that is, "by Moses." And λαῷ is dative, the case of personal interest. We may note the dative "to the people" (λαῷ) here whereas later in the sentence in the subordinate clause "which God commanded to you. . . ." πρός with accusative appears, translated "to you." The difference may be slight but there is a difference. Basically it is the difference between the dative and accusative cases. Of course the preposition πρός adds its particular touch too. The element of *personal interest* indicates that the laws were spoken by Moses directly to the people in person. And they responded in a personal commitment. The personal element is intensified by the dative. In the accusative ὑμᾶς that personal element is absent. πρός literally means "facing toward." The accusative case limits an idea in "content, scope, or direction." When God was dealing with the problem of a covenant for his people, facing in their direction, as it were, he came up with the "blood of the covenant which he commanded *in your direction*." The content of the problem was paramount in the accusative; the personal relationship and commitment is more prominent in the dative.

Besides the initial genitive absolute only two clauses appear in this complex sentence of vss. 19-20. With a compound object the main clause says, ". . . he sprinkled both the book itself and all the people. . . ." The subject "he" is described by two circumstantial participles. First the aorist λαβὼν, "having taken the blood." The context suggests this to be temporal, "when he took. . . ." The *kind* of blood is specified by genitives of "heifers and goats." English "amidst" is about the equivalent of Greek μετά. He mixed the blood "amidst" water, scarlet wool and hyssop.

λέγων is another circumstantial participle modifying subject "he." It gives the surrounding circumstances accompanying the sprinkling of the book; ". . . saying, This is the blood of the covenant. . . ."

The only dependent clause in the sentence springs off of "covenant" and is inserted by ἧς = "which." It is an adjective clause descriptive of "covenant."

Though it does have a compound direct object of the verb, the sentence of verse 21 is simple in structure having but the one clause. ὁμοίως is an adverb meaning "in similar fashion." αἵματι is instrumental case indicating the instrument or means with which the sprinkling was done. λειτουργίας is genitive case specifying the *kind* of "vessels" that were sprinkled. They were vessels of the official public religious ministry.

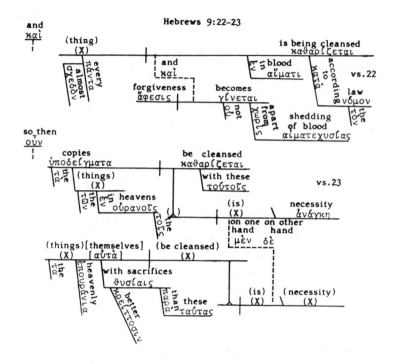

Hebrews 9:22-23

THE DIAGRAM OF HEBREWS 9:22-23

Two independent clauses certify the sentence of verse 22 to be compound. The first clause is positive, "everything is being cleansed." The second is negative, "and forgiveness does not become apart from blood-shedding."

σχεδὸν is an adverb; when referring to *place* it means "near" but when referring to *degree* it means "almost," "nearly." Its root is to be traced to ἔσχον, second aorist of ἔχω = to have, get. "According to the law" (the Jewish Torah) as suggested in 9:19 almost everything. . . ." There are some exceptions though not many! The phrase ἐν αἵματι tells *how* everything is cleansed and so is adverbial.

257

Here "in blood" means "in connection with blood." It seems that in some way or other blood was used in ritual cleansing of "almost all things." One should not overlook that "the life is in the blood." Blood is efficacious because it carries life.

Subject of the second clause is ἄφεσις. The root of this word is ε to which is prefixed the preposition ἀπό = off. All -σις words are action words and hence the word means a "sending off." Forgiveness is a sending away of sin and guilt, a blotting from the memory. The use of γίνεται, "become" rather than a form of εἰμί, "be" is significant. Forgiveness is not represented here as a state of "being" but a "becoming." To "become" is the unfolding of a vital energy. True, forgiveness of sin is a divine gift but it is a condition within that thrusts itself up and out into one's life. ἄφεσις is an action word, a process going on that "becomes" as life inherent in a plant pushes itself out into stake, leaf and fruit. And this happens "not without bloodshedding," that is, the giving of *life* through the shedding of the life-blood.

The sentence of verse 23 is a compound-complex of four clauses, two independent and two dependent. By use of μὲν and δὲ the basic ideas are placed in striking contrast. The subjects in both clauses consist of rather ornate noun clauses. The first says, ". . . the copies of the (things) in the heavens are being cleansed with these (is) a necessity. . . ." Present tense καθαπίζεται is iterative in force. The copies are repeatedly being cleansed. The demonstrative pronoun τούτοις is anaphoric pointing back to those things mentioned in verse 19. It is instrumental case.

Much of the subject and all of the predicate of the second independent clause is borrowed, implied from the first. αὐτὰ is reflexive pronoun "themselves" referring back to

258

"things," subject of this noun clause. "With sacrifices" (θυσίαις) is instrumental. The preposition παρά followed by accusative cause is a normal way of expressing comparison.

A glance over 9:19-23 leads to a summary outline of the thoughts suggesting:

Forgiveness "Becoming!"

1. Covenants, old or new, established by blood-shedding.
   (a) Almost all "things" are thus ritually cleansed.
   (b) Forgiveness "becomes" by blood-shedding.
2. "Better" blood from "better" sacrifice cleanses the heavenly realities themselves.

Hebrews 9:24-26

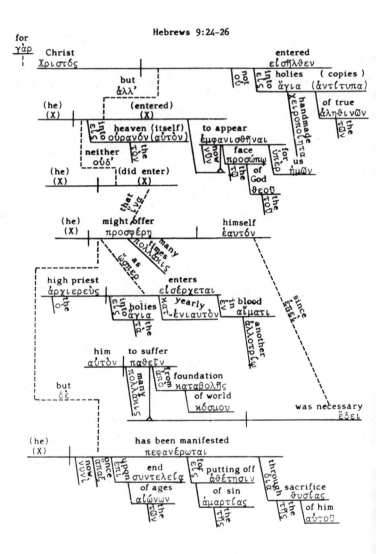

260

THE DIAGRAM OF HEBREWS 9:24-26

This is a compound-complex sentence of seven clauses, four of which are independent. The first independent is a negative idea, "Christ did not enter. . . ." The place into which Christ "did not enter" is described in the prepositional phrase "into handmade Holy of Holies." ἀντίτυπα (copies) is in apposition with ἅγια (holies) and defines "holies" as being antitype, that is, that which is symbol of the real thing. It answers to or is counterpart of the actual Holy of Holies. It's a copy.

The next two independent clauses (except for modifiers) are entirely elliptical being implied by the context. They say, ". . . he entered . . ." and ". . . neither did he enter. . . ." There is strong adverse contrast between the first and second clauses underscored by ἀλλ'. "Christ did not enter . . . *but* he did enter. . . ." Again we have an εἰς phrase acting adverbially to tell *where* he entered, "into heaven itself." ἐμφανισθῆναι is aorist passive infinitive expressing purpose, "now to appear in the presence of God in our behalf."

The purpose for which Christ "did not enter" is stated in the ἵνα clause: ". . . that he might offer himself many times. . . ." Stemming from that purpose clause is another adverbial dependent clause introduced by ὥσπερ. It sets up a standard of comparison. As the highpriest enters "according to each year (annually)," so by that standard Christ did not enter! Yet another adverb dependent supports the idea that Chirst did not enter "many times." This time a causal (implied condition) clause heralded by ἐπεί, since. ". . . since that he suffer many times from the foundation of the world was (would be) necessary." The ἐπεί actually introduces an implied conditional idea. One might translate, ". . . since (if that were true) then that he suffer etc. . . ." It would be a second class condition determined as untrue.

The fourth of the independent clauses has as its verb the perfect πεφανέρωται = has been manifested. The tense suggests that his manifestation was permanent. The adverb ἅπαζ "once for all" reinforces that idea. The three prepositional phrases ἐπί, εἰς, and διά introduce adverbial ideas. The first answers the question *when*: "upon the end of the ages." The second pictures the *purpose*, "for putting off of the sin." And the third inserts the *agent* through whom the "putting off of sin has been manifested," that is, "through the sacrifice of himself."

A Summary Outline of 9:24-26

1. Christ's entrance into the sanctury.
   (a) Not the one made with human hands.
   (b) Into God's presence in heaven itself.
2. Christ's a decisive, effective, once-for-all offering.
   (a) Negatively stated: Not like Aaronic priests.
   (b) But one permanent sacrifice.
3. When, for what, and how!
   (a) Upon the "end of the ages."
   (b) For "putting off of the sin."
   (c) Through sacrifice of himself.

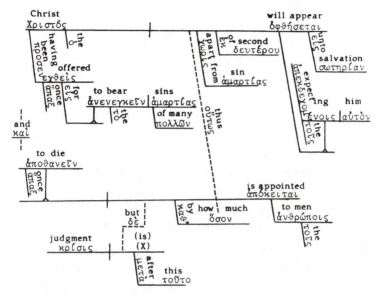

THE DIAGRAM OF HEBREWS 9:27-28

These final two verses of chapter nine incorporate a complex sentence of three clauses. The independent declares: "The Christ will appear. . . ." ὀφθήσεται is future indicative passive, "he will be seen." In other words, "he will appear."

The presence or absence of the definite article is always of some significance in Greek. Originally it was a demonstrative and it never entirely lost that trait. It points out! It points attention to an earlier reference to the person or thing with which it is used or it points with special emphasis to that person or thing that is "the" well known one. Here it is used in the latter sense. "The" Christ, heralded of old, taught among men, crucified and risen, preached and hoped for—*that* Christ will appear a second time.

Also modifying "Christ" is the aorist passive circumstantial participle προσενεχθείς, "having been offered." It presents certain circumstances that occurred antecedent to the action in the main verb. Adverb ἄπαξ fastens the mind on the fact that it was a once-for-all offering. The infinitive phrase introduced by εἰς portrays the purpose for which he made the one decisive offering. ἀνενεγκεῖν is aorist infinitive of ἀναφέρω. The idea here is kin to Isa. 53:12, "he bore the sin of many. φέρω means to "carry to some definite end in contrast to βαστάζω which gives emphasis to the weight of what is carried. Jesus offered himself once "for to carry to the cross the sins of many."

But this "second time" he will appear "apart from sin." The first time he came in order to "carry" sins to the cross and get rid of them. The second time he will appear "for (εἰς) salvation" and without having to be preoccupied with the elimination of sin. Those for whom he will appear are designated by the attributive present participle ἀπεκδεχομένοις. The present is durative action calling attention to the continuously unabating watchful expectation of "the ones expecting him."

The adverb οὕτως brings in the dependent clauses. It says, ". . . thus . . . by thus much (καθ' ὅσον. A quotation from Westcott (Heb. pg. 276) is of special interest: καθ' ὅσον . . . οὕτως καί expresses a conclusion drawn from an identity between two objects in some particular respects . . . while ὥσπερ . . . οὕτως . . . describes a complete correspondence. . . ." One particular point of parallel lies between men and Christ as a man. It is: "To die once is laid away (ἀπόκειται) for men but after this comes judgment." So with the man-Savior, the Christ. He dies once! After that, in his case, judgment comes, that is, the righting of the horrible wrong of his death at the hands of sinful men. For Christ as sinless man judgment is a blessing; a total exoneration; an acquittal.

The Second Appearance!

1. Christ died once: His acquittal (judgment) follows.
2. He will appear a second time.
   (a) Having carried sin to the cross.
   (b) Unto salvation apart from sin.
   (c) To those awaiting and expecting him.

A Translation

Hebrews 10:1-18

For the law, having a shadow of the coming good things, not the image itself of the things, is never able to perfect the ones coming with the same yearly sacrifices which they are perpetually offering, since they would not have ceased offering, because once having been cleansed the ones serving would no more be having conscience of sins. For impossible it is that the blood of bulls and goats be taking away sins.

Wherefore he, coming into the world, says, Sacrifice and offering you did not wish, but a body you prepared for me; in whole burnt offerings and (sacrifices) for sin you did not delight. Then I said: Behold! I come—at the head of the book it stands written about me—to do, O God, your will.

Saying earlier, 'sacrifices and offerings' and 'whole burnt offerings and (sacrifices) for sin you did not wish, neither did you delight,'—which they are offering according to law,—then he has said, 'Behold! I come to do your will.' He takes away the first in order that he may establish the second.

Indeed, on the one hand every priest is standing day by day officially serving and offering many times the same sacrifices which, by their very nature, are never able to take away sins. But on the other hand, this (one) having offered one sacrifice for sins forever, sat down on the right hand of

God, confidently awaiting, as to the rest (of history), until his enemies be put as footstool under his feet. For with one offering he has made perfect forever the ones being sanctified. And the Holy Spirit testifies for us; for after having said, "this is the covenant which I will covenant with them after those days," (The) Lord says, ". . . giving my laws upon their hearts and upon their mind I will write them. And their sins and their lawless deeds I will not remember any more." And where forgiveness of these (is), offering for sin no longer (is needed).

AN OUTLINE OF HEBREWS 10:1-18
THE VALID SACRIFICE FOR SIN

Where may man look for a valid sacrifice for his sin?

I. THE OLD SACRIFICES WERE PROVISIONAL. 1-4

    1. Repetition of animal sacrifices a sign of inadequacy. 1-2

    2. Repetition was a reminder of sin, not of forgiveness. 3

    3. Animal sacrifices irrational, hence deficient. 4

II. THE GENUINE SACRIFICE. 5-10

    1. Perfect obedience the only real acceptable sacrifice. 5-7

    2. Christ's sacrifice of obedience abolishes the old. 8-9

    3. Man shares in his obedience. 10

III. PERMANENT POWER OF CHRIST'S SACRIFICE. 11-14

   1. Repetitious sacrifices contrasted with Christ's. 11-13
   2. Power of Christ's sacrifice is permanent. 14

IV. FORGIVENESS BRINGS FULFILLMENT. 15-18
   1. Prophetic word: "I will not remember their sins...." 15-18
   2. Where forgiveness is, need for sacrifices eliminated. 18

To turn from forgiveness to remembrance of sin is wicked, not wise!

SOME EXPOSITORY THOUGHTS ON HEBREWS 10:1-18

The author of Hebrews ever recognizes the need for sacrifice for sin. But with equal force he faces the impossibility that "the blood of bulls and goats should take away sin." Shadow can never be substituted for substance. Half measures can not replace a full cup. Nor can a pattern be worn as a dress.

10:11-13 detail what 14 summarizes. First, "every priest stands daily officially serving and offering many times the same sacrifices." The "sameness," the "daily" repetition, the "standing" reflect the fatal weakness in the old covenant. If a key, after repeated efforts, won't open the lock, it isn't very clever to use the same key on the same lock! Yet this is precisely what the priests of the old covenant did. Their offerings gave no relief from guilt. They only dramatically pantomimed what was needed. And that with no real help in abolishing sin and its concequences.

They were "standing day by day." That sacrifices had to be repeated daily was a confession of the impotence of the oblation. "Standing" suggests lack of grandeur that belongs to the authority of a throne. He who "sits" is ruler; he who stands is servant.

No human being is without the need of an efficient, effective, capable sacrifice for sin. Guilt burdens everyone. Wrongdoing eats like termites at each man's soul. Repeated efforts to forget, cover up, and "make up for" testify to the failure of our efforts to get rid of our sense of evil. Repetitious religious rituals universally witness to this weakness of all human struggle to rid itself of guilt. Even the relief of scientific psychology demands costly, time-consuming, repeated visits to the counselor. Is there no way, by one stroke of the eraser, to wipe the slate clean? Our text states, "which (sacrifices) by their very nature aren't able to take away sins." The failure of humanity to get rid of its evil, personal or racial, is a fact of life. We are guilty!

In an imposing contrast our author continues, "This one, sat (in royal triumph) at God's right hand, having offered forever in behalf of sin one sacrifice." His offering of himself was the key that unlocked the door the first time he used it. Besides, the door opened permanently that sinners might enter any and all times without hindrance. It reaches conscience and lifts guilt. It breaks the bonds of death and makes me victor over the grave.

His victory is a matter of history. He wrought it at Calvary and sealed it at the open tomb. As to the rest of history, with expectant confidence he waits universal recognition of his conquest. All enemies shall be put under his feet. The issue of history is not determined by a SALT treaty between world powers. It's embedded in Christ's death and resurrection.

For these reasons, "He has, with one sacrifice, brought to perfection forever the ones being sanctified." To "be made perfect" does not refer to a soul's flawless purity. Perfection is not the absence of wrong-doing. It means that because of Christ's one sacrifice on Calvary he is able to "forgive" our sin. Thus he can *treat* us as blameless. He's broken death's chains and conquered the end result of sin. How more "perfect" can one be?

If, having asked and received his forgiveness, we constantly go back to fret about, worry over, rehash our evil and deenergize ourselves by insisting on carrying our guilt, we are reverting to the old "daily" human efforts. To lift the burden of sin; we are offering the "same" sacrifice of self-effort.

No doubt about our standing with God should remain. But if there be any, verses 15-18 remove it. Speaking in Jeremiah the prophet the Holy Spirit of God promised a new kind of covenant. The old one approached man with tablets of stone on which were written the prohibitions of holiness. "You shall not murder . . . etc. . . ." By a series of blessings and curses it proposed to force on man a conformity to the ideals of righteousness. Obey this law and you'll be blessed with life. Disobey and the curse of death will be yours. Results depended on the punishment of police action.

But the appeal of the promised new covenant was from a totally different kind of approach. Two distinctive features of the new covenant our text mentions. First, "I will give my laws on their *hearts* and I will write them on their *understanding*." The new has righteousness rising from within the heart; it isn't forced by any exterior power pressing upon a man. The water of life doesn't overwhelm like a flood. The water springs from within as an artesian well. Under the old, men were whitewashed. Their guilt was covered, painted over, hidden, pushed away. The new presents man with a reborn soul, a newly-created heart, a cleanly washed mind, a renewed spirit. The old painted petals on an artificial rose. The new plants seed in the good soil of faith in Christ from which righteousness thrusts up into a new rose bud. The old conformed to life; the new *is* life! The old was obeyed because of fear of police punishment; the new by the power of growing life.

A second distinctive feature of the new is that the end results are different. Verse 17 says, "Their sins and their rebellions I will *not remember* any more." What strength the new has! How weak the old is! In the old every time a man offered sacrifice his sins were brought to mind. He had to face them daily and agonize over them annually. He must *remember* his wrongs. Not so in the new! God forgets guilt forever! And God expects us to do exactly what he has done with our sins; forget them. Even though scars are left and practical living is affected, as a barrier to fellowship guilt is not to be retained in memory.

Only God can forgive sin. If he says that he never remembers our sins or iniquities, then any further sacrifice has no point. To "do penance" or go on carrying forgotten guilt is an impertinence, a reflection on God's promised word of forgiveness. Verse 18 sums up God's opinion on the matter, "Where (God's) forgiveness is, offering for sin no longer has any place."

Faith in God's word demands forgetting of forgiven sin! *My* sin!

271

Hebrews 10:1-2

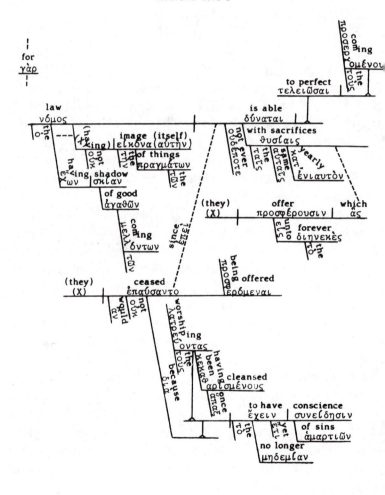

272

THE DIAGRAM OF HEBREWS 10:1-2

The sentence of 10:1-2 by classification is complex. It has one independent clause. And though it has but two dependent clauses that appear, a third one is clearly implied.

The independent clause is negative declaring, "the law is never able to perfect. . . ." The infinitive τελειῶσαι completes the idea of "able" (δύναται). And the infinitive has its own direct object in the form of attributive participle translated, "the ones coming." The reason why "the law is never able to perfect the ones coming" is stated in two circumstantial participles. One (ἔχων) is stated, the second implied from the context. Both participles suggest cause. First is the positive, ". . . having a shadow of the coming good things" and the second is negative, ". . . not (having) the image itself of the things. . . ." Modifying the verb of the main clause is the locative θυσίαις "with sacrifices." αὐταῖς is identical pronoun meaning "same" used here adjectively to modify "sacrifices." The preposition κατά with accusative ἐνιαυτὸν is the distributive use, that is, "year by year by year. . . ."

The relative ἃς inserts a dependent adjective clause which describes "sacrifices." They are sacrifices "which they are offering perpetually. . . ."

The other stated dependent clause is introduced by πεί. But it is really an apodosis (conclusion) of a second class condition that has a protasis suppressed but implied by the context. "(If those same yearly sacrifices really did perfect the worshipers), then they would not have ceased being offered. . . ." The participle translated "being offered" is supplementary to "ceased."

διά with the articular infinitive is classed as an infinitive phrase. But it has all the force of a full dependent clause.

273

The attributive participle λατρεύοντας is adverbial (accusative of general reference) presenting the ones performing the action of the infinitive (the subject so-called). This attributive participle is itself modified by a causal circumstantial participle κεκαθαρισμένους "having been cleansed." The tense is perfect suggesting the permanancy of the cleansing, had they been able to cleanse at all. "Because the ones worshiping have once been cleansed, they no longer have need to be having conscience of sins."

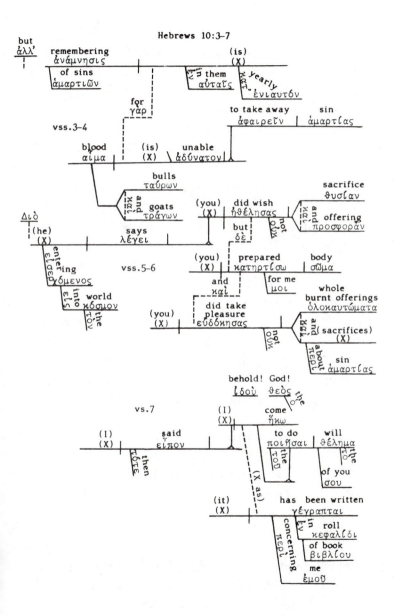

Hebrews 10:3-7

275

THE DIAGRAM OF HEBREWS 10:3-7

Deposited in 10:3-4 is a compound sentence of two clauses. Subject of the first is the action noun ἀνάμνησις = remembering. The verb ("is") is not stated but is implied by the context. But the meat on those meager bare bones is supplied by three modifying expressions. Genitive "of sins" (ἁμαρτιῶν) specifies the kind of "remembering." "In these" (αὐταῖς) tells *where* the remembering took place. The prepositional κατά phrase indicates *when*. The second clause has αἷμα for subject. The predicate is the adjective translated "unable" which in turn is completed by the infinitive "to take away." ἀδύνατον is one of those adjectives that needs an infinitive idea to complete its meaning.

Verses 5-6 embody a complex sentence. It has the one independent to which is subjoined three dependent noun clauses. "(He) says" is the main clause. A temporal circumstantial participle describes the subject "he" by saying, "entering into the world. . . ." The content of what he says follows in the three noun-object clauses. The first is negative, "(you) did not wish sacrifice and offering. . . ." Then a positive statement comes: ". . . you prepared for me a body. . . ." κατηρτίσω is aorist middle indicative second singular from καταρτίζω = make ready, equip, prepare. That is followed by a second negative remark, ". . . you did not take pleasure in whole burnt offerings. . . ."

Verse seven encases another complex sentence with the independent clause stating, "I said. . . ." Direct object of εἶπον is the noun clause "I come." τοῦ ποιῆσαι is the articular infinitive in genitive case, a quite normal way of expressing purpose. From the noun clause hangs an adverbial clause of comparison, ". . . (as) it has been written. . . ." The perfect tense γέγραπται = "as it stands written." It stands as a permanent part of the eternal plan of God. It had been written and it still stands as a written promise in God's enterprise.

Hebrews 10:8-10

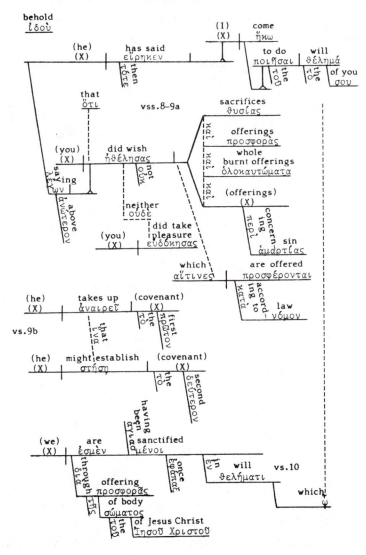

278

THE DIAGRAM OF HEBREWS 10:8-10

One independent clause appears in the sentence of 10:8-9a, "he has said." Perfect tense εἴρηκεν reminds the readers that what Christ ("he") said stands as a permanent certainty. The content of what "he has said" is expressed in the noun clause, object of "has said." "I come to do your will." The articular genitive infinitive ποιῆσαι expresses purpose. Adverb τότε modifying εἴρηκεν tells *when* and aids in contrasting the repeated many "sacrifices and offerings" with the one sacrifice of obedience, "to do your will." Descriptive of the subject "he" is circumstantial participle λέγων. Object of that participle is the noun clause, "that you did not wish sacrifices. . . ." An additional negative object noun clause is, "neither did you take pleasure. . . ." Constantly repeated external, irrational "sacrifices and offerings . . ." was never God's objective "wish" as a solution for man's sin. Neither was it his subjective "pleasure." That's the reason Christ came "to do your will." Such repeated "sacrifices etc. . ." are those "which (αἵτινες) are offered according to law." That is, such sacrifices are by their very nature external, legalistic, statutory. Such is the force of the qualitative relative αἵτινες and the absence of the article with νόμον.

The result of these contrasting methods of sacrifice is expressly stated in the complex sentence of verse 9b. "He takes away the first (covenant) that he might establish the second (covenant)." He takes away the weak repetitious that he might install the final permanent; he gets rid of the outward in order that he might decree the one that fulfills by its inward sacrifice of rational self-surrender. ἵνα with aorist subjunctive expresses purpose. It is a subordinate adverbial clause.

Verse ten classifies as a simple sentence. It has but the one clause, "We have been sanctified. . . ." The perfect passive participle ἡγιασμένοι is predicate supplementing ἐσμέν. Together they form a perfect periphrastic verb which gives extra emphasis to the continuing effects of past action. "We have been sanctified and we still are. . . ." Adverb ἐφάπαξ ("once") increases the sense of permanency involved in the perfect tense. Relative pronoun ᾧ agrees in case, gender and number with its antecedent θελήματι. And we note that the antecedent is incorporated into the locative case from the accusative as it appeared in verse eight. The broken line indicates a connection in thought though not in grammar.

Hebrews 10:11-13

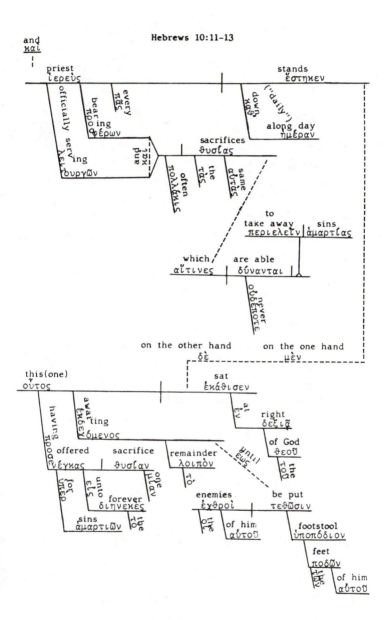

281

THE DIAGRAM OF HEBREWS 10:11-13

The sentence of 10:11-13 is compound-complex. It displays two independent clauses. From the subject of each clause hangs two circumstantial participial phrases. From each of these flows a dependent clause.

The two main clauses state, "every priest stands" and "this (one) sat." Prepositional phrase καθ' ἡμέραν is used adverbially telling when every priest stands, that is, "daily." In balanced contrast a similar adverbial phrase ἐν δεξιᾷ . . . indicates where "this" one sits; "at God's right. . . ." Subject of the first independent clause ἱερεὺς has for its modifiers the present active participles λειτουργῶν and προσφέρων. Their linear action is iterative. The priests "stand ministering officially and bearing day after day many times (πολλάκις) the same sacrifices." The adverb ("many") adds its emphasis to the iterative idea.

The qualitative relative pronoun αἵτινες thrusts in an adjective clause describing θυσίας; "which by their nature are never able to take away sins." The present tense of δύναται with strong negative οὐδέποτε gives a picture of a continuing inability to accomplish the punctiliar action presented by the aorist active infinitive περιελεῖν. The inability is constant: to "take away" is conceived of as a single point.

Again we note sharp contrast by use of μὲν with the first clause and δὲ with the second; "on the one hand . . . but on the other hand. . . ." The daily repetition of inadequate sacrifices reveals a fatal weakness in contrast to the once-for-all finality of the one efficient sacrifice of "this one."

Another pair of circumstantial participles modifies οὗτος. Perfect tense in προσενέγκας points up the definitiveness and finality of the "one sacrifice." And to add emphasis the adverbial phrase εἰς τὸ διηνεκὲς "forever" is inserted. Adverbial ὑπὲρ ἁμαρτιῶν "over sins" explains why the single sacrifice was made. Present ἐκδεχόμενος is linear of continuous action, "expectantly awaiting" as to "the rest" of time.

ἕως introduces a subordinate clause. It expresses a temporal idea, "until his enemies shall be placed as footstool under his feet." The first aorist passive subjunctive τεθῶσιν looks to a climactic point at which the enemies of the Christ shall be "put" as "footstool of his feet." ὑποπόδιον is adverbial accusative to tell where the enemies will be put as well as the manner in which they will be treated, "as footstool."

The author is manifestly anxious that his readers feel his own sharp contrast between the picture of the first clause and that of the second. Particles, tenses, phrases, participles are all designed to impress this contrast between the weak imperfections of the repeated sacrifices versus the authoritative finality of the one sacrifice. Even the number of dependent modifying ideas gives sharpness to this balanced contrast between the weak old and the strong new.

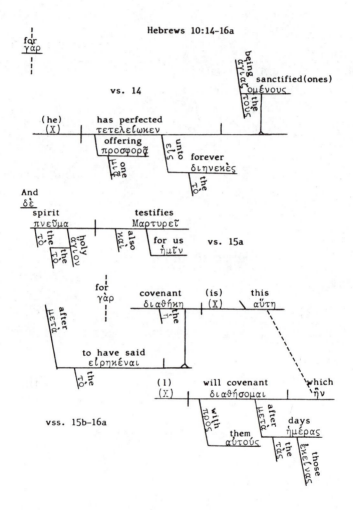

Hebrews 10:14-16a

284

THE DIAGRAM OF HEBREWS 10:14-16a

The sentence of verse 14 is simple in construction. It is attached in thought to the preceding sentence by the co-ordinating conjunction γὰρ. It is illative here; it introduces the *why* that the preceding is true. ". . . for he has perfected. . . ."

The perfect tense of τετελείωκεν calls attention to the permanent completion of the action involved. "He has made perfect once and for all and that perfection is still a continuing reality." The English word "perfect" can be deceiving when used as a translation for τελειόω. At bottom the verb means "to bring to an intended end." When a runner in a foot race comes in first and thus wins the race he has attained his "intended goal." That doesn't include any suggestion that the race was run without some flaws. It simply means that the racer successfully attained the goal which he set before him. "Perfect" does not mean faultless. It simply means "to bring to successful completion." So, by his sacrificial offering "this one" brought to God's intended goal those who are the object of the action. That is, "the ones being sanctified." The attributive present participle ἁγιαζομένους serves as direct object of the verb "has perfected." Though the "making perfect" is a permanent act, finished and completed, the present tense in the participle signals to the reader that sanctification is a continuing process. προσφορᾷ is instrumental case, "with one offering." εἰς διηνεκὲς is adverbial telling how long, "forever."

From a structural point of view verses 15-17 represent broken, irregular sentences. In fact they could hardly be called sentences. It is with some degree of arbitrariness

285

that they are divided into three sentences. Taking 15a as a complete idea it forms a simple sentence. "The Holy Spirit also witnesses for us."

As they stand verses 15b-16 are not grammatically sentences. But the idea seems clear. Though no independent clause appears the prepositional infinitive phrase μετὰ εἰρηκέναι in sense serves as one. It may be paraphrased, "After (formerly) he said. . . ." More literal: "For after the to have said. . . ." A practical accommodation might read, "He has formerly said. . . ." Perfect infinitive εἰρηκέναι gives emphasis to the fact that what was "said" stands permanently said. "It stands said!" The infinitive has as its direct object the noun clause, "the covenant is this."

An adjective clause more completely describing "this" covenant is introduced by the relative pronoun ἥν. The prepositional phrase πρὸς αὐτούς "to them" is used here instead of the original "to Israel." The covenant is not limited to the physical, historical Israel but "to them." That is, to those whose minds and hearts receive it. That would be the new Israel of God.

Note once again the illative γὰρ connecting the idea of this sentence back to the preceding. However, here the "for" gives the reason why the author *believes* "the Holy Spirit testifies."

If we take this sentence of 15b-16 as completely separate it appears as complex with one main clause and two subordinates.

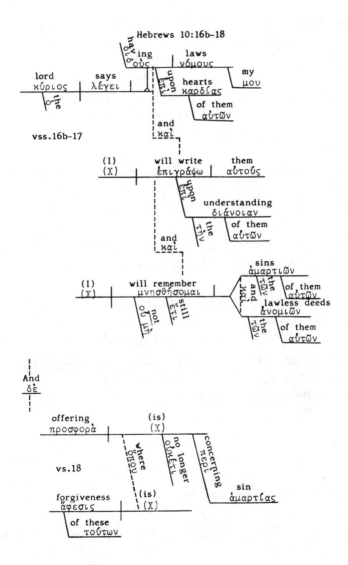

Hebrews 10:16b–18

lord κύριος — says λέγει — having ἔχων — laws νόμους — my μου — upon ἐπί — hearts καρδίας — of them αὐτῶν — the ὁ — those οὓς

vss.16b–17

and καί

(I) (X) — will write ἐπιγράφω — them αὐτούς — upon ἐπί — the τήν — understanding διάνοιαν — of them αὐτῶν

and καί

(I) (X) — will remember μνησθήσομαι — not οὐ μή — still ἔτι — sins ἁμαρτιῶν — the τῶν — of them αὐτῶν — and καί — lawless deeds ἀνομιῶν — the τῶν — of them αὐτῶν

And δέ

offering προσφορά — (is) (X) — no longer οὐκέτι — where ὅπου — concerning περί — sin ἁμαρτίας

vs.18

forgiveness ἄφεσις — (is) (X) — of these τούτων

287

THE DIAGRAM OF HEBREWS 10:16b-18

As diagrammed verses 16b-17 exhibit a complex sentence. In the original quotation from Jeremiah "The Lord says" are words of the prophet. But here the author of Hebrews appropriates them as his own statement. They provide the main clause. The remainder of the quotation from the prophet appears as three clauses, objects of λέγει of the independent clause. Though διδούς is present active participle it may be translated as if it were a finite verb used as parallel to ἐπιγράψω and μνησθήσομαι of the following clause. "(I) give my laws upon their hearts and I will write them on their understanding and I will not remember. . . ." It is possible to treat διδούς as circumstantial participle modifying the subject of verb ἐπιγραφω ("I"). If that be preferred the translation would be, "in as much as" or "because."

In the third of these dependents our author alters the quote from the original of Jeremiah and from the same text as quoted in 8:12. So we observe that the writer does not use other scripture mechanically or by simple rote. He adapts scriptures to his own emphasis and purpose. Biblical authors in drawing upon other scripture writings seek the *meaning* of their sources rather than an unthinking automatic recitation of the text. And at times they even adapt that meaning to their own use!

The future indicative μνησθήσομαι with strong negative οὐ μή furnishes sharper emphasis than the subjunctive μνησθῶ in 8:12. Furthermore, his adding ἀνομιῶν ("lawless deeds") gives a definite explanation of what is contained in the more general ἁμαρτιῶν ("sins"). The genitive case after verbs of memory is normal.

This sentence unscreens a solid affirmation that the new covenant provides the all-out removal from memory of our rebel deeds. The older covenant brought them to mind time after time, year after year. The new covenant blots them out as a barrier to restored fellowship with God. The third dependent clause is a strong negative statement which affirms a very positive idea about the power of the new covenant in the Christ.

The sentence of verse 18 is complex with one independent and one dependent clause. "Where forgiveness of these (is) offering concerning sin (exists) no more. . . ." The dependent idea links up to the independent by ὅπου "where." It's an adverbial idea indicating place. This subordinate fact supports the independent statement, "offering for sin is no more necessary." Where actual forgiveness is accomplished any offering for sin is of no worth.

A Translation
Hebrews 10:19-25

Having, therefore, brethren, bold confidence for entrance into the holiest sanctuary in the blood of Jesus, which (entrance) he inaugurated as a way, freshly made, through the curtain, that is, his flesh, and (having) a great high priest over the house of God, let us come near (to his person) with a true heart in fullness of faith, having our hearts sprinkled from an evil conscience and having bathed the body in pure water; let us be holding fast the confession of the hope unyielding, for the one who promised is faithful, and let us consider one another for (the purpose of) stimulating one another to love and the works of good quality, not forsaking the assembling of yourselves together as the habit of some is, but offering encouragement and by so much more by howsoever much you are beholding the day drawing near.

AN OUTLINE OF HEBREWS 10:19-25
LET US CONSIDER

"Therefore!" In view of the weakness of the "many" and the perfect power of the "one sacrifice" three exhortations are in order:

> Let us come near.
> Let us hold fast.
> Let us consider one another.

I. LET US COME NEAR TO GOD AND HIS THRONE OF GRACE.

    1. Why we should come near:

        (a) Because of Jesus' human experience. 19-20

        (b) Because we have a "great high priest." 21

        (c) Conscience has been relieved of guilt. 22b

        (d) Our "bodies bathed," that is, committed to him. 23c

    2. How shall we come? 22a

        (a) With true heart; genuine, honest, sincere!

        (b) In fullness of faith; absolute trust!

II. LET US HOLD FAST. vs. 23

    1. To what shall we hold? The "confession of the hope."

    2. Why hold fast? His is trustworthy. 23b

III. LET US CONSIDER ONE ANOTHER. vss. 24-25

    1. Consider the word "consider." To "put your mind down on one another." Think thoroughly about each other!

    2. Consider each others' attitudes and habits toward stated assemblies; "not forsaking the assembling . . . ."

    3. Positive consideration:

        (a) Encouraging one another in mutual support!

        (b) Consider the motive: "inasmuch as you see the day approaching. . . ."

    4. The purpose of this considering one another:

        (a) The stimulation of "love."

        (b) The stimulation of "works" the character of which is "good."

Such is the divine way of "provoking" one's friend, neighbor and brother. Let us provoke one another!

SOME EXPOSITORY THOUGHTS ON HEBREWS 10:19-25

Like three peaks in a mountain range three ideas thrust up in the diagram of 10:19-25. (1) Draw near, (2) hold fast, (3) carefully consider. These form the marrow of the exhortation.

A variety of modifying, subordinate ideas support and amplify the three basic counsels. How should we draw near? In two ways: (1) with true hearts. That is, hearts that aren't phony, two-faced, or evil-motivated. Hearts that are genuine, real, tested for loyalty, firmness and faithfulness. (2) In a fullness the character of which is faith, trust, devotion. When true hearts of people with a sense of fulfillment in faith draw near to Christ, our perfect priest, power results, conviction grows, character stabilizes.

Why should we "draw near?" Because "in the blood of Jesus" we have bold confidence to approach God. The awesome holiness of the very presence of God has been put within my reach. As an ordinary person, a humble and humiliated sinner, the blood of the perfect sacrifice, the perfect priest, has opened free access even to me. Christ in his humanity, his human nature, has torn down the veil which in the past has separated me from God. Nothing need now bar my way unto the holiest person of the universe. For the "way" he inaugurated "for us" is "freshly made" and "living." "Fresh" because God himself in the person of Jesus removed the veil and opened the way at a point in history. It's not an idea but an event. It's not a theological speculation; it's death to conquer death, a life given that life may be gained. It's a new, fresh, history oriented way to God. Furthermore, it's "living" in contrast with all the "dead" ways men have tried. It is living because Christ himself is the "way and the life." He *is* life! Therefore, he gives life. I live because he lives. This is my confidence!

The second mountain peak in this triad of urgings says, "let us continually hold fast the confession of the hope unyielding." The pressure to forsake the faith was relentless, constant, daily, so the exhortation is to equalize that by a relentless, continuous, unyielding, unbending, unwavering resistance. "Be holding *fast*!" That to which we are to hold fast is "the confession of the hope." That hope has been defined in previous chapters as entrance into the *real* sanctuary where God himself is. The great high priest, the efficient sacrifice, genuine forgiveness, the better promises are all a part of the "confession of the hope" we have in Christ. Why return to the old when the new is so rich and full of such reality? Why turn to the unreal when the real is mine for the "holding"? And I should hold it "without any yielding," without compromise or unwavering determination. As added incentive remember, "the one who promised is faithful." That is to say, God is trustworthy. You can count on his doing what he has said he will do. He will forgive; he will raise me from the dead; he will crown with the victor's crown. By "holding fast" I have everything to gain and nothing to lose. By failing to "hold fast" I have everything to lose and nothing to gain.

"Be putting your mind on each other" and that "for inciting love and good works." This is the third mountain peak. In the face of constant pressures to forsake faith these Hebrew Christians are urged to "think on one another." Not on the ill points but on ways and means to support in weak or wayward tendencies. My thought, plans, actions are to be with the purpose of stimulating my brother to love and good works. We can live for one another only as we intelligently plan for one another.

How we may thus encourage one another is stated negatively and positively. First, by not forsaking the regular announced gatherings of the people of God. Strength in the Christian conflict cannot come to maturity in isolated withdrawal. There are times when one must seek solitude and individual meditation. But to walk alone without the strength of the assembled community is fatal to faithfulness. Neglect of the supportive power of the gathered church is the first step toward apostasy. It's habit is a guarantee of apostasy. There *is* strength in numbers; in numbers who gather in common faith. And it's not the holy place but rather the holy people who make the assembly an agency of redeeming energy.

The positive side of this social encouraging is the bringing of comfort in sorrow, hope in despair, light in darkness, strength for weakness, forgiveness for sin. Moral strength lies in the knowledge that we do not walk the weary path alone. Spiritual power comes when we share the burdens with one another!

Why should we share life's labor? And in what measure? "By so much the more as you see the day coming near." The day of Christ's coming again is sufficient motive for mutual encouragement. Christians are living in "the last times." We have been in these "last times" since Jesus ascended. Christ's urging is "to watch, for you know neither the day nor the hour." We help one another "watch."

A son inherited the care of a large estate whose owner had not been on the grounds for over a quarter of a century.

In fact the young caretaker had never personally seen the owner. His instructions had been, "Keep the estate clean and productive, ready for the master's return!" Once when a visitor inquired about the impeccable care after so many year's of the master's absence he replied, "I want to be ready when he comes. Should he come today I am ready for his inspection!"

Hebrews 10:19-25

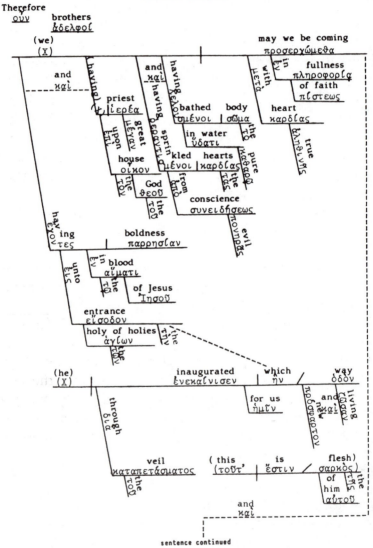

THE DIAGRAM OF HEBREWS 10:19-25

These verses form one compound-complex sentence. It has three independent clauses and four subordinate clauses. The independents publish three exhortations. (1) Let us come near, (2) let us hold fast, (3) let us consider one another.

Four circumstantial participles expand the first of the three exhortations: (1) having boldness, (2) having a great priest, (3) having been sprinkled as to the hearts, (4) having bathed the body. These may be classed as casual since they suggest reasons why we should be "coming near."

Modifying the first of these participles are two important prepositional phrases having the force of adverbs. "For entrance" (εἰς εἴσοδον) suggests either purpose for "having boldness" or a result of such bold confidence. The phrase "in the blood of Jesus" advances the basis for having boldness for entering. The work of Jesus at the cross makes it possible to enjoy bold confidence.

An adjectival clause describes "entrance" (εἴσοδον), which he inaugurated (as a) way, newly (made) and living." Another adverb prepositional phrase modifies ἐνεχαίνισεν, the verb of this dependent clause. It is "through the veil." Preposition διά (through) with genitive is a normal way of expressing agent through which a given thing is accomplished. Christ is the agent "through" whom this freshly made and vitally living way into God's presence was made. The χαταπετάσματος (veil) is defined specifically by the appositional expression, "this is, his flesh." The curtain which separated the Holy Place from the Holy of Holies of the temple symbolized man's separation from the real presence of God. Christ's "flesh" removed not only the symbolic curtain but also that which it symbolized. Christ's

297

experience while he was in the flesh, most especially his death and resurrection, ripped away all barriers between man and his access to God.

In the English translation that appears above the Greek diagram the present subjunctive προσερχώμεθα is rendered "may we be coming." Subjunctive at this point is kin to the imperative mode in that it offers an exhortation or entreaty. Here the most useful translation would be the exhortation "Let us be coming near." But because "let us" may suggest "permission" the translation here uses "may we be coming." The author of Hebrews is not giving permission to come as though someone might be resisting their coming. On the contrary, he is urgent! He is pressing hard in a plea that his readers give high priority to "coming near." Modifying προσερχώμεθα are two adverb prepositional ideas both of which suggest the manner in which we should "be coming near." First, "with true heart." Adjective "true" (ἀληθινῆς) means "made of truth," the essence of what is real, genuine, not hypocritical or about which there is anything which smacks of make believe. The idea "in fullness of faith" would suggest a trust that is absolute one in which doubt cannot find any good or permanent lodging.

A continuation of the diagram and explanation of 10:19-25 is on the following pages.

298

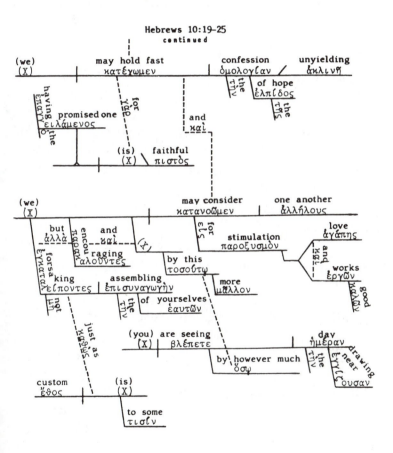

299

THE DIAGRAM OF 10:19-25
(continued)

In this continuation of 10:19-25 are the second and third of the independent clauses. The second exhorts, "Let us hold fast the confession of the hope unyielding." Again we note the present subjunctive. The tense indicates that we "go on holding fast." Do not ever let up "holding fast!" The preposition κατά which combines with ἔχω to form the verb is the intensive perfective idea of a preposition prefixed to a verb. From κατά comes the enriching stress = hold fast, tight, secure, clinched, firmly anchored. That which we are to hold tight is seen in the direct object ὁμολογίαν translated "confession." It derives from a compound verb meaning "to say the same thing," that is, a compact or agreement. The genitive ἐλπίδος characterizes the confession as one of "hope." The predicate adjective adds the idea that the tightly-held hope be held "without bending." Don't yield to environmental pressures.

Though conjunction γάρ normally introduces a coordinating idea, here it connects to the main clause an adverbial dependent clause. It gives a reason *why* one should hold fast the confession. "For the one who promised is faithful." The subject of the clause is the aorist attributive participle ἐπαγγειλάμεωος, "the one having promised."

The third exhortation pleads, "Let us consider one another." Once again it's important to note the perfective use of preposition κατά on a verb νοέω. The root idea is "to think with the mind." The perfective use of the preposition gives stress to the urgent intensity with which one is to think. Combined with the direct object ἀλλήλους (one another) it signifies to "hold your mind down with vigor on one another."

300

Three circumstantial participles help expand the action of the main clause. First a negative way to "consider each other." "Don't forsake the announced assembling." Present tense ἐγκαταλείποντες urges that one shouldn't ever entertain the practice of missing the stated assembly of the brethren. This negative part of the exhortation is enhanced by the adverbial comparative dependent clause introduced by καθὼς, "just as to some (such a) habit is already being practiced."

A second participle is on the positive side, "encouraging," (παρακαλοῦωτες). The degree to which this supporting encouragement should go is pictured in an implied repetition of "encouraging" to which is added the τοσούτῳ . . . ὅσῳ, subordinate adverb clause of degree. "By this much more by howeversomuch as you see the day drawing near." This dependent clause sets before the readers a strong motive for offering one another encouragement.

The point toward which the entire exhortation has been moving finds expression in the adverbial accusative παροξυσμὸν with its preposition εἰς, "for (the purpose of) stimulating. . . ." This (παροξυσμὸν) is an action noun having ἀγάπης (love) and ἐργῶν (works) as objective genitives. καροξυσμὸς means to sharpen, spur on, stimulate, incite. It's a compound word built off of the adjective ὀξὺς = sharp and the perfective use of παρά. We get our word "paroxysm" directly from it.

A Translation

Hebrews 10:25-39

For willingly sinning after (we) get the full knowledge of the truth, no longer concerning sins is there left (any) sacrifice but a certain expectation of judgment and jealousy of fire being about to consume the adversaries. Anyone, having disregarded Moses' law, dies without mercies upon (the testimony of) two or three witnesses. By how much worse do you suppose he shall be deemed worthy of punishment, the one having trodden down the son of God and has considered common the blood of the covenant in which he was sanctified, and who insulted the Spirit of grace? For we know the one who said, To me (belongs) vengeance, I will repay; and again, The Lord will judge his people.

But remember the former days in which you, having been enlightened, endured great conflict of sufferings, being made a public spectacle in both reproaches and afflictions, and also having become sharers with the ones so living. For you also sympathized with the prisoners and with joy accepted the plundering of your possessions knowing you yourselves to be having better possession and one that abides. Therefore, don't cast off your confidence which has great reward. For you have need of patience that, having done the will of God, you may receive the promise. For yet a little while the one coming will come and he will not tarry but

302

my righteous (one) shall live by trusting and if he
shrink back my soul does not take pleasure in him.
But we are not shrinking back unto destruction,
but (are) of faith unto preserving of (the) soul.

AN OUTLINE OF HEBREWS 10:26-39

WARNING OF APOSTASY AND ENCOURAGEMENT OF HOPE!

Threat of judgment and hope of reward are ever-present
companions in a world such as this. The danger of falling
and the hope of rising are both possibilities.

I. PERILS OF APOSTASY. 26-31
1. Persistent, willful apostasy a present possibility. 26a
   (a) It eliminates any and all sacrifices. 26b
   (b) It brings a consuming judgment. 27
2. Pattern of punishment. 28-31
   (a) O.T. pattern reveals the moral nature of punishment. 28
   (b) Greater revelation brings greater punishment. 29
       (1) The rebellious deed.
       (2) The rebellious thought.
       (3) The rebellious personal assault.
3. The nature of God and people of God require judgment.

II. ENCOURAGEMENT OF HOPE. 32-39
1. Former faith the basis for present power. 32-34

    (a) You endured affliction.
    (b) You shared affliction with others.
  2. Exhortation to press on to the end. 35-39
    (a) Don't abandon confidence or faith.
    (b) Motives for pressing on.
      (1) There is One coming!
      (2) Faith is the power for living.
      (3) Shrinking back displeasing to God.

The power of positive thinking! "We aren't of those who shrink back unto destruction but of those who believe unto the preservation of the soul!"

SOME EXPOSITORY THOUGHTS ON HEBREWS 10:26-39

The harvest of heaven is better than a cash crop. Fear of hell has turned some men's thoughts away from wickedness. To a change in conduct hope and fear move mightily the hearts of men.

The author of Hebrews exclaims, "If we are sinning wilfully after we receive the knowledge of the truth. . . ." But it's not just sin as sin of which he writes. The context makes clear that he refers to a specific sin. He has in mind a contemptuous abandonment of faith. Even more particularly, the disdainful rejection of the person of Jesus a God's Christ. It is done "wilfully." That is, it is a voluntary conscious choice. Nor is Jesus denied once in an obscure manner. It is repeated; done in open public; and with scornful disregard of the faith of others. It takes the form of personal attack upon Jesus, his life, his claims, his church. It's the sin of apostasy!

304

A star shortstop on a championship baseball team may commit an error. But he isn't thereby expelled from the group. In fact, he may fall into a batting slump yet still be a vital part of the team. His dedication to the game, his team, his manager and his own future is not questioned. *But* should he deliberately, wilfully, with malice commit errors, should he curse the owner, vilify the team and reject the game as unworthy of his loyalty, then he himself would be rejected. He would be eliminated from baseball forever. It is just such a kind of sin of which the author of Hebrews is warning his readers. Christians may and do commit errors in their effort to live the redeemed life. They are not thereby expelled from the squad. In the upward climb weakness may repeatedly overtake us but as long as personal commitment to Jesus is present we are still a part of the family of God. But if we openly, repeatedly, publicly and vociferously renounce our faith in the person of Jesus as God's son, by such sin we eliminate ourselves from God's people. We are no longer a part of the team.

Such apostasy brings at least two specific results. First, no redemption is possible. To reject the world's only Savior is to have no savior. "If we sin wilfully after we receive the knowledge of the truth, there remains no more sacrifice for sin." If there's only one mechanic in town available and if I repudiate that mechanic as competent to repair my car, then I will have to do without any mechanic, at least in that town. He who rejects the only one of its kind is left empty-handed.

A second result of repudiating Jesus is that a consuming judgment awaits. "A fearful expectation of judgment and a fury of fire" consumes the adversary. The result of apostasy from Jesus is not an artificial punishment imposed by an impulsive, outraged, bitter deity. No! It's an aggressive, progressive, cancerous eating at the soul which brings its own decay. There's nothing more putridly rotten than to have to live in the foulness of one's own self when that self has sinned against light, abused love, and forsaken truth. Such fire is a torment of judgment built into the nature of the sin. On him who is condemned to die the slow death of cancer there is no need to inflict punishment. The nature of the disease carries its own painful punishment.

Could there be any sin greater than "trodding down the Son of God" or "treating common the blood of the covenant," or "insulting the Spirit of grace. . . .?" Even the shadowy old covenant brought precise moral retribution. The same God who would not temporize with violation of that moral code is the God of the greater covenant. Will he not expect the same quality of obedience to the greater revelation? The Old Testament pattern of punishment reveals the moral nature of punishment. Retribution is not optional. It is a reflection of the undeviating moral nature of God. It is built into the quality of human life as a man echoes the divine nature in which he was created. So punishment returns on the violator as measured by the magnitude of the sin committed. Rejection of the greater revelation brings greater punishment. Particularly after one tastes the power of the greater! The rebellious deed done, "tramping down the Son of God"; the rebellious thought felt, "considered unclean the life's blood of God's Son"; the violent personal assault, "insulting the Spirit of grace";—these greatest of sins demand the ultimate in retributive justice. The nature of God requires it. The fact that we are "the people of God" expects it for we enjoy higher blessings.

But apostasy need not be our lot. We have tools with which to avoid this final of all sin. Memory is a sword that can kill. But it also protects and preserves life. Three things had already happened to these Hebrew Christians that revealed their latent strength. And that moral power, experienced in the past, could be recycled in the present crisis. You endured being a public spectacle in former years. That very experience demonstrates present potential. You *can* endure! You even felt the joy of God's presence when your personal possessions were vandalized. You experienced the peace of God amidst the storm of being dispossessed of your material wealth. The joy and peace of that past can again be experienced now.

But yet more, beside your own suffering, you found strength to share the afflictions of others. You even entered into prisons to offer the strength of your own faith to that of those shackled because of Christ. The very memory of such personal power lends muscle to present spiritual crises. Therefore, lay hold on this reservoir of might. You've shown great confidence in the past. Don't cast away this bold assurance. That very boldness is itself a stimulant to rise to new heights of victory. Confidence "has great reward." It generates patience under duress, it sustains through storm, it generates obedience to the "will of God" when disobedience is the popular way.

Besides all this you have strong motives to move forward by the power of faith. It's only a "little while the one coming will come and he will not tarry." In the days of the prophets God always came in time to help his own. He now stands at the door and will not forsake you. His presence is as sure as your faith in him and his coming. Faith motivates! "My righteous one shall live by trusting."

Besides, to shrink back through the faltering of faith doesn't arouse God's admiration, to say the least. God honors him who trusts. God prizes faith and faithfulness. But he shrinks from the soul that shrinks back in behalf in him.

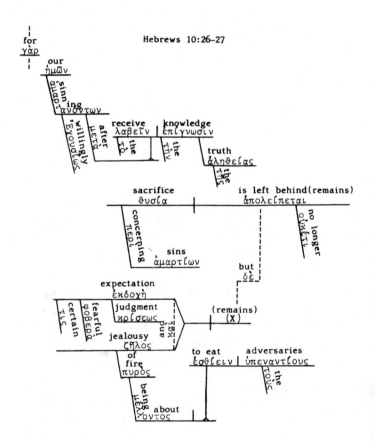

Hebrews 10:26-27

THE DIAGRAM OF HEBREWS 10:26-27

Strictly speaking the sentence of verses 26-27 is compound. It has but two full clauses connected by the coordinate conjunction δὲ. The genitive absolute at the beginning of the sentence is, by definition, not grammatically related to the rest of the sentence. Yet it really furnishes a conditional thought which for all practical purposes supplies a dependent clause supporting the first of the independent clauses. The literal translation would read, "For our sinning willingly after the to receive the full knowledge of the truth. . . ." But for the English reader it may be put as a conditional dependent clause. "For if we are sinning willingly after we receive the full knowledge of the truth. . . ." So, technically this is surely a compound sentence. Yet practically it might be called compound-complex.

Ἑχουσίως is an adverb, emphatic by position, which calls attention to the voluntary will involved in the apostasizing sin. And present tense of the participle ἁμαρτανόντων underscores the prodigal habit of repeating the sin. The infinitive λαβεῖν is aorist. It looks to the fact and point of "getting" the knowledge. The thoroughness of the knowledge is emphasized by the choice of ἐπίγνωσις rather than the simple γνῶσις. This is full, mature knowledge from which they are about to fall away. The genitive ἀληθείας specifies the kind of quality of knowledge. The "truth" isn't truth in general but the truth as embodied in the Christ who once said, "I am the truth."

The sin of which the author here speaks is apostasy, the rejection of the one perfect sacrifice. It's done openly, with full knowledge, and voluntarily. The inevitable conclusion is that no other sacrifice is available. He who rejects the only one of its kind is left empty-handed. So the first main clause asserts, ". . . no longer concerning sins is being left any sacrifice. . . ." Present ἀπολείπεται linear of continuous action, "is being left."

The second of the independent clauses borrows its verb from the first, "remains." The subject is compound suggesting two ideas. ἐκδοχὴ is the judgment (χρίσεως) that man may expect; ζῆλος represents the abused love which must come upon the one abusing as "fire" (πυρὸς). That the fire is a consuming fire comes out in present circumstantial participle μέλλοντος with its infinitive phrase "to eat the adversaries." Both participle and its object infinitive are present tenses. They give a moving picture of an aggressive, devouring, tormenting ordeal of judgment. Of the pronoun τις Wescott makes (pg. 328) a pertinent observation: "The rhetorical use of the indefinite τις gives a solemn awe to the statement. The fact that the expectation cannot be exactly defined necessarily makes it more impressive."

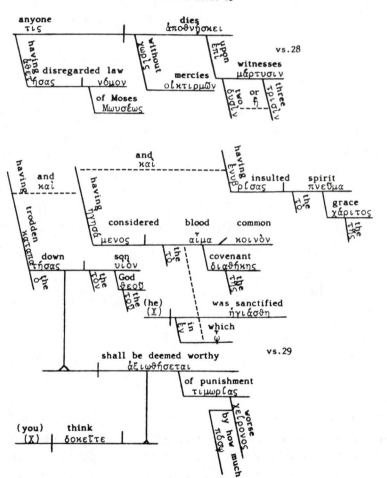

311

THE DIAGRAM OF HEBREWS 19:28-29

As punctuated in the Nestle's text 10:28-29 constitutes one sentence. But the diagram presents verse 28 as one simple sentence. That leaves verse 29 as a complex sentence of three clauses.

"Anyone dies" is the clause of the sentence of verse 28. ἀποθνήσκει is present tense, probably best thought of as gnomic in force. It was a law of universal application whether consistently enforced or not. Modifying the subject is circumstantial participle ἀθετήσας an aorist active of ἀθετέω "to set at nought." It is built from alpha privative plus the familiar τίθημι to place or put. Here it means to "put aside" or render "null." Its aorist tense focuses attention on the point of rebellion rather than the process. The plural οἰκτιρμῶν seems to draw attention to the fact that in Old Testament practice *all* the people were involved in afflicting the punishment.

The independent clause in verse 29 is a question, ". . . do you think. . . .?" Object of "think" is the noun clause, ". . . shall be deemed worthy by how much worse. . . .? πόσῳ is instrumental case of degree or measure. χείρονος (worse) is comparative of κακός. The subject of the verb ἀξιωθήσεται is a three-pronged compound subject. It is a forceful indictment of the dreadful nature of the sin under consideration. First comes καταπατήσας "having trodden down the son of God. . . ." It reflects a deed done, an act committed. There follows an opinion adopted, ". . . having considered the blood of the covenant (as) common (unclean). . . ." Attached to this second prong of the subject is an adjective phrase describing αἷμα; "in which he was sanctified." The adjective κοινὸν is used here as an objective complement which describes the "blood" as "common" in the sense that it was deemed "unclean." That is to say, the shed blood of Christ was really not "innocent blood" as remorse-stricken Judas declared but actually was deserved. Jesus really got what he deserved because he was guilty of offense to God and man!

The final fragment of the three-pronged subject represents an open assault and personal attack by the rebel apostate; "having insulted the spirit of grace." All three of these participial phrases are attributive coming under the sway of the article ὁ appearing with καταπατήσας.

This threefold subject pictures with vivid force the nature of the sin to which the Hebrews were being tempted. It was a determined and open repudiation of their original confession of faith in Jesus as the Messiah of hope, the son of God and their Savior. And there was a certain contemptuous rejection of him whom they had once held in reverent high esteem. Thus this is no ordinary sin but an open disavowal and defection from their former faith.

Hebrews 10:30-31

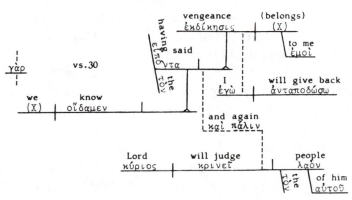

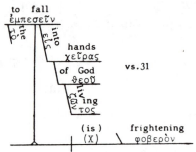

314

THE DIAGRAM OF HEBREWS 10:30-31

Two quotations from Deuteronomy 32:35-36 form the content of three subordinate clauses in the sentence of 10:30. They are noun clauses, direct objects of the attributive participle εἰπόντα. In turn that participle is direct object of οἴδαμεν of the independent clause. The sentence is to be classed as complex.

The coordinating γὰρ ties the thought of this sentence to the certainty of retributive justice as stated in the preceding sentence. This current thought explains why punishment must inevitably come. It is because of the nature of God and of the people of God.

"We know . . ." is the assertion of the main clause. And it's the knowledge that is intuitive and absolute (οἴδαμεν). The first two of the noun object clauses reflects (1) the justice of God, "vengeance (belongs) to me." And (2) the necessary requital that springs inevitably from his nature, "I will repay the precise due." The third object clause turns attention to God's people as another basis on which retributive judgment must come. By virtue of their favored position and privileges they will be held accountable. Those more highly blessed must expect a judgment that reflects such high privileges. Thus it is particularly true that "the Lord will judge *his people*." λαὸς is a word most frequently used for the peculiar "people of God."

Verse 31 reveals a simple sentence. "To fall into the hands of the living God (is) frightening!" Infinitive ἐμπεσεῖν is aorist and thus calls attention to the point at which the apostate feels the judgmental grip of God clasp him. The perfective use of the preposition ἐν (appearing as ἐμ before πεσεῖν) combines with the aorist tense to emphasize further

315

the awesome experience of feeling the judgmental vengeance of the "living God." ζῶτος is circumstantial present participle describing "God." He is not a dead god; he is not an impersonal force; he is not a creation of human imagination or the result of the artisan's skill. He is "living!" Living in the sense that he actively enters into the affairs of man; living in the sense that he is constantly projecting himself into the events of history; living in that he thinks, feels, wills as any other "living" person does. The present tense of ζῶντος reminds that this activity is constant; going on all the time.

φοβερὸν = "frightening" is a true picture of him of whom it is said, "God is love." Love in the presence of sin appears as severe judgment wrath. At least to him who is committed to sin. Love is not love if it ignores wrong. Against sin love appears as judgment.

Hebrews 10:32-34

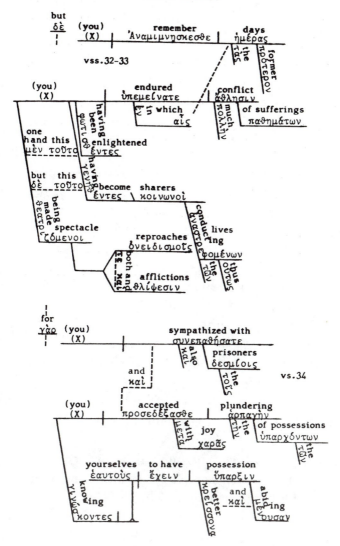

317

THE DIAGRAM OF HEBREWS 10:32-34

These verses encompass two sentences. The first is complex, the second compound. They are closely related in ideas; the flow of thought slips easily from one into the other. In fact the clauses of the compound (vs. 34) express ideas parallel to that of the subordinate clause of the complex of vss. 32-33.

The independent clause is an exhortation: "be remembering the former days. . . ." The verb translated "remember" is present middle. The present tense calls for maintaining a conscious awareness of earlier injuries. The middle voice magnifies the part the subject plays: "*you*" exercise your memory. You don't need to *be reminded* for you yourselves remember. Preposition ἀνά on the verb is the perfective use intensifying the idea of remembering. Remember every single pain and loss. The entire clause is expressive. Rightly used, memory can be a useful stimulant to arouse action that will help avoid apostasy.

The dependent clause attached by ἐν αἷς is adjectival in function. It describes the "former days" they "endured much conflict of sufferings. . . ." Those sufferings, no doubt, extended over a long period but the author gathered them all up in one graphic snap shot by the aorist ὑπεμείνατε. Looking back on them they could appear as a single unpleasant experience. Three participles bring out certain circumstances which surrounded their "endurance" of former trials. Aorist φωτισθέντες reminds them that their Christian faith had brought "enlightenment." The light of truth might even have been a contributing cause to their "conflict." There follows θεατριζόμενοι, "being made a spectacle." Its present tense jogs memory to repeated times they were publicly afflicted. But they not only were made a shameful exhibit they themselves voluntarily became "sharers" (γενηθέντες κοινωνοί) with others who were "so conducting their lives."

The sentence of verse 34 has two clauses of equal rank. They say: "You sympathized with . . . you accepted plundering of possessions. . . ." Furthermore, μετὰ χαρᾶς tells in what manner they did it; "with joy." The underlying cause *why* they accepted such abuse finds expression in circumstantial participle γινώσκοντες with its object infinitive phrase ἔχειν. ἑαυτοὺς is accusative of general reference (so called subject) with infinitive. μένουσαν is present circumstantial participle describing "possessions." Present tense of the infinitive as well as the participle contribute to a subtle reminder that true possessions are abiding while that of which they had been plundered weren't really possessions. They were things held in trust.

These verses (10:32-34) form a natural unforced outline.

> Memory can stimulate high resolve!
> I. The conflict of suffering.
>   1. You were a spectacle.
>   2. You shared other's afflictions.
> II. You sympathized with prisoners.
> III. You accepted plundering.
> You have better, more permanent possessions.

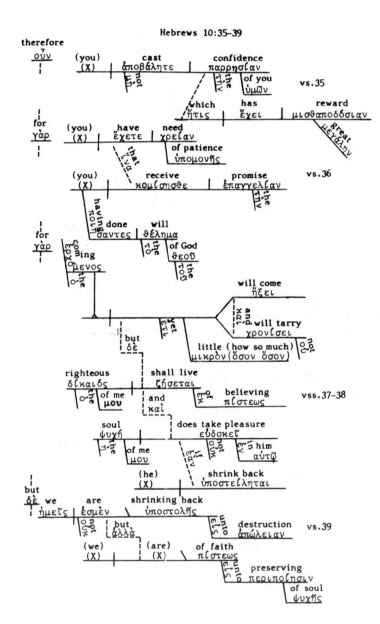

320

THE DIAGRAM OF HEBREWS 10:35-39

"Don't cast off your confidence" is the exhortation of the independent clause of the complex sentence of verse 35. The verb ἀποβάλητε is an effective aorist. It focuses on the actual end achieved, the throwing away one's bold confidence. The ἀπό prefixed to the root verb is perfective. It adds a note of finality to the total verb idea. Don't make a corpse of your confidence so as to bury it as in reinforced concrete. ἥτις is a qualitative relative pronoun meaning "which by its very nature." The adjective clause it introduces declares, "which by its very nature has great reward." Bold confidence is half the battle in any venture of faith. Carelessly casting it away is a stride toward defeat.

Verse 36 entails another complex arrangement. γάρ relates this sentence to the previous one by presenting a reason why we shouldn't dispose of boldness. "You are having need of patience" and "bold confidence" will sustain patience. The ἵνα clause is adverb of purpose, "in order that you may receive the promise." The definite article τὴν with "promise" points to a specific promise. That originally given to Abraham and repeated in various forms in the centuries through patriarch, prophet, priest and king. That which finds fulfillment in the Christ they were tempted to abandon. Circumstantial participle ποιήσαντες is either causal or conditional or a combination of both.

Three independent clauses, the last of which has a conditional dependent tacked on, furnish the frame for a compound-complex sentence in verses 37-38. The subject of the first clause is the attributive participle ὁ ἐρχόμενος, "the one coming." The phrase is taken from Hab. 2:3 and referred there to God's coming to destroy the Chaldeans, the enemy of God's people. The author of Hebrews applies

321

the idea to the Christ from which his readers were tempted to turn away. Men of faith have always had to wait patiently for the coming of God's relief. And it doesn't come in the manner men expect it; but it does come. The doubling of the verbs gives emphasis to the certainty of his coming: ". . . will come and will not tarry. . . ." The second clause continues, with slight alteration, the thought of Habbakkuk. "My righteous (one) shall live by faith." πίστεως is not so much a reference to the content of faith but the power that comes in the process of believing. The third of the independent clauses is the apodosis of a third class conditional. It is supported by the ἐάν dependent adverbaial idea "if he shrink back." The "if" leaves the condition undetermined but with likelihood that it will happen. "If he shrink back, and he just might though it's not sure that he will. . . ." The verb "shrink back" is point action aorist; Present "does take pleasure" is iterative. God's displeasure takes expression any or every time a shrinking back happens.

Verse 39 is compounded of two clauses. Personal pronoun ἡμεῖς as subject is very emphatic. "We on our part aren't shrinking back. . . ." ὑποστολῆς and πίστεως are predicate genitives. It's a possessive idea in the predicate. The εἰς phrases indicate direction toward; "unto destruction" and "unto preserving. . . ."

A Translation
Hebrews 11:1-40
The nature of faith. 1-2

But faith is of things being hoped for a title-deed, of things not being seen a conviction. For in it the ancients have been testified to (approvingly).

Faith and the unseen world of origins. 3

By faith we perceive that the worlds have been created by God's word so that the thing which is being seen has not risen out of things appearing.

Faith in the pre-flood world. 4-7

By faith Abel offered a better sacrifice than Cain, on account of which it was testified that he was righteous, God testifying upon his gifts, and through it, though having died, yet he speaks.

By faith Enoch was changed so as not to see death, and he was not being found because God changed him. For before his change it had been witnessed that he had pleased God. But without faith, to please is impossible. For it is necessary that the one coming to God believe that he exists and that to the ones seeking him he becomes a rewarder.

By faith Noah, having been warned concerning the things not yet seen, having acted with reverence, prepared an ark unto the saving of his house, through which (faith) he condemned the world and became heir of the righteousness (which is) according to faith.

Faith and the patriarchs. 8-22

By faith Abraham, being called, obeyed to go out unto a place which he was about to receive for an inheritance, and he went out not knowing where he was going. By faith he sojourned as an alien stranger in a land of promise, having dwelt in tents with Isaac and Jacob, the one inheriting the same promise; for he was expecting the city having the foundations of which God is architect and builder.

By faith even Sarah herself got power for founding of seed and (she got power) beyond season (of childbearing) since she counted faithful the one who promised. Wherefore from one (man) they became, and these from (one) having become dead, just as the stars of heaven (are) in multitude and as the sand along the lip of the sea (is) innumerable.

According to the standard of faith these all died not having received the promises but from afar having seen them and having saluted (them) and having confessed that they were strangers and sojourners upon the earth. For the ones saying such things as these are declaring that they are seeking a fatherland. And if indeed they were remembering that (land) from which they went out they were having time to return; but now they desire a better, that is, a heavenly. Wherefore God is not ashamed, as to them, to be called their God, for he prepared for them a city.

By faith Abraham being tried offered the Isaac, and the one having received the promises, to whom it was spoken, 'In Isaac your seed shall be called,' he was offering the only begotten, calculating that God (was) able to raise him even out of the dead, from whence also he did receive him in parable.

By faith also, concerning things to come, Isaac blessed Jacob and Esau. By faith Jacob, dying, blessed each of the sons of Joseph, and worshiped on the top of his staff.

By faith Joseph, as life was drawing to its end, mentioned concerning the exodus of the sons of Israel and he commanded concerning his bones.

Faith for fighting conflicts. 23-31

Having been born, by faith Moses was hidden three months by his parents because they saw the child (to be) goodly and they did not fear the command of the king. By faith Moses, when he became great, refused to be called the son of Pharaoh's daugher, choosing rather to be ill-treated with the people of God than to have the enjoyment of sin for a season, for he was looking unto the recompense. Not getting afraid of the king's anger, he left Egypt by faith for he got strong as (one gets strong) as he sees the unseen. By faith he performed the passover and the sprinkling of the blood in order that the one destroying the firstborn might not touch them.

By faith they passed through the Red Sea as through dry land, of which the Egyptians, having made an attempt, were swallowed up.

By faith the walls of Jericho, having been encircled seven days, fell.

By faith Rahab the harlot, having received with peace the spies, did not perish with the ones who disobeyed.

Faith in the later history of Israel. 32-34

And what shall I say further? For the time will forsake me if I should describe concerning Gideon, Barak, Sampson, Jephthah, and both David and Samuel, and the prophets, who through faith conquered kingdoms, wrought righteousness, obtained promises, stopped lions' mouths, quenched power of fire, fled mouths of sword, from weakness were made strong, became mighty in battle, turned armies of aliens; women by resurrection received their dead, but others were tortured, not having accepted their release so that they might get a better resurrection; but yet others took trial of mockings and scourgings, but further, bonds and prison. They were stoned, they were tempted, they were sawn asunder, they died in slaughter of sword, they went around in sheepskins, in goatskins being afflicted, being ill-treated, of whom the world was not worthy, wandering upon deserts and mountains and caves of the earth.

And these all, though having been witnessed to through their faith, did not receive the promise, God having foreseen something better concerning us in order that without us they might not be perfected.

AN OUTLINE OF HEBREWS 11:1-40
THE FULFILLMENT OF FAITH

Presuppositions are not the creation of feverish fantasies of over-heated brains. They are the bread of life; the basis upon which human beings think, act, and maintain a measure of social order. Science, practical affairs, and religion rest on assumptions that lie beyond "proof." Men "believe!" So they live, build institutions, conduct business, and die in hope! Because men had faith "they were approved by the testimony" of God!

I. THE NATURE OF FAITH. 1-2

    1. Faith is as "title-deed of things hoped for." 1a
    2. It is "conviction of things not seen." 1b
    3. The ancients' faith stands "witnessed to." 2

II. FAITH AND THE UNSEEN WORLD OF ORIGINS! 3

　1. Creation and the "word" of God. 3a
　2. Things "which appear" and unseen spiritual. 3b

III. FAITH IN THE PRE-FLOOD WORLD. 4-7

　1. Faith in worship; Abel. 4
　2. Faith in fellowship; Enoch. 5-6
　3. Faith and righteousness; Noah. 7

IV. FAITH AND THE PATRIARCHS. 8-22

　1. Faith and obedience; Abraham "went out." 8
　2. Faith and patience; "he sojourned." 9-10
　3. Shared faith. Sarah "got power." 11-12
　4. Faith's testimony to the spiritual quality of human life. 13-16
　5. Faith and absolute surrender; Abraham "offered" his son of the "promise." 17-19
　6. Faith and God's choice; "Isaac blessed. . . ." and "Jacob worshiped. . . ." 20-21
　7. Faith and the beginning of the "people of God." Joseph mentioned "the sons of Israel. . . ." 22

V. FAITH FOR FIGHTING CONFLICTS. 23-31

　1. Faith at the birth of Moses. 23
　2. Moses and his conflict of faith. 24-26
　3. Faith and Moses' choice to forsake Egypt. 27
　4. Moses' faith and the institution of Passover. 28
　5. Faith of Israel in conflict. 29-30
　　(a) Against natural obstacles. 29
　　(b) Against opposing peoples. 30
　6. Faith shared with a gentile "enemy." 31

VI. FAITH IN THE LATER HISTORY OF ISRAEL. 32-38
    1. Faith in typical leaders of theocratic kingdom. 32
    2. Faith and various kind of victories. 33-35a
    3. Victories from the endurance of faith. 35b-38

Failure of the fathers to find perfecting of God's promise. 39-40
    1. They failed to find fulfillment in their lifetime. 39
    2. Something "better" to be consummated with "us." 40

SOME EXPOSITORY THOUGHTS ON HEBREWS 11:1-40

Presuppositions are essential to thinking! They are the staff of life, the basis upon which human beings can think with logic. Without presuppositions our actions would be meaningless, helter-skelter, without purpose. There would be social chaos. The most exact science rests on some basic assumptions that lie beyond empirical proof. A scientist can no more "prove" the eternity of matter than a religionist can "prove" the existence of God. Under any world view lie premises on which the superstructure of thought and action rests. He who deposits money in a bank "believes" that the banker is honest and the bank will fulfill the promised services. And he who comes to God must "believe that he exists and that to the one seeking him he is a rewarder." Assumptions are vital to human life.

The nature of faith

What is faith? Some versions of Hebrews 11:1 say that "faith is the *substance* of things hoped for." That is, it is

329

that which "stands under," gives an element of reality to things for which the human spirit longs; that which enables him to plan actions as if the hoped for things were present realities. What a title-deed is for real estate faith is for "things hoped for." A title-deed is the guarantee that the property on which I hope to build is mine. And therefore I live my day to day life on the expectation that the property is already in my possession.

Faith is also "the conviction of things not seen." As sight, sound, touch, produce evidence of things *visible,* faith is the faculty in human beings which fits them to see what cannot be seen! Faith sees beyond sight. It enables us to plan and live life as though the invisible were now present before our eyes.

Without exception all men who have found the meaning of life, enjoyed the guidance and blessing of God's unseen world, not to mention this present world, have been men whose faith has determined their actions. Without faith no one at any level of life has ever succeeded. History is a demonstration of the energizing power of faith. For in faith "the ancients have been witnessed to" and found divine approval.

Faith and the unseen world of origins

"By faith we perceive that the worlds have been created by God's word. . . ." Did the might, beauty, precision of this visible world and universe appear because of unintelligent chance or by the rational purpose of a discerning Creator? Either view rests on an act of believing. Men have a choice of that which they will believe. Evidence is too slim for anyone to say "I know the origins are this or that!" So the author of Hebrews details his presupposition

330

by saying, "WE perceive that the worlds have been *created* by God's word so that the thing being seen has not risen out of things appearing." By faith we may proceed with life in the assured conviction that the world and human history responds to a divine purpose; that the "will of God" explains all things. God created; God guides; an intelligent goal is to be reached.

Faith in the pre-flood world

"By faith Abel offered a better sacrifice than Cain." Both brothers offered the best they had. Cain was a successful farmer; Abel a good shepherd; his cattle the sleekest and best. A man can offer to God only what he has. So Cain offered the choicest fruit from his orchards and the ripest grains from his fields. Abel gave to God the best of his herd, the most faultless of his flock. The difference did not lie in *what* each presented but *within* him who gave it. Hebrews says Abel offered in "faith" and thus "through it he was testified to that he was righteous." Furthermore, "though he died he still bears witness" to the value of faith.

It is said of Enoch that he "walked with God." And though his length of life was less than half that of his peers yet his was a life of quality. Instead of death he was "translated." Though they searched for his remains "he was not found." He obviously "pleased God" for his association with God was one of intimate personal fellowship. He walked on the same terms, walked unquestionably in the same path, was sensitive to the spiritual quality of divine purposes. He did it "by faith." One who walks with God like that eliminates death as a thing to be feared. Fellowship with God empties death of its power!

331

Faith is an inward conviction about "things not seen." When Noah was "divinely warned" about the unseen judgment to come he took God at his word. He believed the warning and allowed it to affect what he did. He prepared for the unseen catastrophe; he "prepared an ark." Faith regulated his actions. Hence he "became the according-to-faith righteousness." He did what was "right" because he believed God. He saved his own house through faith and condemned the world by that same exercise of faith.

Faith and the patriarchs

From verse eight through 22 four factors about Abraham are mentioned. He "went out," "he sojourned," his wife "got power," and "he offered the son of the promise." Faith led him first to "obey" by going out "not knowing where." He trudged toward the unknown future. To "sojourn" means that he kept uprooting himself as each stage of life proved not to be that secure city for which he hoped. That requires patient endurance. But faith was equal to the task. His faith inoculated his wife with enough trust to nullify her doubt and gave her strength to conceive seed against all the experience of nature. Abraham's faith was shared by Sarah until her action was as "of one." But above all the patriarch's faith rose to the sublime height of absolute surrender when it led him to give up his son of the promise. He who withholds anything from God has a weak link in the chain of his faith. Abraham met that ultimate test. And thereby became the father of all those who believe.

His faith was imitated by his son and grandson. "Isaac blessed . . ." and "Jacob worshiped. . . ." In each instance the faith of the patriarch gave God his opportunity of freely *choosing* him through whom the divine destiny would move. Isaac blessed Jacob, not Esau. Jacob blessed Ephraim, the younger, not Manasseh, the older. Faith reversed the expected order. Faith always enables God's will to move freely along the channel *he* wills.

Faith for fighting conflicts

The life of Moses and the history of Israel are interwoven as thread in fabric. Moses and his work stands like a mount Everest in Israel's history. And faith is the dominant ingredient in Moses' life. It encircled him at birth for "by faith his parents hid him three months." They believed the unseen destiny of God's purpose in their child. So they defied the threat of the Pharaoh. Moses himself, "when he had become great" made his own choice of faith. "He refused" kingship, rejected the temporary "pleasure of sin" and identified with "the people of God" and their suffering. He preferred "the reproach of the (unseen, future) Christ" than the pleasure, power and palliative of this-world culture. Faith with the people of God in conflict with the opposition that Egyptian world power could muster sealed its triumph by a religious festival. Moses "by faith has made the passover and the sprinkling of the blood that the destroyed of the firstborn might not touch them." That passover feast still stands as memorial to the force of faith over sin and its power as embodied in world-empire.

Moreover, Moses' faith became Israel's faith in its conflicts. The power of Israel's faith versus the power of armed evil is quite manifest at the crisis of their flight from Egypt. "By faith they passed through the Red Sea . . ."

which "the Egyptians trying were swallowed up." After
forty years of wandering and in another generation that
power of faith in conflict had not diminished. "By faith
the walls of Jericho fell. . . ." The strategy of war-lord
generals, the strength of walled defenses, cannot stand
against God's power when unleashed by faith in his people.
Even an "enemy" of God is transformed into a tower of
power by the force of faith. "By faith Rahab the harlot
was not destroyed. . . ."

To recite all the names and events in Israel's later history
would push beyond reason. Suffice it to remind that both
kings and commoners have shared in the sure victories
of faith. Kingdom, righteousness, wild animals, fire,
sword, weakness, alien armies, torture, scourgings, lonely
vigils, homeless hungers, and death have all been subdued
by faith. Where faith is, victory is! The endurance and
triumph of faith is not even recognized for what it is.
Faith's standard of "success" appears unreal to this world.
The victors of faith are those "of whom the world is not
worthy." The triumphs of faith are counted failures by
the measuring sticks of this world.

The final fulfillment

Yet with all the victories of faith the ancients "all" failed.
With each mountain climbed another horizon arose. The
fulfillment of each promise revealed that it was not the
fulfilled of *the* promise! "These all died in faith not having
received what was promised but having seen from afar . . .
if they remembered that from which they went out they
had time to return; but they desire a better, a heavenly
(fulfillment). . . ." Any victory in this world is a sign of

an ultimate victory of and in another world. Something "better" awaited them in connection with "us." Their faith and our faith are united in God's Christ and the destiny he won for all men of faith. "This is the victory, even our faith!"

Hebrews 11:1-4

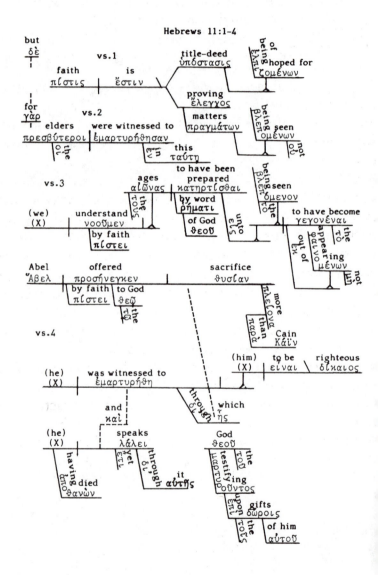

THE DIAGRAM OF HEBREWS 11:1-4

The sentence of verse one is simple in structure. It declares "But faith is (of the nature) of a title-deed of hoped-for (thing), a proving of things not being seen." Both ὑπόστασις and ἔλεγχος are predicate nominative. And they are without the article thereby calling attention to the nature or quality. Each of these two words has both a subjective and objective meaning. ὑπόστασις may mean either *substance* or *assurance*. ἔλεγχος may mean either *evidence* or *confidence*. ὑπόστασις as "title-deed" is amply verified in papyri examples in koine Greek. Each of the two words is described by a genitive present attributive participle, "of things being hoped for . . ." and "of things not being seen. . . ." It ought also be noted that πίστις is an *action* noun; "faith" is more than just a state of mind; it is a process going on. It works itself into inward energies and outward acts.

Verse two occasions another simple sentence. Its introductory γάρ binds it closely to verse one. The article οἱ suggests that the author has a particular set of "elders" in mind, the patriarchs and saints of Old Testament history. Our fore-fathers lived under the need of two factors: (1) future hopes; (2) a world of forces invisible to the physical senses. Faith was the factor that enabled them to regulate their lives as though the future were present and the invisible were seen. "The elders were witnessed to in connection with this (faith)."

By classifying infinitive expressions as phrases rather than clauses verse three is left with but one clause. So it is classed as simple. "We understand . . ." is the one clause. The means with which we gain understanding is in the instrumental πίστει. The content of what we understand is in aorist passive infinitive κατηρτίσθαι with its accusative of general reference αἰῶνας. "By faith we understand the ages to have been prepared. . . ." Instrumental case ῥήματι expresses the instrument by which the ages were prepared. The εἰς infinitive phrase expresses result (not purpose). Articular present participle βλεπόμενον is accusative of general reference with perfect infinitive γεγονέναι. "So that the things being seen to have become. . . ."

Verse four contains a complex sentence of three clauses. The independent says, "By faith Abel offered . . . sacrifice. . . ." The degree to which his offering surpassed Cain's is expressed by comparative πλείονα with παρά, "more than Cain." The relative clause ushered in by δι'ἧς is adjectival describing "sacrifice." The sacrifice Abel offered was the agency "through which he was testified to that he was righteous. . . ." εἶναι is accusative case object of ἐμαρτυρήθη. All infinitives are in fixed forms; their case is determined by usage in context.

The second dependent clause is also adjective in function. It also describes "sacrifice." "Through it (the sacrifice) he still speaks though he has died." ἀποθανὼν is aorist circumstantial participle of concession, "even though having died. . . ."

The diagram concludes with the genitive absolute, "God, upon the basis of his gifts, testifying."

Hebrews 11:5-6

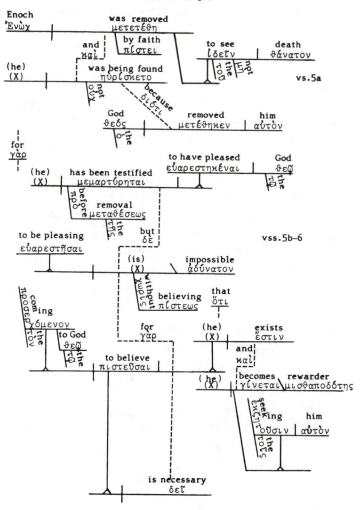

THE DIAGRAM OF HEBREWS 11:5-6

Verse 5a encloses a compound-complex sentence. It has two independent ideas. To the second is attached a causal clause.

The bare first clause is, "Enoch was transferred . . ." μετετέθη is aorist indicative passive constructed from the preposition μετά = "after" and τίθημι "put" or "place." The compounded verb indicates to "change" or "transpose." Infinitive with its object, "to see death" signifies purpose. Instrumental πίστει indicates the means by which Enoch was "removed."

The second independent clause includes a conative imperfect ηὑρίσκετο with negative οὐκ. "He was not being found. . . ." It implies efforts were made to find him but were unsuccessful. The reason why no one could find him is stated in the διότι adverbial clause. "Because God removed him." The point of God's transferring Enoch is presented in aorist μετέθηκεν which contrasts vividly with the anxious searching as pictured in the imperfect ηὑρίσκετο.

Verses 5a-6 unfold into another compound-complex. Three independent clauses form the backbone of the sentence. Without its modifiers the first clause affirms, "he has been witnessed to." When that witness was made is detailed by the πρό phrase functioning adverbially, "before his translation." It was witnessed to Enoch "before he was removed from this world. . . ." Some interpreters would place this phrase as modifying the object infinitive "to have pleased (εὐαρεστηκέναι)." And that is a possibility. It seems better to place it where the diagram has it. The position in the sentence of μεταθέσεως favors its modifying "has been witnessed to." Perfect tense of εὐαρεστηκέναι draws a picture of Enoch's life as one that not only learned how to please God but having done so once he went right on pleasing God.

The second independent clause has for its subject infinitive εὐαρεστῆσαι. "To be pleasing (is) impossible." But the qualification or limits of this "impossibility" is set forth in the phrase "without faith." By faith is not meant the doctrinal content of belief although that may be included. It's the deeds, process and power of believing that pleases God. In fact, the two dependent clauses, objects of πιστεῦσαι in the subject phrase of the third independent clause, fill out in some detail what faith pleases God. It's not only faith "that he exists" but especially that he is "rewarder of the ones seeking him." God rewards a faith that trusts, not just an acceptance of a doctrine about God's existence.

The verb of the third independent clause is δεῖ. Subject of that verb is aorist infinitive πιστεῦσαι. Accusative of general reference with that infinitive is the present attributive participle προσερχόμενον. That "the one coming to God believe is necessary." As stated above, *what* he believes is stated in the two noun clauses objects of the infinitive in the subject. The present tense of the attributive participle ἐκζητοῦσιν is suggestive. To know God one must seek God. And he must seek God with unflagging insistence. To make an effort and then quit will not bring the experiential knowledge desired and needed. One must come, believe, seek! It's all quite logical. δεῖ is logical not moral necessity!

341

Hebrews 11:7-8

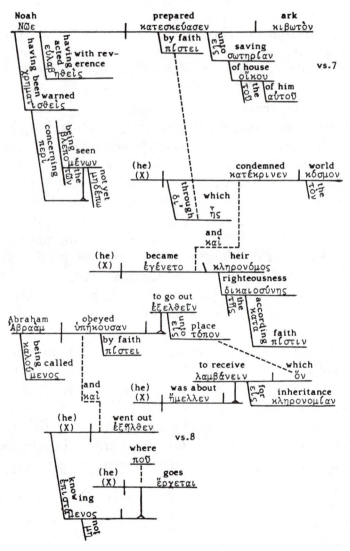

342

THE DIAGRAM OF HEBREWS 11:7-8

Two dependent adjective clauses describing πίστει of the independent clause make 11:7 a complex sentence. "Through which" (διά with genitive) informs of the agent (in this instance "faith") that enabled Noah, not only to perform the action stated in the verb of the main clause, but also that of the dependent, "condemned." It was by means of faith "through which Noah condemned the world" as indeed it was through that identical faith through which "Noah prepared the ark." Another subordinate clause is added as a further demonstration of the place and power of faith in Noah's life. ". . . and (through which) he became heir of righteousness according to faith."

Modifying "Noah" in the first clause are two circumstantial participles. χρηματισθείς suggests both cause and time; "because he was warned" and "after he was warned. . . ." εὐλαβηθείς suggests the manner in which he acted in preparing the ark. Prepositional εἰς phrase proposes the purpose of his preparing the ark. The finite verbs of two of the clauses as well as the circumstantial predicate participles mentioned are aorists. Though Noah took 120 years in actually getting the ark "prepared" the entire action is treated as a single point: "he prepared." But κατέκρινεν is imperfect drawing a picture of the extension of the condemnation as going on over the extended period of 120 years. Then in the next verb ἐγένετο he returns to the point action aorist, "he became heir. . . ."

Verse eight embodies a compound-complex sentence. The two independent clauses, when denuded of all modifiers, say, "Abraham obeyed. . . ." and "he went out. . . ." The aorist infinitive ἐξελθεῖν is placed on a pedestal after the main verb as if it were a direct object. But it might be thought of as adverbial expressing result. "He obeyed so as to go out. . . ." The relative ὅν introduces an adjective clause describing τόπον. This "place" unto which he went out is not named for at the time it was "not seen" and was unknown to the patriarch. He only had the word of God that it was there and he was to go. In fact it was the fact that it was in the future, "unseen" and unknown that gave value to his faith.

Modifying the subject of the first independent clause is the present circumstantial participle καλούμενος, "being called." The linear action of the present followed immediately by the aorist of "obeyed" suggests that his obedience took place while the calling was going on. His obedience was immediate.

Another present circumstantial participle (ἐπιστάμενος) modifies the subject "he" of the second independent clause. It too is used in connection with an aorist finite verb. The "not knowing" was going on during the entire experience of his "being called" during which "he went out."

The final clause of the sentence is a noun clause direct object of the participle "knowing." It is an indirect question, "where he goes." Abraham's "not knowing where he is going" but in the light of his "being called" is the quality of faith which impressed itself on his contemporaries and his heirs.

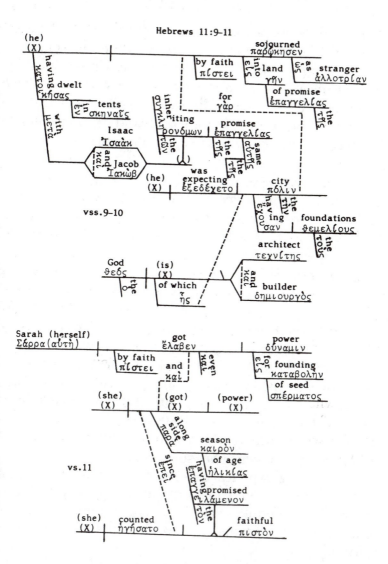

345

THE DIAGRAM OF HEBREWS 11:9-11

In the previous sentence it was reported that "Abraham went out." In this sentence of verses 9-10 the author points out that "he sojourned. . . ." But he adds a second independent idea, "for he was expecting the city. . . ." Then to this clause he adds an adjective dependent idea describing that city as being one "of which God (is) architect and builder." So the sentence is to be catalogued as compound-complex.

The finite verbs of the two independent clauses show a sharp contrast by means of their tenses. Aorist παρῴκησεν looks to the many years of wandering without any settled home and brings it all together into a focused point. The aorist emphasizes the fact without decoration or description. Imperfect ἐξεδέχετο with linear import draws a moving picture of an ongoing mood of expectation. Every time Abraham lingered somewhere during his "sojourn" he pondered whether this might be "the" expected city for which he looked! He "sojourned!" That's a fact. But he repeatedly "expected." That was a recurring experience.

The whole experience of his "sojourn" and its oft-repeated "expecting" forced one thing into Abraham's consciousness. It was that this city which he constantly expected to discover was one "of which God was architect and builder." All of the cities in which he "sojourned" were built by men. Thus this long experience in life taught him clearly that God's promise would not be realized by any tangible, touchable, material ownership. The promise, given in terms of things material, was to find fulfillment in things spiritual.

Verse 11 encompasses another compound-complex. The finite verb in the first independent clause is aorist indicative

346

ἔλαβεν from λαμβάνω = receive. When the idea of "receive," the Aktionsart of which is linear, is transposed into aorist the resultant idea is "get." Abraham's faith came immediately and without hesitation. But Sarah had to "get" faith for at first she doubted. But through the strong influence of her husband's faith she "herself got. . . ." The "power" which she got as a result of faith was "for" the purpose of "casting down of seed." καταβολὴν is compounded from κατά "down" and βάλλω, "throw," "cast."

The preposition παρά literally means "along side." Here it is used with accusative καιρὸν = season, time. The word for season is itself described by genitive ἡλικίας characterizing the "season" as being one "of age." When the time of childbearing is put alongside of Sarah's impotence it is manifest that she "got power beyond the age of childbearing." It's an adverbial expression modifying the understood "got."

The ἐπεὶ clause is an adverbial dependent of cause. "Because she "counted faithful the one having promised she got power. . . ." Perfect participle ἐπαγγειλάμενον is attributive, object of the verb. Perfect tense indicates that once she arrived at faith it was that God who promised was constant in honoring his promised word. πιστὸν is objective complement. ἡγήσατο is aorist. Once Sarah figured it all out she arrived at a conclusion; this is an effective aorist looking to the conclusion of her calculation.

Hebrews 11:12-14

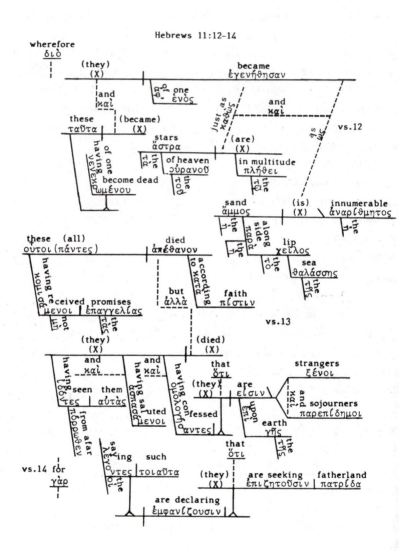

348

THE DIAGRAM OF HEBREWS 11:12-14

Hebrews 11:12 accommodates a compound-complex sentence of four clauses, two independent and two dependent. The two main ideas say, ". . . they became . . ." and "these became. . . ." The dependent clauses stem off of the "became" of the first clause. They are both adverb clauses of comparison, ". . . just as the stars of heaven (are) in multitude and as the sand along the lip of the sea is innumerable. . . ."

A matter of textual criticism affects the verb ἐγενήθησαν. As it stands in Nestle's text it is aorist passive of the defective verb γίνομαι. Westcott-Hort's text follows the variant ἐγεννήθησαν = they were born, from γεννάω = to beget, bear; in the passive: to be begotten. The structure of the sentence remains the same. And textual problems lie outside the scope of this work.

The Prepositional expression ἀφ'ἑνός serves as an adverbial idea answering the question from whence. "They became (sprang) from one man as source. . . ." Abraham's faith was completed and made effective by Sarah's faith. Thus it was "from one." The perfect participle νενεκρωμένου is attributive even though it lacks the article, "of one having become dead." Of course, that is a hyperbole. Neither Sarah nor Abraham were dead but in the matter of child-bearing they were both as productive as those who were. And the perfect tense emphasizing this very point. He and she were permanently "dead."

Verse 13 adopts the compound-complex as its structural form. The second of the two independent clauses states practically the same thing as the first but is put in a strong adversative relation by ἀλλά. These all died *but* they died.

The πάντες is in apposition to the subject of the first clause. The "all" refers to the patriarchs, Abraham, Isaac, Jacob inclusive Sarah as "one" with Abraham. But in one particular they were "all" very much alike; "not having received the promises." These "all" received many manifestations of God's care, concern, guidance, and oversight. But each "fulfillment" left them lacking in realizing the ultimate meaning of God's oft-repeated promises.

Three circumstantial participles describe the subject "they" of the second independent clause; "having seen from afar them (the promises), having saluted (them), and having confessed that they were strangers and sojourners upon the earth." In other words, the totality of their human experience was one unending experience of faith, walking toward an unseen, though promised, anticipated future. The sum total of life's meaning is that life in this kind of world is one of "strangers and sojourners." If life is to be successful, of necessity, it must be one of faith.

The sentence of verse 14 is complex of two clauses. Subject of the independent clause is articular attributive participle λέγοντες. ἐμφαννίζουσιν is present indicative = are declaring. This declaration was repetitive. Each time life brought them to a dead end of disappointment they would make such a declaration. The content of what they declare is in the noun clause object of the verb of the main clause; "that they are seeking a fatherland."

350

Hebrews 11:15-16

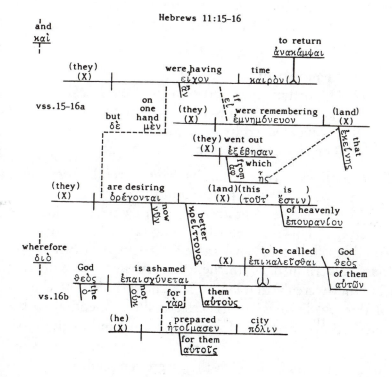

351

THE DIAGRAM OF HEBREWS 11:15-16

Two sentences are encompassed by 11:15-16. The first (15-16a) is compound-complex having two independent clauses and two dependent. The second is compound with two independent elements. In thought they confirm what the author has said in verse 13 about "not having received the promises etc." An outline of the thought might be:

"Seeking the City of God!"

1. Memories of the past. 15a
2. Opportunities to return to that past. 15b
3. Looking to the unseen, heavenly future. 16a
4. Acknowledged by God. 16b
5. The city of God. 16c

Such outlines spring naturally from careful observation of sentence analysis as pictured in the diagrams.

The first independent idea states, "they were having time to return." This is the conclusion (apodosis) of a 2nd class condition. It has untranslatable ἄν to help identify it as 2nd class, determined as untrue. "If they were remembering (but they weren't) that land. . . ." The verbs in both clauses of this conditional are imperfect calling attention to the repeated opportunities for remembering and many possibilities for returning. To return was an ever-recurring siren song. That land to which they were tempted to return is described by the relative pronoun expression ἀφ'ἧς, "from which they went out."

The second independent clause presents quite a strong contrast (μὲν . . . δὲ) and relates how they turned from the seduction of the past to the allurement of the unseen future. ὀρέγονται is present indicative of a word meaning strong "desire." It is a stretching forward with eagerness to something lying beyond. It's not selfish ambition but it is virile and tenacious.

The conjunction διὸ connecting sentence 16b to the preceding is a combination of δι'ὅ = on account of which. Because "all these" patriarchs resisted temptations to return to the past and were eagerly stretching forward toward a heavenly future, "God is not being ashamed. . . ." They hadn't let God down in his expectations of them. "On account of this" he wouldn't let them down in their expectations of him! Epexegetic present infinitive ἐπικαλεῖσθαι completes the main verb, ". . . is ashamed to be called. . . ." αὐτοὺς is accusative of general reference with ἐπαισχύνεται, "as to them."

The final clause states, "for he prepared for them a city." Their faith was to be honored, for a city has been prepared. Like a title-deed to property faith deals with "things hoped for" and "things not seen." In this case a sure secure city prepared by God!

353

Hebrews 11:17-20

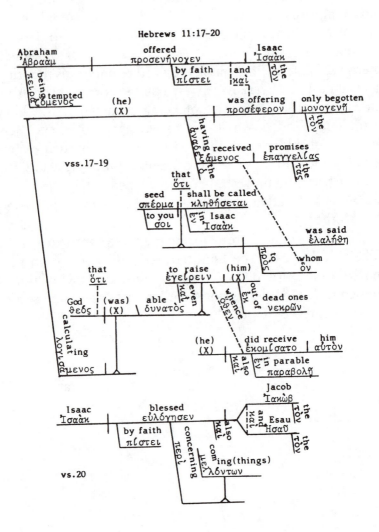

354

THE DIAGRAM OF HEBREWS 11:17-20

Five clauses furnish the framework for the compound-complex sentence of verses 17-19. The first two are independent. Both have to do with Abraham's offering of Isaac. "By faith, being tempted, Abraham offered Isaac and, having received the promises, he was offering his only begotten. . . ." The present circumstantial participle πειραζόμενος modifies "Abraham." The temptation was a continuous pressure on the patriarch right up until "he offered Isaac." The perfect tense προσενήνοχεν shows that as far as Abraham was concerned the offering of his son was already permanently settled.

In the next clause προσέφερον is a conative imperfect. That is, it was an offering begun but interrupted while in process. Participle ἀναδεξάμενος is circumstantial which reflects the ground support which Abraham received. It gave him strength to perform the sacrifice of his son; "having received the promises." The tense is aorist, looking to the point at which Abraham got assurance and therefore was able to plan ahead accordingly.

The prepositional phrase πρὸς ὅν refers ultimately back to Isaac, "the only begotten." But the immediate antecedent is the implied "one" in the attributive participial ἀναδεξάμενος, "the (one) having received." The subject of this dependent clause is a noun clause introduced by ὅτι, "that your seed shall be called in Isaac." The personal pronoun σοι is dative of possession modifying "seed."

A circumstantial participle of cause (λογισάμενος) modifies the subject "he" of the second independent clause. Abraham's being "tempted" was an ongoing continuous (present) thing; the "calculating" was an accomplished conclusion (aorist). The patriarch figured "that God was able even to raise him (his son) from the dead. . . ." The ὅτι inserts a noun clause, object of the participle. The ὅθεν clause is adverbial answering the question from whence. Abraham's calculation, in effect, was correct. God "did raise him" in a parabolic, symbolic sort of way.

Verse 20 encases a simple sentence. "Isaac, by faith, blessed Jacob and Esau also concerning coming things." εὐλόγησεν is aorist looking to the point of blessing. After all, both sons were blessed by their father. But, contrary to what Isaac had planned, the younger got the blessing of the "coming things" not yet seen which were involved in the plan of God. Isaac "blessed" them beyond the present; it extended into the future beyond which either son might realize in his own life-time. The act of blessing was a point in history; the result extended far into the unknown unseen future.

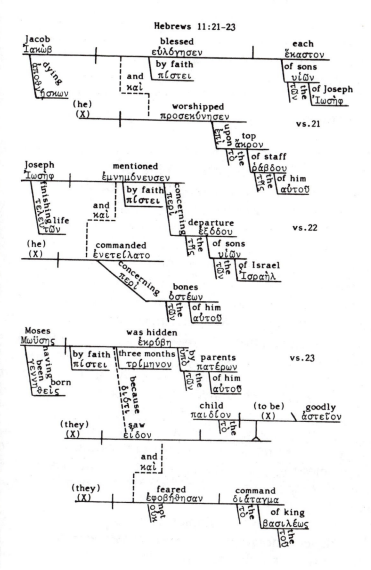

Hebrews 11:21-23

Jacob Ἰακὼβ / dying ἀποθνῄσκων / blessed εὐλόγησεν / by faith πίστει / and καὶ / (he) (X) / worshipped προσεκύνησεν / each ἔκαστον / of sons υἱῶν / the τῶ / of Joseph Ἰωσὴφ / upon ἐπὶ / the τὸ / top ἄκρον / of staff ῥάβδου / the τῆς / of him αὐτοῦ

vs.21

Joseph Ἰωσὴφ / finishing τελευτῶν / life / mentioned ἐμνημόνευσεν / by faith πίστει / and καὶ / (he) (X) / commanded ἐνετείλατο / concerning περὶ / concerning περὶ / departure ἐξόδου / the τῆς / of sons υἱῶν / the τῶ / of Israel Ἰσραὴλ / bones ὀστέων / the τῶ / of him αὐτοῦ

vs.22

Moses Μωϋσῆς / having been born γεννηθείς / by faith πίστει / was hidden ἐκρύβη / three months τρίμηνον / because διότι / by ὑπὸ / the τῶ / parents πατέρων / of him αὐτοῦ / (they) (X) / saw εἶδον / child παιδίον / the τὸ / (to be) (X) / goodly ἀστεῖον / and καὶ / (they) (X) / feared ἐφοβήθησαν / not οὐκ / command διάταγμα / the τὸ / of king βασιλέως / the τοῦ

vs.23

357

THE DIAGRAM OF HEBREWS 11:21-23

In Hebrews 11:21 and 22 may be found two compound sentences each having two clauses. Verse 21 says, "Jacob blessed . . . and . . . he worshiped. . . ." Verse 22 reports, "Joseph remembered . . . and . . . he commanded. . . ." Each of these sentences demonstrates the faith of the patriarchs involved as he anticipated the future of the unfolding purpose of God.

All four of the finite verbs involved in these two sentences are aorists reflecting historical events drawn to a focused point. But modifying the subjects "Jacob" and "Joseph" are linear action presents ἀποϑνήσκων "dying" and τελευτῶν "finishing life." In general the difference between punctiliar versus linear action is that between a snap-shot and a moving picture. One is still; the other is motion! The main verbs report facts as events which happened; the circumstantial participles paint vividly the human interest particulars surrounding the action snapped by the finite verbs.

In the clause "Jacob blessed each . . ." the pronoun ἕκαστον is more specifically described by the genitive "of the sons of Joseph" (τῶν υἱῶν . . .). This is an important item because Joseph married the Egyptian Asenath. So there entered into the blood line of the "people of God" this Gentile ancestry. And even in blessing these two sons a selection was made as to which one should receive the greater blessing. Faith led Jacob not only in blessing the "sons of Joseph" but also as to how to distribute the blessings.

Verse 23 portrays a complex sentence of three clauses. The independent simply declares, "Moses was born. . . ." γεννηϑεὶς is a circumstantial participle of time and may be translated, "having been born" or "when he was born."

358

The point action of the aorist looks to the point of birth; it is antecedent action. But at the point of birth he was immediately "hidden." During pregnancy the parents antici- pated hiding him. So the moment he was born he was hidden. τρίμηνον is an adverbial accusative of extent of time. ὑπό with ablative of "parents" expresses the "agents" who did the hiding. It was they also who had the faith al- though it was the birth of Moses that drew that faith out to full demonstration.

διότι is a subordinating conjunction compounded from διά and ὅτι = "on account of that. . . ." Here it introduces two dependent causal clauses. These clauses present two reasons that led the parents to hide the baby Moses. ". . . because they saw the child (to be) goodly and they did not fear the order of the king." The direct object of εἶδον is the infinitive phrase, "the child (to be) goodly." παιδίον is accusative of general reference with an implied present in- finitive εἶναι = "to be." ἀστεῖον is an adjective in the predi- cate in accusative case referring back to the accusative of general reference. We call this an infinitive phrase yet it has all the practical force of a full clause when translated, ". . . that the child was goodly."

Hebrews 11:24-28

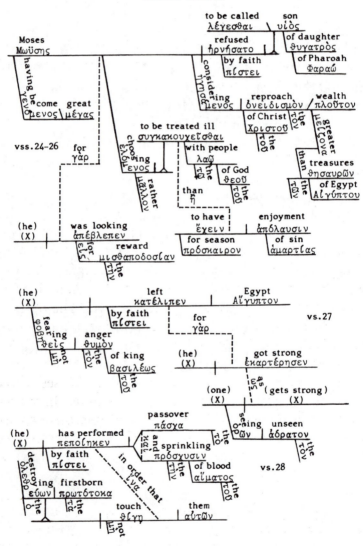

THE DIAGRAM OF HEBREWS 11:24-28

The sentence of verses 24-26 has two independent clauses that say, "Moses refused . . ." and "he was looking. . . ." Though a number of infinitive and participial patterns emerge no other full fledged clauses appear. So this would be classed as compound.

Three circumstantial participles in the first clause fill out the description of the subject "Moses." First comes aorist γενόμενος "having become great." This is temporal and might be translated in the form of a temporal dependent clause, "after he became great. . . ." The "becoming great" obviously took place over a period of time but the aorist treats the whole process as a point in history. It's a fact to be reported, not an event to be described. The second aorist participle follows ἑλόμενος "having chosen." Once again the punctiliar action looks to the moment of choice rather than a sketching of the methods used in making the choice. This is a participle suggesting cause. The object of the participle is the present passive infinitive συγκακουχεῖσθαι "to be ill-treated." The point action of the participle reflects the determined finality of the choice. But the linear action of the present infinitive shows that Moses' choice envisioned a repetition of ongoing afflictions. In making his choice he balanced the anticipated ill-treatment against the manifest "enjoyment of sin." This is expressed by another present infinitive ἔχειν. But the fact that such "enjoyment" was temporary is brought out by the adverbial accusative πρόσκαιρον "for a season." λαῷ is instrumental case, the case which expresses agent when referring to "things" but association when used with "people." Another participle modifying the subject, it too aorist and also cause, is ἡγησάμενος "having considered." It sets forth another reason why he "refused." That which Moses refused is set forth in the present infinitive λέγεσθαι "to be called." It is direct object of the verb "refused." He "refused to be called. . . ." υἱός is predicate nominative.

Two independent clauses and one dependent establish verse 27 as compound-complex. The two main clauses say, "He left Egypt for he got strong. . . ." When it comes to its subject and verb the subordinate clause is elliptical, ". . . as (one gets strong). . . ." But then the implied subject has a circumstantial present participle ὁρῶν "seeing the unseen." So the entire sentence would read, "By faith he, not fearing the anger of the king, left Egypt for he got strong as (one) seeing the unseen (gets strong)."

Verse 28 embraces a complex sentence of two clauses. The main clause states, "He has made the passover and the sprinkling of the blood. . . ." Perfect tense in πεποίηκεν accents the sustained nature of the passover and sprinkling. ἵνα brings in an adverbial purpose clause with aorist active θίγῃ with negative μή; ". . . in order that . . . might not touch them." The subject of this dependent clause is the articular attributive participle ὁ ὀλεθρεύων "the one destroying. . . ." αὐτῶν is direct object in genitive cause after verb of sensation, "touch."

Hebrews 11:29-31

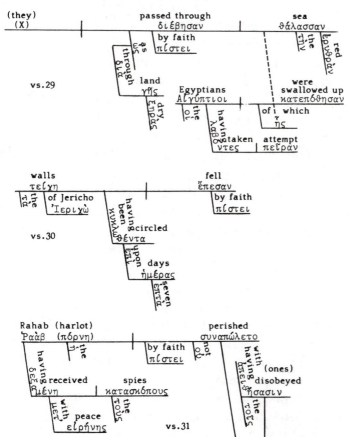

THE DIAGRAM OF HEBREWS 11:29-31

As diagrammed the sentence of verse 29 represents a complex arrangement. The ὡς expression wears the aspect of an adverbial phrase. It could have been diagrammed with ὡς as an adverbial conjunction joining the independent clause to an implied dependent idea. In that case "through dry land" would then be modifying the understood verb "pass through." The sentence would have read, "By faith they passed through the Red Sea *as* (they pass) through dry land. . . ." But it seems simpler to treat the expression as a phrase modifying the one main verb.

The sentence has a single dependent clause, ". . . of which the Egyptians, having made an attempt, were swallowed up." The diagram shows this clause as adjective attached to and describing θάλασσαν, sea. It really refers back to the total idea of the main clause. But it seems most closely related to "sea." The Egyptians attempted to do that which the Israelites had done. They "took trial of the sea." But they failed from the simple fact that they didn't move forward motivated by faith in the leadership of God. The familiar πίστει refers to the faith of the people. Their faith was drawn out by and was a response to the faith of Moses. All verbs in this sentence are aorists including the circumstantial participle λαβόντες. Aorist is the normal tense to be used in historical narrative unless strong reasons demand a more vivid descriptive style.

Verse 30 involves a simple sentence. Here again it's the faith of the people that became the instrument of victorious conflict. "By faith the walls of Jerich fell. . . ." κυκλωθέντα is aorist passive circumstantial participle indicating the manner in which the walls were brought down. ἡμέρας is accusative extent of time.

Verse 31 is also a simple sentence. "Rahab the harlot
. . . did not perish . . . " is the single idea. The subject,
Rahab, is expanded by the appositional πόρνη. It is also
described by circumstantial participle suggesting cause,
δεξαμένη, "having received." "Because Rahab the harlot
received with peace the spies. . . ." The faith of Moses
generated faith in the sons of Israel. And the faith of the
two spies of Israel helped breed faith in this outcast, gentile,
harlot. God honors faith in *people* as human beings not
some special class of people. μετ' εἰρήνης "with peace" is
adverbial in function telling how or in what manner the
spies were received by Rahab. ἀπειθήσασιν is an aorist passive
attributive participle in the instrumental case, "with the
ones having disobeyed." This refers to the other inhabitants
of Jericho who had similar opportunities to get faith which
Rahab had. They had heard the reports of the incoming
Israelites but rejected the God of Israel. The harlot believed
in the future of Israel and Israel's God. Faith may be immature, burdened with ignorance and superstition but as
long as it is genuine and moves toward the true object God
responds favorably to faith in any human being. Lack of
faith checkmates God's advances of grace.

Hebrews 11:32-34

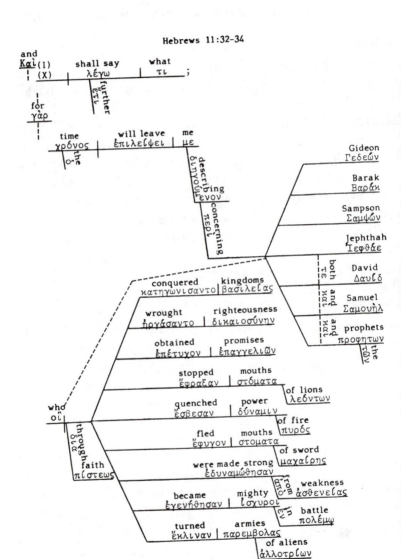

366

THE DIAGRAM OF HEBREWS 11:32-34

Verse 32a presents a rhetorical interrogative question, "And what shall Is say further?" It is a simple sentence that clearly implies it's own answer. "There really isn't anything I could add to what I've already said!" But the author does proceed to give a summary of faith as it appears in the subsequent history of Israel. λέγω, though having the same form in the indicative, here it is a deliberative present active subjunctive. "Shall I go on or shall I not go on saying . . . .?" It's the pondering of a possible question that gives to a subjunctive its classification of deliberation. It's a literary device; a means of altering and lightening the style.

In structure the sentence of verses 32b-34 is complex. To its one independent clause is attached a circumstantial participle (διηγούμενον) describing με. It suggests condition; ". . . if I go on describing. . . ." ἐπιλείψει is further indicative, punctiliar action, ". . . the time will leave me describing about. . . ."

περί with genitive means "concerning" or "about." Here it appears with six historic leaders of Israel plus "prophets." They sum up the whole theocratic, prophetic order of Israel. Then with the advent of the relative οἵ a long adjective clause is inserted to describe the victories of faith which these leaders achieved. They represent various types of opposition which sought to thwart their efforts in behalf of the redemptive program of God. διὰ πίστεως is a change from the usual instrumental πίστει. διά with genitive indicates the agent through which a given menace is overcome.

Hebrews 11:35-36

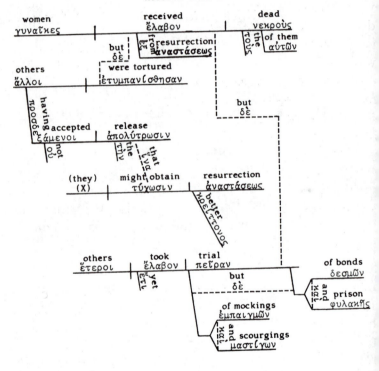

368

THE DIAGRAM OF HEBREWS 11:35-36

According to the punctuation in Nestle's text one sentence extends from 11:35 through 38. But the diagram is treating verses 35-36 as a single sentence. It has three independent clauses and but one dependent. So it may be classed as compound-complex. A very striking note of victory is sounded in the first independent clause when it declares, "Women received their dead. . . ." But the victory is pictured in the prepositional phrase ἐξ ἀναστάσεως. It was "out of resurrection" that the women "received their dead." ἐξ with the ablative is a clear cut indication of "source" or "origin." That's the meaning of both case and preposition. A resurrection is viewed as the source from which they got their dead back again. It is not a figurative reference but apparently alludes to historical events in which faith conquered the claims of the grave. See II Kings 4:17ff, I Kings 17:17ff.

δὲ is a coordinating conjunction that normally is adversative "but." It is used to set one thing over against another. In contrast to those women who with joy "received their dead. . . ." there were "others" who "were tortured. . . ." They were beaten to death. The circumstantial participle προσδεξάμενοι with the negative οὐ adds the description that these women were offered the opportunity to deny their faith in exchange for their "release" from torture. But their faith led them not to accept such compromise. The participle is probably causal though it could be temporal. It may suggest both ideas. From this second independent clause there hangs a ἵνα adverb clause of purpose. τύχωσιν is second aorist active subjunctive of τυγχάνω, "reach, get, obtain." It takes genitive ἀναστάσεως after it as direct object.

369

Yet another adversative (δέ) independent clause is injected into the sentence; "others got trial. . . ." Two pairs of genitives identify what kind of trials they "took." They were: "of mockings" and "of scourgings." But in addition some "of bonds" and even the trial "of prison."

It is not without significance that these extremes of sufferings were endured by *women*. Faith is not a matter confined to the male sex. It was equally effective to lead women to attain victory over death or, what may be worse, suffering that is just short of death. Faith doesn't inquire as to what sex it empowers!

Hebrews 11:37-40

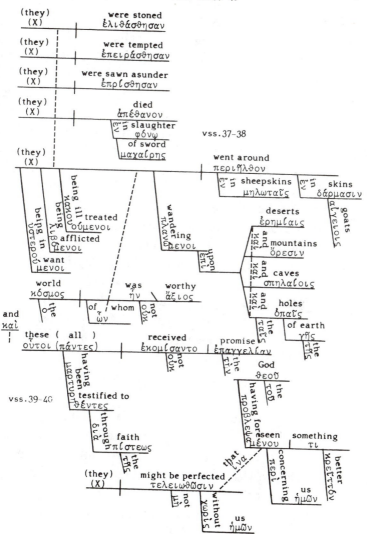

vss. 37-38

vss. 39-40

371

THE DIAGRAM OF HEBREWS 11:37-40

Asyndeton is the omission of formal conjunctions between the words, phrases, or other parallel parts of a sentence. It can be a very effective stylistic tool. It is quite impressive in the sentence of verses 37-38. This is a compound-complex sentence having five independent clauses not one of which is joined by a conjunction. And besides these five clauses two prepositional phrases appear without conjunction and four participial expressions lack couplings.

When read aloud the five short statements with the same subjects, same tenses of the verbs and with minimum of modifying elements are most forceful. "They were stoned, they were tempted, they were sawn asunder, they died in slaughter of sword, they went around. . . ." Modifying this last are two prepositional phrases without formal connection, ". . . in sheepskins, in goat skins. . . ." Besides this the four participles pile up their effective asyndeton: "being in want, being afflicted, being ill-treated, . . . wandering. . . ." That's a total of eleven elements not one of which has a formal stated connection but all of which are very vitally related. This use of asyndeton gives a powerful effect.

The one dependent clause is adjectival. It describes the "they" which is the subject common to all five of the main clauses. It affirms that these heroes of faith were those "of whom the world was not worthy."

Verses 39-40 is a concluding summation covering "these all" mentioned from verse two through 38. The sentence is complex. Besides the one independent it has one dependent clause hanging off of a genitive absolute. The ἵνα with first aorist passive subjunctive τελειωθῶσιν and μὴ is a negative adverb purpose clause.

The independent clause has aorist active indicative with strong negative οὐx. "These all did not receive the promise. . . ." The verb of the clause translated "received not" is aorist middle of xομίζω. In the middle it means to "bear for oneself" hence to "receive." This whole chapter would seem to make this statement inconsistent with reality. For every one of them did receive a fulfillment of a God-given promise. But each fulfillment was merely a new uncovering of the fact that the real and ultimate fulfillment would never come "apart from us." As a matter of fact the aorist passive circumstantial participle μαρτυρηθέντες and its prepositional (διὰ) modifier makes clear that they got God's approval "through their faith." They got fulfillment of "a" promise but not of "the" promise.

The basic difference between a circumstantial participle and a genitive absolute is its grammatical tie to some word within the sentence. The genitive absolute *is* a circumstantial but one that is *not* grammatically yoked to anything. It stands off alone! It is "absolute." But for that very reason it is even more emphatic. He who stands by himself separate from the crowd yet obviously a part of that crowd by the standing alone calls attention to himself. God had a purpose in that "these all did not receive the promise." A purpose for "them" and "us."

A Translation
Hebrews 12:1-13

Therefore we also, having such a cloud of witnesses around us, putting aside every weight and the easily encircling sin, through patience let us run the race lying before us, looking unto the leader and perfecter of the believing (experience), Jesus, who, facing the lying-before-him joy, endured cross, despised shame and has sat at the right hand of God's throne. For yourselves consider what sort of gainsaying by sinners he endured against himself that you get not weary, fainting in your souls. For you didn't resist up to blood striving against sin; and did you forget the exhortation which reasons with you as with sons?

> My son, quit regarding lightly the Lord's discipline,
> Neither be fainting while being reproved by him;
> For whom the Lord loves he disciplines,
> And he scourges every son whom he receives.

For reason of discipline continue enduring; as with sons God is bearing himself toward you. For which son is there whom a father does not discipline? But if you are without discipline of which all have become partners, then are you bastards and not sons. Furthermore, indeed we are having our fathers of the flesh as chasteners and we were reverencing (them). Shall we not much more subject ourselves to the father of spirits and live? For they for a few days according to what seemed good

374

to them were disciplining, but that one on the basis of what is profitable (disciplines) in order that we might share his holiness. Indeed, each disciplining does not seem for the present joyful but grievous, but later it gives peaceable fruit to the ones being exercised through it. Wherefore, straighten up the relaxed hands and the paralyzed knees, and make straight tracks with your feet that the lame be not twisted out of joint, but rather be healed.

AN OUTLINE OF HEBREWS 12:1-13
GOD'S DISCIPLINE OF HIS SONS!

Man expects and respects discipline. "Spare the rod and spoil the child" was true in Eden and is true now. A delinquent becomes so because he loses respect for his authority figure. Trains wreck and run wild when not restricted to tracks for which they have been made. So does man!

I. MOTIVES FOR DISCIPLINE. 1-2
    1. A cloud of witnesses. 1
       (a) Who give active testimony.
       (b) Who are spectator witnesses of our race.
       (c) Strip for action.
    2. The perfect witness. 2
       (a) He is "leader" going ahead to demonstrate how.
       (b) He is "perfecter" as example of true trust.
       (c) His reward answers to his measure of suffering.
II. THE GOAL OF DISCIPLINE. 3-13
    1. Suffering as chastisement. 7-8

2. Suffering as parental chasetisement. 7-8
3. Earthly and heavenly chastisements. 9-11

Exhortation to respond to God's discipline in life. 12-13

SOME EXPOSITORY THOUGHTS ON HEBREWS 12:1-13

Man was created to "have dominion." And he was made to respect dominion. Respect for authority is built into him. To rebel against that respect for authority is sin. So at bottom a human being expects and respects discipline. A delinquent becomes that way if he sins without consequences. When he can disregard "right" and suffer no retribution he loses respect for that authority figure to which he looks whether God or man.

Constraint does not mean lack of freedom. It means one is free to perform. The restrictions of the musical scale don't mean one is not free to play melody. On the contrary, they guarantee that if he follows the pre-determined notes he is free to play rich harmony. When a train is restricted to tracks it is free to run to its destiny. But if it jump the tracks it will wreck itself and all it meets. Man is made for discipline!

Motives for discipline.

By "having such a great cloud of witnesses" Christians have every incentive to run well in the race set before us. We are like athletes in a stadium. Row upon row of spectators encircle us. The competition of the race, the desire to be "best" is sufficient motive for running. But the presence of such a vast cloud of spectators adds excitement. Their presence in such numbers prods us on to beat our own records. Besides, these innumerable "witnesses" rising tier upon tier are more than mere spectators. They have themselves run the same race. They have experienced the agony of weary muscles, bursting lungs, bleeding feet. They have known the tingling thrill of victory. They have endured the agony of defeat. They can identify. They've been through it all. In addition, when called upon, they come to the podium and give active testimony. They declare that "faith" gave them the power and drive to press on in the face of the agony of training. They encourage by personally testifying, "We did it; you can too! We did it with less on which to hope than you. Don't be defeated by the pain of discipline or power of opposition. By faith press on!

With such encouragement sounding in our souls we strip for action. We "lay aside every weight." Each encumbrance is set aside. Clothes that hamper rapid movement. Weights that have a place in training are set aside when we go to the starters' line. Jobs, social obligations, possessions, or other such things are set aside as hindrances to running a winning race. Things that under other circumstances are harmless must be discontinued as millstones. Then, too, the "easily encircling sin" must be laid aside. Especially sin that weakens our hold on faith in Christ. But jealousies, hatreds, lusts that have clung like leeches are to be disowned, set aside, thoroughly killed. To the Christian who plans on winning the race sin is not just a burdensome weight it is totally destructive to the racer. It's a deadening drug that paralyzes muscles, that blurs and distorts vision and dulls effort. Sin is a de-energizing force that destroys ambition, drains stamina, kills vitality.

Sin is not a winner! Set it aside with a once-for-all decision.

But the supreme motive is the pattern of faith set by Jesus. Turning from every rival we look unto Jesus, "the leader and perfecter of faith." Jesus didn't go through Gethsemane or win victory on the cross or vanquish death in the tomb without personal faith. From him we learn what faith is. Faith is not a creed to be believed; it is trust in a Person who controls the invisible world of my hope! Jesus was the ultimate believer! He too looked beyond the seen to the unseen; beyond the present to the future. And because he was such a "leader and perfecter" of faith his recompense equalled his investment of faith. He captained the whole host of believers. He depicted faith in its finest form. He carried faith to its ultimate triumph. Death became a victim to his faith. Thus he is the purest pattern for our faith. Consequently he reigns "at God's right hand."

The goal of discipline

And so you suffer?? "Don't faint while being reproved by him; for "whom the Lord loves he disciplines." Suffering is blessing in disguise. Suffering is the divine schoolroom; suffering is a chapter out of God's textbook. Suffering is an assigned lesson on the moral quality of life in a wicked world. Suffering isn't "sent" by God but it is certainly controlled by our divine pedagogue. God is teacher; we are students; suffering is the lesson. As learners we are to study the lesson!

Besides, suffering is part of family discipline. "Which son is there whom a father does not discipline?" We ought not marvel that God permits us to suffer. On the contrary, when we go astray we should marvel if he does *not* allow us to suffer. Suffering is proof of sonship! God loves enough that he will hurt us with punishment rather than abandon us to perdition. Suffering is not abuse; it is parental chastisement. And just how much wiser is God's divine chastisement than that of a faulty earthly parent who is himself in need of the same lesson? If we respect a human parent's discipline, how much more God's loving reproof?

Besides all that, the *result* of pain and punishment is the measure of its value, not the anguish of the moment. It's the "peaceable fruit" that's plucked from the pain that makes the suffering worthwhile. Who's to say that a young mother's breaking heart as she lays her five year old son into the open grave hasn't learned more of the meaning of life than had that son lived? The tuition is high but the lesson is vital! Faith says that if a hair cannot fall without his notice a son can't die without his love! Suffering "does not seem for the present joyful . . . but later it gives peaceable fruit."

The real test in life is not what happens to me but how I handle what happens. The real test is what I do with what happens to me. How I react to it! How I grow from it! Or wither under it! Wherefore, the believer in trouble must "straighten up the relaxed hands and the paralyzed knees, and make straight tracks for the feet. . . ." Afflictions need not maim me. They make me! The heavier the burden the stronger I become. The greater the pain the greater the power. He, with the trial, makes a way of escape!

Hebrews 12:1-2

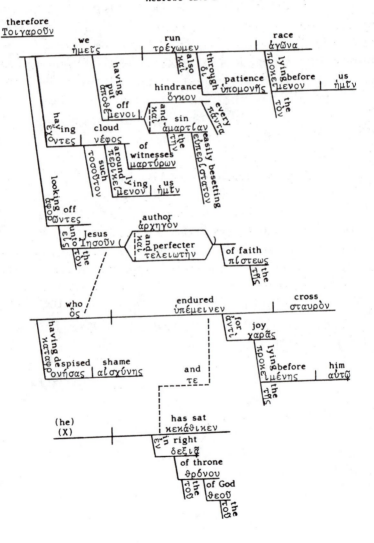

380

THE DIAGRAM OF HEBREWS 12:1-2

This sentence is complex in structure. Besides its independent clause it has two dependents. Describing the subject of the main clause are three circumstantial participles. The basic idea is an exhortation, "let us run. . . ." That urging is introduced by the very strong inferential particle Τοιγαροῦν "therefore." In other words, "In view of the many witnesses in the arena in which life's race is run, *therefore, . . .*" The insertion of the personal pronoun ἡμεῖς as subject spotlights the "we"; "therefore let *us* run...." Present tense in the verb translated "run" calls attention to the fact that the race is a continuing effort. There's to be no let up. And it's to be run, not "with" but "through (διά) patience" as a means of successfully finishing the course.

Of the three circumstantial participles the first, ἀποθέμενοι, "having put off . . ." is aorist expressing once-for-all point action. Every encumbrance that distracts from the Christian race plus the ever-present besetting sin that destroys the very vitals of our strength must be decisively stripped away. That's what the aorist declares. But the other two participles by their present tenses contrast the action. ἀφορῶντες "looking off . . ." shows the manner in which the race is to be run. It is with uninterrupted concentration on Jesus as "author-leader" and "perfect examplar" of what faith is. "Continue to look . . ." ἔχοντες "having a cloud . . ." depicts a situation in an athletic arena that is continuous and that offers an unceasing motive to run the race well. περικείμενον "lying around us" modifies "cloud" and is probably attributive. It too is present tense contributing its linear action moving description to the flow of thought.

The two subordinate clauses are both adjectival describing "Jesus." And the tenses of the verbs in the two clauses show a sharp contrast. Aorist "endured" (ὑπέμεινεν) centers attention on the event as an historical fact. Perfect "has sat" (κεκάθικεν) points out not only that it was an event of the past but that it is also a continuing reality. He took his royal seat "on the right hand of the throne of God" and he still sits there in kingly triumph with royal authority.

καταφρονήσας "having despised" is point action. To the wise of the world a cross is debasingly shameful. Jesus could have allowed the shame to hinder his obedience to God's assignment of suffering. But with a firm decisive resolve he put the shame out of mind; he "thought it down," "despised" it. One factor that helped him make that determination was the "joy" that stood "over against" (ἀντί) the shame. Besides, the joy was constantly "lying before him" (present tense). The joy in what the cross would achieve offset the disgrace which men place on the criminal form of death on a cross. The coordinating conjunction τε is significant. Both τε and καί mean "and." But τε implies an intimate connection between the items joined. The context must decide what that inward relationship is. Here it suggests an inwrought kinship between cross and crown, between suffering for men and ruling over men. Christ reveals that in this kind of world there is no crown without a cross.

Hebrews 12:3-6

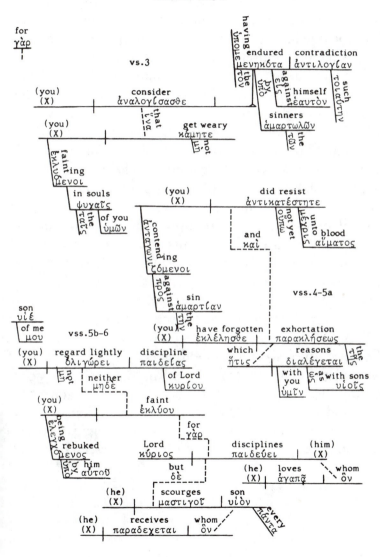

383

THE DIAGRAM OF HEBREWS 12:3-6

The complex sentence of verse three proposes a method by which one may gain endurance under pressure. "Consider the one having endured such kind of contradiction of sinners against himself. . . ." ὑπομεμενηκότα is perfect of a verb which literally means to "remain under." The tense looks on the action as abiding in its consequences. τοιαύτην is qualitative demonstrative = "of such kind as this." ὑπὸ with the ablative expresses the agents through whom "such kind" of contradiction took place. The main finite verb ἀναλογίσασθε is aorist, "consider." The greatest antidote to getting sick and weary of strong opposition is to fasten attention on Jesus and the contradictions he met. Such kind of opposition was far more than anything any believer must endure. The ἵνα inserts a negative adverbial purpose clause, ". . . in order that you don't get weary. . . ." κάμητε is aorist. Getting weary comes all at once but there was a gradual enfeebling as suggested by the present of circumstantial participle ἐκλυόμενοι, "fainting."

Verses 4-5a embody a compound-complex sentence. "You did not resist unto blood as yet . . ." is the first of two independent clauses. The verb "did resist" is aorist of a double compound verb formed of ἀντί, κατά and τίθημι, "to stand down (up) against." The prepositions are perfective intensifying the idea. It's a strong negative expression; an effective aorist. Participle ἀνταγωνιζόμενοι is present. The "contending" was continuous and repetitive but at no point did they "resist unto blood." The tense of the verb of the second main clause is perfect ἐκλέλησθε, "you have forgotten." You not only forgot but you never remember the exhortation! Genitive παρακλήσεως is normal after verbs of remembering or forgetting. ἥτις is *qualitative* relative = "which by its nature" and it brings in an adjective clause modifying "exhortation."

The sentence of verses 5b-6 has four independent clauses. Two of them have a dependent tagged on. The first two independents are exhortations. Present imperative with negative μὴ means either "quit what you are doing" or "do not have the habit of. . . ." It is a bit more pointed and personal to say, "Quit regarding lightly. . . ." If "quit regarding lightly" be correct then the present of the verb in the second clause also would be "quit fainting. . . ." Circumstantial particple ἐλεγχόμενος is also present, probably iterative; every time you are rebuked "quit fainting. . . ."

The seond two independent ideas give positive reasons which should encourage the readers to accept the discipline of suffering. First, "the Lord disciplines." Discipline of suffering is under the positive control of the Lord and therefore should be acceptable. Particularly when you take into consideration that it is love that admits it. This idea of love is expressed in the dependent clause introduced by relative ὃν, "whom he loves." It modifies an understood "him."

A companion independent clause declares, "he scourges every son." To this is added another adjective dependent idea, "whom he receives." All four verbs in the final four clauses are linear action presents representing habitual repeated behavior.

Hebrews 12:7-9

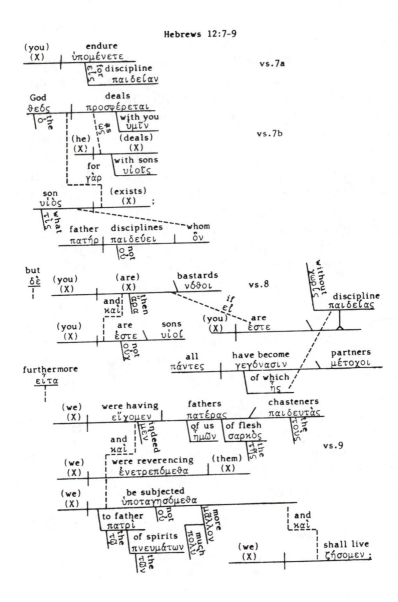

386

THE DIAGRAM OF HEBREWS 12:7-9

Verse 7a is a simple sentence. ὑπομένετε may be either indicative or imperative so it's either a statement or an exhortation. In any case it is linear action; "you are enduring . . ." or "keep on enduring. . . ." The purpose is set forth in the εἰς prepositional phrase, "for discipline." God's use of suffering is disciplinary. Yet, the end result depends on the human attitude. Suffering can be a text for learning, a method for teaching, a beneficial experience. Be looking on it in that way!

Verse 7b is compound-complex. The first main clause says, "God deals with you. . . ." προσφέρεται is present middle indicative of verb meaning "carrying oneself toward" and is used with dative. An adverbial clause of comparison (ὡς) follows, "as (he deals) with sons." Subject and verb are implied by the main clause. A second independent clause uses its own dependent clause to make clear the underlying reason for God's dealing as with sons. The clause is a rhetorical question, "What son (exists)?" The added ὅν clause is adjectival filling out the idea of "son." The obvious answer to the question is that no father exists who does not discipline a son. παιδεύει is present tense involving a gnomic idea. That good fathers always discipline sons is universally true.

Verse eight is also compound-complex. It enjoys two basic independent elements; "you are bastards" and "you are not sons." The "if" (εἰ) clause is the protasis for a first class condition. It assumes the condition to be true. "If you are without discipline (and you are). . . ." Then the conclusion necessarily follows, "you are bastards." A second dependent idea appears as an adjective clause springing from the "if" clause. It describes παιδείας, ". . . of which

387

all have become partners." γεγόνασιν is perfect tense = "have become." It calls attention to the fact that "all" those who are sons share partnership in discipline. So, if you are without discipline you have forfeited that which is common to all "sons."

In the diagram of verse nine four independent clauses come into view. All appear as in one compound sentence. They might be divided into two sentences since asyndeton exists between the second and third clauses. But the diagram treats this as one sentence. The first clause states, "We indeed were having our fathers of the flesh as chasteners. . . ." παιδευτὰς is objective complement. The particular aspect of parenthood in view was that of "chasteners." A second statement of fact arises in the next clause, "we were reverencing (them). . . ." Imperfect ("were reverencing") draws a living picture of continued respect for these earthly fathers. The last two clauses combine to ask a question (actually two closely related questions) which expect "yes" for an answer. "Shall we not the more subject ourselves to the father of spirits and live?" ὑποταγησόμεθα is future passive. ζήσομεν is future active. Both are aoristic action. The first looks to the point at which we entered into the "submission." The second looks to the point at which we "get life."

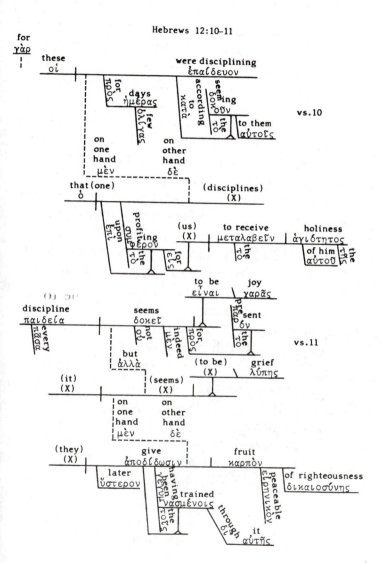

389

THE DIAGRAM OF HEBREWS 12:10-11

By the use of μὲν and δὲ the author places the two independent clauses of verse ten in strong adverse relationship. "On the one hand these were disciplining . . . but on the other hand that one (disciplines). . . ." The contrast is carried on through the modifiers. The κατὰ with accusative attributive participle presents the measure on which "these" earthly parents "were disciplining." That is balanced in the second clause by ἐπὶ with accusative revealing the basis upon which "that one" exercises discipline. The verbs also offer a contrast though both are linear action. These "were disciplining. . . ." That's imperfect expressing iterative action in past time. The implied "disciplines" of the second clause is present and as here used suggests gnomic, iterative, as well as distributive ideas. The heavenly Father universally disciplines, repeatedly disciplines, and he disciplines each separate "son" in his own time. The πρὸς phrase under the first clause does not have an expressed phrase matching it in the second. But the very absence entails a contrast. πρὸς with accusative is extent of time. The absence of a comparable phrase indicates that there is no limit of time on God's disciplining.

Being an infinitive, μεταλαβεῖν and the words surrounding it are categorized as a phrase rather than a clause. Hence this is a compound sentence. Yet when translated this phrase turns into an adverbial purpose clause. Preposition "for" becomes "in order that," the implied accusative of general reference "us" becomes the subject "we," the infinitive becomes a finite verb "may receive." ἁγιότητος "holiness" remains as direct object. So for all practical purposes this infinitive phrase is used as a dependent clause

Again in the sentence of verse 11 infinitive phrases appear that might be treated as clauses. But strictly speaking the three full clauses are all independents of equal rank. No actual dependent clauses are present. So we class this as compound. The three clauses offer a double contrast. The first clause contrasts that which discipline "seems not to be" with what it "seems to be" as recorded by the second. Then by μὲν and δὲ the author makes an even stronger contrast between what it "seems to be" with what it actually is; at least what it does. The first clause says, "Every discipline does not seem to be joy." The second clause gives the adverse side by saying, "but (it seems to be) grief." Then the third declares, . . . "they (the repeated disciplinary times of suffering) give peaceable fruit. . . ." Disciplinary experiences are to be measured by their helpful results, not their pain.

The πρὸς phrase with its attributive present participle is accusative extent of time. And so is ὕστερον in the third clause. γεγυμνασμένοις is perfect passive attributive participle with an article. It is an indirect object in dative = "to the ones having been trained. . . ." Object καρπὸν has two modifiers, accusative "peaceable" and genitive "of righteousness." "Peaceable" is attributive adjective; "of righteousness" more sharply defines what the fruit is. It's not "righteous fruit." It is the fruit which *is* "righteousness." It's a qualitative genitive.

Hebrews 12:12-13

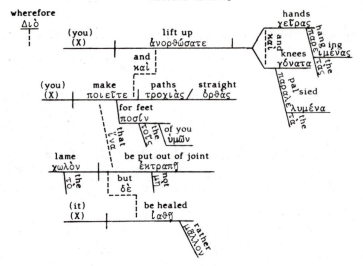

THE DIAGRAM OF HEBREWS 12:12-13

The conjunction Διὸ with which the sentence of verses 12-13 begins is compounded from διά "because" and relative ὅ "which." It means "on account of which" or "wherefore." Here it ties the present exhortation to the preceding teaching about the Lord's discipline. "Because of the chastening straighten up your hanging hands and your palsied knees. . . ." This is a compound-complex collection of clauses. It includes two independent clauses and two subordinates.

ἀνορθώσατε is aorist active imperative of a verb compounded from the preposition ἀνά "up" and ὀρθόω, "to set straight." The idea is to make straight what's crooked, make firm what's drooping, make strong what's weak. The Hebrew Christians had allowed their spiritual arm muscles to grow flabby, their leg and knee muscles to grow feeble. The aorist imperative proposes that the Hebrews make an unqualified absolute decision to firm up their weak-kneed drooping spiritual appendages. And *that* is dependent on a once-for-all definitive decision.

However, the verb of the second independent clause is present imperative. "Be making straight tracks for your feet." To firm up so as to get a fresh start demands a determined decision. But to keep on going forward, especially if one needs to clear a path and fill in rough potholes, takes sustained and continuing effort. So the present imperative exhorts to "keep on making straight tracks. . . ."

The two subordinate ideas are both adverb clauses of purpose using ἵνα as introductory conjunction, ". . . in order that the lame not be twisted out of joint but rather be healed." χωλὸν could refer to the "palsied knees" or "drooping hands" to which the author has already alluded. If that be the reference then the author is trying to arouse his readers not to allow their deadening neglect to go any further. Don't keep on until your muscles will throw your body completely out of joint. Firm things up right away so things won't go from the present bad to a possible worse. However, χωλὸν may refer to other people who are lame. You straighten up your relaxed muscles and weak knees etc. lest your indifferent lazy behavior have a deadening effect on other already weakened Christians. Either meaning makes sense and either suits the context. But the former meaning seems preferable. It is more direct and personal and in keeping with the way he has exhorted them in earlier parts of the epistle.

A Translation
Hebrews 12:14-17

Peace be pursuing with all, and the consecration to purity without which no one shall see the Lord; carefully watching in order that not anyone be falling from the grace of God, and that any root of bitterness, springing up, not crowd in on you and the many be defiled through this; (and that any fornicator or profane person not (exist as (was) Esau who, for one meal, sold his own birthright. For you are knowing that even afterwards, wishing to inherit the blessing, he didn't find place of repentance, even though he sought it with tears.

AN OUTLINE OF HEBREWS 12:14-17
THE PURSUIT OF PEACE AND PURITY

Christians must live in a sinful society, a corrupt culture, a wicked world order. We are "in the world but not o the world."

I. THE PURSUIT. 14
1. The object of pursuit:
   (a) "Peace *with* all!"
   (b) Purity *of* all.
2. The problem of pursuit:
   (a) An impure world won't sacrifice its impurity
   (b) Purity can't compromise without self-destruction.

3. Without purity "no one shall see the Lord."

II. THE NECESSITY OF PERSISTENT PURSUIT. 15-17

1. Lest there be want of progress; "falling away."
2. Lest a blight on the plant; "root of bitterness."
3. Lest the poison spread; the Christian society be defiled.
4. Lest contempt of our sacred heritage be harvested.

Pursue with eager unrelenting regularity. Make purity the purpose of living. Peace with God's purity survives impurity with Satan's servants. Be at peace but not at the price of purity!

SOME EXPOSITORY THOUGHTS ON HEBREWS 12:14-17

Jesus prayed, ". . . the world has hated them because they are not of the world." Christians must live in a sinful society which is opposed to the life style of purity in Christ. Yet the Hebrew letter insists that we "pursue peace with all *and* that dedication to sanctify, without which no one shall see the Lord." This is the perplexity: how pursue peace without spoiling purity.

The pursuit

One of the highest objects of the Christian is to "be at peace" with all. And that means absolutely all men. Of whatever color, race, religion, economic level, peace is important if we are to find a degree of contentment in this world. Constant outward conflict is detrimental to inner tranquility of soul. Peace is a worthwhile object of pursuit.

But if a choice must be made, purity takes priority over peace. We are to live in the world but we are not to be of the world. God is the absolute pure. And we live life in his presence. "As the Lord God lives before whom I stand" said the prophet. Life in God's presence must be uncompromisingly pure. The Christian seeks peace at all times. But he also seeks holiness at any price. Not peace but purity is the highest good!

The problem of peace with purity grows out the uncompromising nature of the moral order. A wicked world won't give up its wickedness. A pure God can't sacrifice his purity without losing his essence. "I am holy therefore you shall be holy!" So God's pure people can't forfeit purity without self-destruction. And the word of God stands unbending, "Pursue . . . sanctification without which no one shall see the Lord."

The necessity of persistent pursuit.

Persistent pursuit of purity is a necessity for the Christian. You either go forward or you drift backward; you grow or die. You either progress or regress, advance or retreat. This is a law of life. So one must be ever alert "watching lest anyone be falling from the grace of God." If we do not keep pace with God's grace then we are severed from that grace.

A blight on the plant of faith becomes a "root of bitterness." A seed lies buried in the ground. But it "springs up" and lo it is a poisoned weed. It's bitter to the tongue and lethal in the stomach. Impurity will kill not strengthen

So we pursue purity even at the cost of peace that God's peace may sweeten our hostile lives. If you want peace with purity eliminate bitterness.

If we sacrifice purity the result will poison the whole Christian community. "The many shall be defiled." Peace at the price of purity brings war not peace; internecine war; a war of the worst kind, that between brothers. Bitterness disrupts the church.

Having spread throughout the Christian society, the final fruit of bitterness is contempt for spiritual values. So be not like Esau whose sensual appetite led him to underprice the spiritual values of God's sacred heritage. He sold his spiritual birthright for one hamburger with french fries!

Hebrews 12:14-16

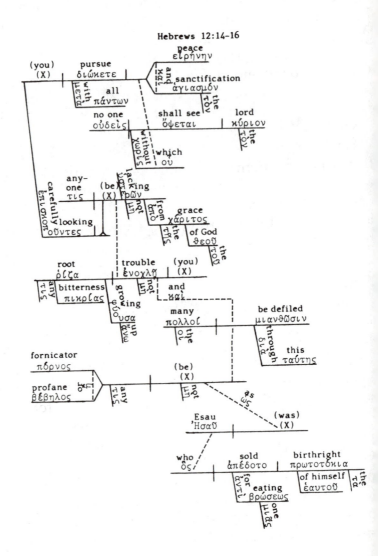

398

THE DIAGRAM OF HEBREWS 12:14-16

Eight full clauses form the frame for the sentence of 12:14-16. But seven of them are dependent and only one independent. So it is to be classed as complex. When reduced to the bare independent the sentence says, "With all (men) be pursuing peace and sanctification. . . ." διώχετε is present active imperative. The pursuit of peace and sanctification is not something that is done once and then effort discarded as though they were permanently possessed. On the contrary, they must be ever and again stalked. Hence the present tense is well suited for this admonition.

The first of the dependent clauses is adjectival. It describes "peace" and "sanctification" by recalling their necessity: "without which no one shall see the Lord." χωρὶς is one of the so-called "improper" prepositions; it is used with ablative case.

The next four of the dependent clauses appear as objects of the verbal element in the participle ἐπισχοποῦντες, "carefully watching. . . ." The participle itself is circumstantial of manner. It describes the way in which we should go about pursuing peace etc. And its present tense is a reminder that we must never cease our careful watching.

The first of the four noun-object clauses is negative purpose, ". . . lest anyone be lacking from the grace of God. . . ." ὑστερῶν is a present supplementary predicate participle, "lacking." It supplements an understood "be" (ἐστί) and thus forms a periphrastic present tense. Periphrasis accents the durative action of the tense. The negative purpose continues into the next dependent (in fact in all these clauses). These noun clauses give four reasons why we should be always "carefully watching." So the second says, "lest any root of bitterness, growing up, be troubling you. . . ." ἐνοχλῇ is present tense descriptive of trouble going on. It is worth noting that the root of this verb is ὄχλος, "crowd" which is compounded with "in" (ἐν). No "root of bitterness" should be "crowding in" sapping strength from healthy roots of righteousness.

The negative purpose extends to the next clause, ". . . lest the many be defiled through this (bitterness)." μιανθῶσιν is aorist passive subjunctive of μιαίνω, "to dye, stain, defile." Sin does more than stain the surface; it becomes part of the fabric. The fourth of the noun-object clauses needs two dependent clauses to fill out its thought. The clause itself says, "lest any fornicator or profane (be). . . ." Be what? That is answered by an adverbial ὡς clause of comparison, ". . . as Esau (was). . . ." And how "was" Esau? That question is answered by an adjective clause describing Esau, at least that element in Esau that is pertinent to the exhortation at hand; ". . . who, for one eating, sold his birthright." ἀπέδοτο is second aorist indicative middle of ἀποδίδωμι, "give off." In the middle voice it means "to give up of one's own" and hence "sell." The preposition ἀντί with genitive may suggest, and here does, the idea of substitution. The preposition means "against" or "opposite." Esau put "one eating" "over against" the birthright He substituted one for the other.

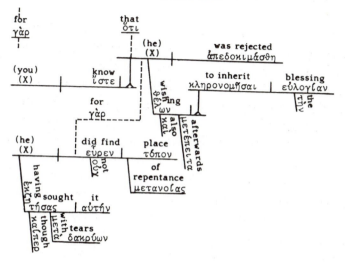

THE DIAGRAM OF HEBREWS 12:17

Verse 17 is a warning based on the "root of bitterness" which Esau allowed to warp his life. So the sentence begins with an explanatory conjunction "for" (γὰρ). The verse presents a compound-complex sentence of two independent and one dependent clauses.

The first clause states "you know. . . . " It introduces indirect discourse. The object of "know" (ἴστε) is a noun clause "that he was rejected." οἶδα is the usual koine form of the perfect of this verb "know" but here the older classic form ἴστε appears. It is probably the indicative mode although it could be imperative. We take it here as indicative. The present participle θέλων "wishing," modifying "he" is circumstantial, probably concessive, "even though wishing (linear continuously wishing) afterwards to inherit the blessing." The infinitive κληρονομῆσαι "to inherit" is aorist. Inherit is seen as an act to be done, not a process of attainment. Hence, even though the "*wishing* to inherit" was an

401

ongoing longing of Esau's, the point action here is appropriate. An infinitive is a verbal-noun. That is, a verb while at the same time a noun. As a noun it is accusative case (fixed form) object of the verbal aspect in the participle. As a verb it not only has tense and voice but it takes cases as other verbs may. Here the word rendered "blessing" is object of the infinitive.

The second independent clause emphatically underscores the irrepealable nature of the consequences of Esau's bitterness; "for, having sought it with tears, he did not find place of repentance." The circumstantial participle ἐκζητήσας "having sought" is without question concessive in force. The adverbial particle καίπερ "though" used with it assures that. Note that the tense of both the participle and the finite verb is aorist. Even though no doubt he made repeated attempts to "seek" a change in his father's blessing those repeated attempts are lumped together as a single effort. As the author of Hebrews viewed Esau's attempts he reduced them to one concentrated struggle.

It is worth taking special note that the last word in the sentence, the pronoun αὐτήν "it" has for its antecedent εὐλογίαν "blessing" and not either "place" or "repentance."

A Translation
Hebrews 12:18-29

For you have not come to (a mountain) being touched and having been burned with fire, and to blackness and to dark gloom, and to whirlwind and to a trumpet's peal, and to sound of words which the ones who heard begged that not (a further) word be put to them for they were not bearing the thing being commanded that even if a beast should touch the mount it shall be stoned. And the thing appearing was so frightening (that even) Moses said, "I am terrified and trembling." But you have come to mount Zion and to (the) city of God who is living and to thousands of angels, a festal assembly, and to (the) judge, God of all and to spirits of just who have been made perfect and to Jesus, mediator of a new covenant and to blood of sprinkling speaking better than the (blood) of Abel (has spoken). You be on the watch; don't refuse the one speaking. For if those having refused the one warning upon the earth did not escape, much more (shall) we (not escape), we, the ones turning away from the one warning from heaven whose voice then shook the earth but now has promised, saying, "I yet once will shake not only the earth but also the heaven." But the phrase "Yet once" makes clear the removal of the things being shaken as things having been made, in order that the things which cannot be shaken may remain.

Wherefore, in as much as we are receiving an immovable kingdom, let us have grace through which we may acceptably be serving God with reverence and awe for our God is indeed a consuming fire.

AN OUTLINE OF HEBREWS 12:18-29
SINAI AND ZION: THE EARTHLY AND THE HEAVENLY

Sinai and Zion represent stages of revelation, the skeleton and the heart.

I. THE TWO MOUNTAINS. 18-24
1. Mount Sinai, the type. A "real" mountain.
   (a) Experienced by the five senses.
   (b) Frightening to those who experienced it.
   (c) It even terrified Moses.
2. Mount Zion, the antitype. The ultimate "real."
   (a) The eternal city of the living God.
   (b) The festal assembly of God 's creations.
   (c) Those still in the struggle.

II. THE MOUNTAIN THAT REMAINS. 25-27
1. The voice which shakes Sinai.
2. But leaves Zion unshaken and unshakable.

III. THE CHRISTIAN'S RESPONSIBILITY. 25a and 28-29
1. Be watching! 25a
2. Be gracious and thankful. 28
3. Be serving God. 29

Our God of love is a "consuming fire." He "saves" his people who trust: he "consumes" those who fall away. Be on the alert!

SOME EXPOSITORY THOUGHTS ON HEBREWS 12:18-29

We live in a world of sight and sound. What we see, hear, and touch, largely determines human life. It's difficult to think of the "spiritual" as consisting of the hard stuff of life. Most men relate to a quick fix with a smoke of pot or a high on a pill than to the biblical exhortation to "be filled with the Spirit." Being "spiritual" is all right for an occasional visit to the church house but in the dog-eat-dog world that isn't very realistic. "Real estate" refers to land and houses, not speculations about God. The Deity is a nebulous, foggy idea, not an every day tool with which to wage war in economic and social life. God is to be "worshipped" but he's not to interfere with the daily exercise of my business. What I see and touch I understand. But the mysteries of religion and the secrets of God I leave to clergymen, children and old people. Dollars and battleships settle disputes in the hard world of facts. Neither God nor religion have made wars to cease!

The two mountains

"You have not come to a mountain being touched and having been burned with fire . . . you have come to Mount Zion. . . ." The two mountains signify stages in revelation, levels of truth, degrees of reality. They point to the physical and the spiritual, the outward and the inward, the external form and the internal verity, the bony skeleton and the beating heart. They do not represent truth versus falsehood. They are more like seed-time and harvest, childhood and manhood, the curses of law and the liberty of gospel. Mount Sinai is shadow; Mount Zion is susbtance. Without Zion, Mt. Sinai breeds fear and death. Mount Zion fulfills the promise of Sinai by bringing hope, joy, security and eternal life.

When Israel came to Sinai the people approached a "real" mountain. They saw it belch forth fire; they smelled the sulphuric smoke that enveloped the craggy height. The land was darkened with a thick black pall of gloom. The winds whirled, the rocks cracked like the sound of trumpets and the voice of God sounded in words of rolling thunder. So frightening were the cumulated sights and sounds that the people begged that not another word be spoken. So overwhelming was the revealed holiness of God that these sinful people despaired of life. Even Moses, who had personally spoken with God, cried, "I am terrified and trembling."

The scene at Sinai is a parable. The "freedoms" we think we have turn out to be frightening illusions. We work for financial independence. We build a bank account pay off the mortgage on the house; invest in real estate stocks and bonds. We plan to fish, hunt, go golfing, and play with the grandchildren. But forces over which we have no control invade our well-planned lives. The four horsemen of the apocalypse, famine, sickness, war, and death. If we escape the clutches of violent crime, storm accident, fire and earthquake, eventually death overtake us. All our worried work and anxious planning go down the drain. Even our approach to religion has been ver

406

much that of buying an insurance policy. To be used in case of emergency but of not much practical value in maintaining the security of life's status quo!

But there is a second mountain. "You have come to Mount Zion and to the city of the living God, to heavenly Jerusalem. . . ." I can't see it, I can't touch it, neither can I smell fire or smoke! But when the author of Hebrews describes that which Zion is and does, then I know that Mount Zion is much more "real" than any Sinai this world can contain. Wherein every other "certainty" which I have pursued in life has turned out to be an illusory fantasy this heavenly Jerusalem becomes the city "whose builder and maker is God." That city that Abraham and all those heroes of faith sought through all the long centuries.

The only abiding security is in the city of God. And we entered it when we were converted to Jesus the Christ. Our Zion gives significance and meaning to Old Sinai. Just as redemption in Christ, the promise of the forgiveness of sin, a clean conscience, the expectation of a heaven of fellowship with God and all his saints, gives meaning to the disappointments we now endure. Mount Zion represents all the true realities of Christian faith. Sinai represents the material externals of this world including the laws and forms of religion. Zion represents the ultimate realities of the inner spirit, the "truth" that gives life and meaning to physical forms. The earth and the heavens will perish . . . they will grow old like a garment . . . thou wilt roll them up. . . . But thou art the same, and thy years will never end." And the Christian is a part of that eternity of God!

Consider what is involved in Zion! "Thousands of angels, a festal assembly, the church of the first-born, ones inscribed on the citizenship rolls of heaven. . . ." What is the meaning of this? What is the Hebrew's author saying? For one thing he is saying that when we become Christians we enter into the most viable fraternity of creatures known to God or man. It's described as a "festal assembly." Its personnel consists of thousands upon thousands of angels. Its membership includes the "church of the first born ones." That is, all who enjoy the inheritance right of the older sons of a gracious, loving affluent heavenly Father. All these sons of God whose names fill the roster of heavenly citizenship. No free citizen of imperial Rome had more or better entitlements than we now possess as redeemed of God.

It is because of a preference to Sinai over Zion, a desire for what we see and touch over that which we believe that the text says, "we have come to a judge who is God of all." Some of "us" prize the sights and sounds of Sinai, the excitements and fanaticism of the stadiums of this world. The festal joy of Christ and his comradery take second place in plans and service. To such Christians who prefer the fires of Sinai to the spiritual reality of Mount Zion there is pledged the judgment of violated love. A judgment far greater than that on those Israelites who, having escaped bondage rejected Moses and longed for the flesh pots of Egypt. They haven't been able to distinguish reality of sacred spiritual values from the bondage of the senses in this world's arena.

Besides that, we have come "to the spirits of just men made perfect." Is the eye of our faith so blinded that we cannot grasp the reality that we have already entered the stadium of eternal life with the believers of all ages? The "spirits of just men made perfect" include the long list of heroes listed in chapter eleven. Enoch, who "walked with God," Abraham, who "went out not knowing where he went," and all the rest of the souls of departed saints. These people are as much alive today as he who sits next to you in the church pew or sings with you in the church choir, or drinks the blood of our Lord with you at the communion table. These are the most real of real people! We don't have to die in order to share fellowship for "we have come to" them. They identify with us and we with them *now*! Is not faith a "conviction of things *not seen*?" Do we not now regulate our lives by the realities of the unseen, hoped-for world as though it were now seen? We live life "by faith." Peter and Andrew, James and John are as real as those howling dervishes in Rupp arena cheering their blue hallucinating phantoms around an arena destined to be an ash heap. I'm in God's eternal stadium cheering with Abraham, Isaac and Jacob. God's hall of fame is as real to me today as any I can see with my eyes or touch with my hands.

In addition Zion obviously includes those yet burdened with the world of sight and sound where the smell of the smoke of Sinai still clings to the garments. But even here, we who struggle to grasp the real world of spirit have come to "Jesus, mediator of a new covenant and a sprinkling of his redeeming blood which speaks volumes more than the blood of Abel." We have a great high priest who redeems and who, though he died, yet he arose and his blood keeps speaking victory and peace to our souls.

The mountain that abides

The less real, the typical, symbolic revelation of Sinai's sights and sounds brought judgment to those who treated

409

it with contempt. That being true, we with the "real" and greatest revelation will be judged with more severe punishment if we play fast and loose with it.

At Sinai God's voice "shook the earth." The people hid from the holiness of God. Sinners can never stand to be in the presence of God's absolute unblemished holiness. When the naked truth is known neither ancient or modern man can stand to face the righteous purity of the Lord. Our "seen" securities crumble to our feet. But that voice which shook Sinai sounds a permanent promise, "Yet once I will not only shake the earth but I will also shake the heaven." But this he declared that he might make clear that his eternal Mount Zion shall remain unshaken and unshakable. The only thing in this life that is really "real" is the spiritual. The permanency of Mount Zion is not dependent on "natural" laws but on the word of the Person of God. For in making the statement "Yet once again I will shake. . . ." God was making plain that this old earth of "real-estate" will be taken away, utterly destroyed. It will be but a cinder on the ash heap of the infinite cosmic universe. Then the divine hand will shape Our Mount Zion into its final perfection. It will be a "new heavens and a new earth" wherein dwells righteousness. "The world is passing away . . . but the one doing the will of God abides forever." The only thing eternally abiding is moral, ethical, and spiritual!

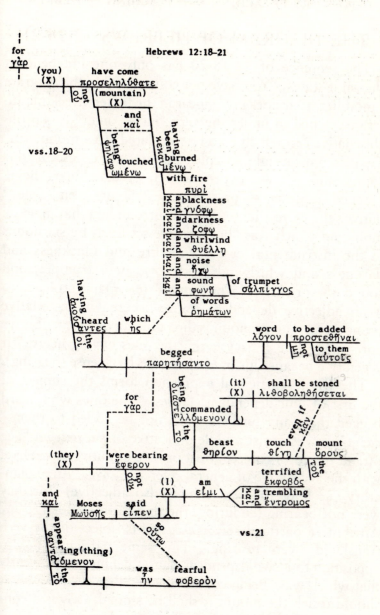

Hebrews 12:18–21

vss.18–20

vs.21

411

THE DIAGRAM OF HEBREWS 12:18-21

The sentence of 12:18-20 has only one independent clause; it states, "You have not come. . . ." In the diagram a modifier, that does not appear in the better Greek manuscripts, is placed under the verb "have come." It is probably dative ὄρει which is to be translated "to a mountain." Two circumstantial particples are inserted to describe this "mountain" as it was experienced by Israel at Sinai. "Being touched" represents a present tense; "having been burned" mirrors the perfect tense. Details surrounding that majestic mountain which was "burned" are set forth by six nouns in the instrumental case: "with fire and blackness and darkness and whirlwind, and noise of a trumpet, and sound of words. . . ." The "sound" (φωνῇ) has attached to it an adjective dependent clause ushered in by relative pronoun ἧς. The pronoun is direct object of the attributive aorist participle οἱ ἀκούσαντες "the ones having heard." It is genitive because it's used after a verb of sense (hearing).

The whole participial expression forms the subject of the first of four dependent clauses. "The ones who heard begged that (any further) word not be added to them." παρῃτήσαντο is aorist middle indicative of παραιτέομαι "beg off." It has for its object aorist passive infinitive προστεθῆναι with the accusative of general reference λόγον. An explanatory γὰρ joins the next clause (also adjective) "for they were not bearing (enduring) the thing commanded. . . ." Attributive participle διαστελλόμενον is object of the verb translated "were bearing." This same participle has in apposition to it two dependent clauses defining more clearly that which was "being commanded," "that even if a beast should touch the mount it shall be stoned." χᾶν is a contradiction of χαί plus ἐάν and it introduces a 3rd class condition, the condition undetermined but with prospect of determination; "even if" leaves open whether any beast would! It might not; then again it is possible that it would. These verses frame a complex sentence.

Verse 21 is also complex in structure. It's base clause attests "Moses said. . . ." The dependent clause inaugurated by οὕτω declares the degree to which Moses was frightened. φοβερὸν is predicate adjective referring back to the subject τὸ φανταζόμενον "the thing appearing." That is a present participle describing the awesome experience at Sinai that led even Moses to be afraid. The fear prompted Moses to say that which is recorded in the noun clause direct object of εἶπεν, "I am terrified and trembling."

413

Hebrews 12:22-24

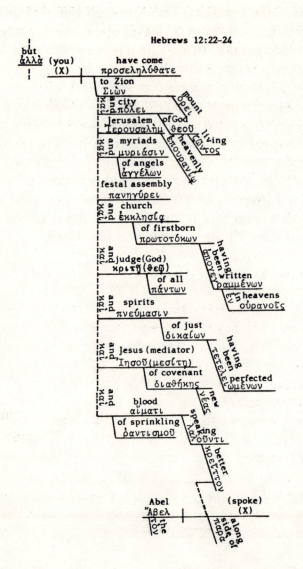

THE DIAGRAM OF HEBREWS 12:22-24

This sentence cannot be classed as simple because of the dependent clause tacked onto the end, ". . . than the Abel speaks." It is an adverbial clause of comparison. Probably the full reading should be ". . . and blood of sprinkling speaking better than the (blood of) the Abel speaks." Preposition παρά means "along side of." When you place "the blood of sprinkling" "along side of" Abel's it is "speaking" better than Abel's speaks. In other words the blood of Jesus speaks more effectively than that of Abel as good as that is. (See 11:4.) The definite article with Abel is anaphoric. That is, it points back to the former use of Abel early in the eleventh chapter.

Though the sentence must technically be classed as complex it is really quite simple since the main clause says, "You have come. . . ." Perfect tense "have come" reminds the readers that they now are involved with a firm, immovable, permanent, mountain. Not such a one as Sinai was.

There then follows a series of ten substantives in the dative case. Of course the dative always involves the personal element in any relationship. Seven of the ten items have modifying words or phrases. The first, "Zion," has the noun "mount" modifying it as an attributive idea; really used adjectively. "City" has genitive "of God" specifying the *kind* of city it is to which they "have come." And in turn that "God" is himself described by the attributive present participle "living." "Jerusalem" has attributive adjective "heavenly" limiting it. When the author comes to the word "church" he uses a genitive plural translated "firstborn" to specify the *kind* of church. It is that kind of

415

assembly (church) the membership of which are "firstborn ones." They are "firstborn" in the sense that they belong to Him who is the only *true* "firstborn" even Jesus. These "firstborn" are further characterized as being "ones having been enrolled (written) in (the) heavens." The next dative ("God") has "judge" in apposition identifying his judicial function; genitive "of all" pictures the extent of his judgments. The word "spirits" uses the genitive to characterize the kind of spirits. "You have come" not just to spirits in general but to spirits "of just" men. These just men are further described by the perfect participle "having been perfected." This is a circumstantial participle. The root meaning of the word says that these men arrived at the goal for which God intended them; the tense adds the fact that they are permanently there. They "have been perfected" and they still are. With "Jesus" the author once again uses apposition to expand his idea. This Jesus is "mediator." Genitive "of covenant" tells what kind of mediator he is. That is, "of new covenant." The last of the ten is "blood." It is described by the genitive "of sprinkling" referring to Christ's blood "sprinkled" on those who "have come" to this new mountain as the Old Testament sacrificial blood was sprinkled on the altar in behalf of those who came to it. The present participle "speaking" introduces the comparison with Abel's blood as mentioned above.

Hebrews 12:25-26

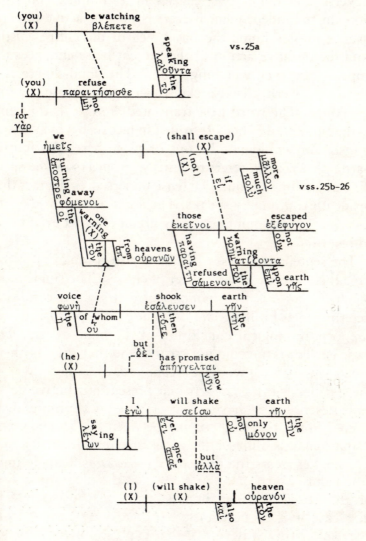

vs.25a

vss.25b-26

417

THE DIAGRAM OF HEBREWS 12:25-26

Verse 25a unites two clauses in a complex combination. In the independent βλέπετε is present active imperative. It presses home the basic plea of the entire epistle
And the durative action of the present tense enhances the
appeal. "Be ever watching. . . ." The subordinate is a
negative adverb purpose clause, "lest you refuse the one
speaking." The word here translated "refuse" is the same
as that in verse 19 "beg off from." In fact such a picturesque
translation would not be out of place here. Attributive
participle λαλοῦντα refers to Jesus who speaks by the shedding of his life's blood. The tense underscores the fact that
his death continually speaks. The aorist παραιτήσησθε with
μὴ brings out its point action by urging, "Don't even begin
to beg off."

The sentence of verses 25b-26 is also complex. But this
time there are six in the cluster of classes. The single independent clause is the apodosis of a first class condition
determined as fufilled. The "if" clause is the protasis which
supports the logical conclusion of the main clause. The
logic is: "For if they did not escape (and they didn't) (then
much more (shall) we (not escape). . . ." Subject "we" of
the independent has an articular present attributive participle describing it (ἀποστρεφόμενοι) "the ones turning away
from." In the text and coming between the article οἱ and
its participle is a masculine accusative definite article τὸν
That either treats the phrase ἀπ' οὐρανῶν as a single unit
"the from heaven one," or it may, as the diagram shows
be the article with an implied participle "warning." In
that case it is to be translated, "the one warning from
heaven." Either way, off of that expression stems an adjective clause describing this "one from heaven"; "of whom

418

the voice then shook the earth. . . ." The adversative conjunction δὲ joins to that another adjective clause, ". . . but he has now promised. . . ." Note the difference in tenses between the two clauses. ἐσάλευσεν is aorist; ἀπήγγελται is perfect. The aorist looks at an historical event. The perfect not only looks back to the promise made but to its present effect. The promise still stands!

The final two dependents are noun clauses serving as direct objects of the circumstantial participle λέγων. "*I* yet once will not only shake the earth but (I will shake) also the heaven." Use of the first personal pronoun ἐγὼ is very emphatic. "I myself will. . . ." The destiny of the earth and heaven is in the hands of a *Person*, not just abstract impersonal laws.

Hebrews 12:27-29

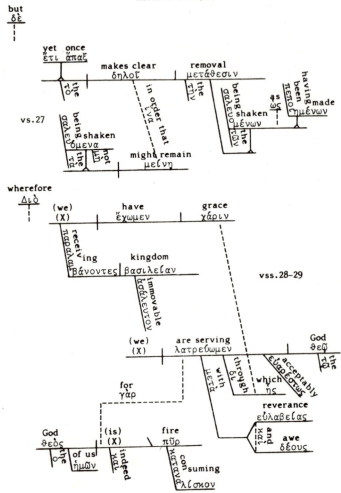

420

THE DIAGRAM OF HEBREWS 12:27-29

Verse 27 projects a complex sentence of two clauses. Subject of the main clause is a phrase ἔτι ἅπαξ "yet once." It is treated as one unit of thought and is made definite by use of the article τό. The article points back to the same phrase as appearing in the preceding verse. The subject might be periphrased, "The expression 'yet once'. . . ." So the opening clause says, "But the 'yet once' makes clear the removing. . . ." An attributive present participle modifies the word rendered "being shaken." It's in the genitive case, "of the things being shaken." ὡς and perfect participle πεποιημένων is for all practical purposes an appositional idea. The expression defines the "things being shaken" "*as things having been made*." One participle is present tense; the other is perfect. The corresponding kinds of action should be noted. God "had made" the things and he established them as permanent as anything material could be permanent. But he "made" them with the intent that they "be shaken," that is, that they be temporary. They were to be removed at the appropriate time. The dependent clause states that the "removing" of those things "having been made" was for the purpose of (ἵνα) "the things not being shaken might abide." This creation is at best temporary. The eternal order is an unshaken, irrevocable, truly permanent order of God's.

The conjunction Διὸ introduces a conclusion, "wherefore." It begins anew sentence based on the revelation of the preceding. Verses 28-29 mold a complex sentence of three clauses. The main clause is an exhortation, "Wherefore, let us be having grace. . . ." Modifying the subject "we" (us) is the present active circumstantial participle

421

παραλαμβάνοντες. It suggests "cause" and may be translated "because we are receiving an immovable kingdom let us be having. . . ." A relative clause, adjectival in force, describes "grace." It is introduced by δι' ἧς "through which." λατρεύωμεν is present subjunctive with dative θεῷ as its direct object. Verbs of serving take the dative. An adverbial idea as to *how* we may serve God is seen in μετὰ with genitives "reverance" and "awe." A reason *why* we serve God is that way is found in the clause announced by γὰρ. "Our God is indeed a consuming fire." The present participle καταναλίσκον "consuming" is probably attributive as used here. Present tense represents God as having this aspect as a continuous quality. This aspect of God brings to mind the thought of 10:31. Such qualities in God are not inconsistent with this essential nature of love. Burning fire is the way love feels when it comes into the presence of rebellious apostate sin. Fire IS love confronting evil. Love consumes evil!

A Translation
Hebrews 13:1-17

Go on exercising brotherly love. Don't forget hospitality, for because of it some have welcomed angels unconsciously. You, as having been bound, be remembering the prisoners; you yourselves, as being also in body, be remembering the ones being ill-treated. Marriage is honorable among all and the (marriage) bed is undefiled for God will judge fornicators and adulterers. Being content with the things being in your possession, your life style (is to be) without love of silver for God has said, "I will not let you down, neither will I forsake you." The result is that we say, "The Lord is my helper; I will not fear what man may do to me."

Continue to remember the ones leading you who spoke to you the word of God; of whom, considering the issue of their behaviour, be imitating their faith. Jesus Christ yesterday and today is the same, and forever! Don't indulge the practice of being carried off with varied and strange teachings. For that the heart be firmed up by grace is good, not with foods in which those living weren't profited. We possess an altar of which the ones serving the tabernacle do not have (the) right to eat. For the beasts, whose blood is carried into the Holy of Holies for sin through the high priest, the bodies of these are burned outside the camp.

Wherefore also Jesus, that he might sanctify the people, suffered outside the gate. Therefore let us go out to him bearing his reproach for we are not having here an abiding city but we are seeking the one coming. So then, through him let's always be carrying sacrifice of praise to God, that is, the fruit of lips confessing his name. But don't forget beneficent deeds and sharing for God is pleased with such sacrifices. Be obedient to your leaders and yield for they are watching over your souls as ones who give an account, that they may do this with joy, not groaning, for that is profitless for you.

A Translation
Hebrews 13:18-25

Be praying for us; for we are persuaded that we possess good conscience, wishing to live rightly among all. But I exhort more abundantly that you do this that we may be restored to you more quickly.

The God of peace, the one bringing from the dead in the blood of the eternal covenant the great shepherd of the sheep, our Lord Jesus, (may this God) who is doing in us through Jesus Christ the thing pleasing before him, perfect you in every good for you to do his will. To (this Christ be) the glory unto the ages of the ages. Amen!

And, brothers, I exhort you: endure the word of exhortation for I have written to you through (these) few words. You know that our brother, Timothy, having been released, with whom I will see you, if he come shortly.

Salute all the ones leading you and all the saints. Those from Italy are saluting you.

Grace (be) with you all!

AN OUTLINE OF HEBREWS 13:1-17
PRAISE THROUGH LIPS AND LIFE

Praising God is always appropriate! Praise with the lips and the life are the kinds of sacrifices pleasing to Him!

I. PRAISE THROUGH THE SACRIFICES OF LIFE. 1-6

    1. By continuing in brotherly love. 1
    2. By "hospitality to strangers." 2
    3. By ministering to the prisoners. 3
    4. By honoring marriage. 4
    5. Contentment with possessions. 5-6
       (a) Lacking in greed.
       (b) Reliance on the promise of God.

II. PRAISE THROUGH RELIGIOUS RESPONSIBILITIES. 7-17

    1. Respecting faithful leaders. 7 and 17.
    2. Christ unchanging versus changing doctrines. 8-9a

3. Our altar is "outside the camp." 9b-13
   (a) Not the "many foods" of Aaronic priests.
   (b) Redemption gained "outside the gate."
   (c) We worship at our altar "bearing his reproach."

Our sacrifice of praise is acceptable and pleasing to God; the "fruit of lips," doing the good; fellowship in sharing!

AN OUTLINE OF HEBREWS 13:18-25
EXHORTATIONS AND SALUTATIONS!

1. Be praying for us. 18
2. May the God of peace perfect you through our Lord Jesus Christ. 20-21
3. Accept these written pleas until Timothy and I come to see you face to face. 22-23
4. Salutations to the "leaders" and "saints." 24
5. "Grace be with you!" 25

SOME EXPOSITORY THOUGHTS ON HEBREWS 13:1-17
Praising God with Life and Lips!

"Let us offer up sacrifice of praise to God, the fruit of lips confessing his name." The goal of creation is the praise of God! God looked on his creation and "saw that it was good." "Let everything that breathes praise the Lord!" (Ps. 150:6). Man, the masterpiece of creative wisdom, is made to praise his Creator. Man's sacrifice of praise is the "fruit of lips."

Praise through the service of life

One can go into the private closet of his soul and "in secret" praise God with his lips. But if it ends there it will be faint praise. Sacrifices of the spirit must find outward expression. I cannot praise God without serving God's people. Praise of lips must find expression in service of life. Man is a social creature. He's not made "to be alone." The text states several ways in which I may praise God in society that surrounds me.

"Continue in brotherly love." A mother of a son going away to college said to an administrator, "Take care of my son." I praise God when I serve his sons. Intelligent good will toward the family of God is pleasing to God as worship.

"Be hospitable to strangers." Travelers on the highways of life need to know that wherever a believer is there is a "hospitality house" for the lonely, the hurting, the sinful. To share one's house and heart with "strangers" is high praise to God.

"Remember the prisoners." God is not locked out when men are locked in the prisons of the world. This is particularly true when the prisoners are God's people. Love must take a risk if it would offer praise. Love risks when it "remembers the prisoners!"

"Marriage is honorable . . . the bed is undefiled." How much greater praise to God can there be than to honor at all costs the marriage vows to be faithful "until death do you part." To do God's will is the greatest praise! Jesus said, "from the beginning God made them male and female . . . and the two shall become one. . . ." Maintaining the sacredness of marriage is to praise God with life.

"Your life style is to be without love of money." Recognize God's place in the providences of material possessions.
To accept God's involvement in this material creation, it
economy and the distribution of material means of liveli-
hood is to praise Him! He has said, "I will not let you
down, neither will I forsake you." It's his gold and silver
We handle it in trust when we "make money" and then
spend it. So we praise God in the market place as we plunge
into the commerce of society.

Praise through religious responsibilities

God guides his people through chosen leaders. Respect
for such leaders is respect to God. Praise God by being
good followers. We learn from their teaching for they
"spoke the word of God." We learn from their pattern
of life. Thus we are to "imitate their behaviour." In matters
of grave dispute we "yield" to their leadership that there
may be order and not chaos in the family of God. To so
yield is profitable to us and makes their burden less weighty.
For they bear the heavy responsibility of having "to give
an account" for our souls. To honor them is to praise God.

Praise God by unfalterable faithfulness to an unchanging Christ. Basics never change. The reason there can be
progress in this world is because there are some things
which never change. Some things are "never the same"
because other things are always the same. Because of a
stable fixed alphabet we can ring the changes on myriad
of words. Because two teams agree on rules that are not
to be altered during the game then both teams have the
opportunity of developing an unlimited number of rapidly
changing plays. Christ is the unchanging One. His "truth"

428

s absolute and unalterable. Therefore we have the opportunity of changing from weakness to strength, from sinner o saint, from moral pigmies to spiritual giants. Because ve know where he is and what his truth is then we have omething stable on which to meet the disturbing changes hat come our way in life.

"We have an altar . . . outside the gate. . . ." Our place of worship is "outside the camp" where sin was defeated and death conquered. We are no longer walled into a debauched society of sin. When we accept "his reproach" and go out to worship him we offer the finest praise to God. We are redeemed from the taboos of custom and traditions of men. We are relieved of the mysteries of priestly rituals and "unclean" foods. Our redemption has been purchased once for all "outside the gate." We are now "free" to bear his "reproach" and enter into his reward.

All these "sacrifices of praise" are acceptable to God and pleasing to him as meaningful methods of worshipful praise. The "fruit of lips" is fulfilled in doing the "good" and in the fellowship of "sharing."

Hebrews 13:1-4

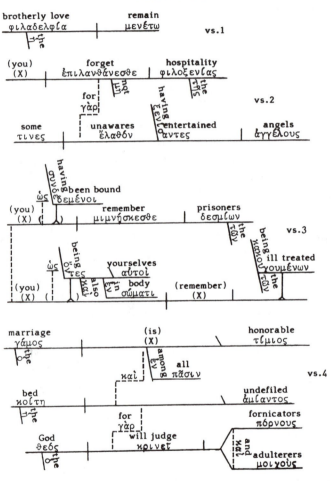

THE DIAGRAM OF HEBREWS 13:1-4

Hebrews 13:1 is a three word simple sentence. The author begins a series of practical admonitions. This sentence counsels, "The brotherly love is to be abiding." μενέτω is present imperative of a verb the aktionsart of which is itself linear. μένω means "to remain." The very root idea in "remain" is durative. Impose on that a linear tense and the emphasis of "going on abiding" is quite impressive to say the least.

Verse two embraces two clauses of equal rank, thus it is compound. The first clause is an exhortation. The second gives a reason for responding to the exhortation. "Do not be forgetting hospitality" uses present middle imperative ἐπιλανθάνεσθε with μὴ "do not be forgetting." Middle voice is to be noted with its stress on the *self*. Love of strangers (hospitality) is at bottom a good way to meet one's own spiritual needs. The present tense urges too that we have the habit of "not forgetting." The verb of the second clause is a periphrastic form. ἔλαθον is aorist indicative active of a classic verb λανθάνω "escape notice," "be hidden." The participle ξενίσαντες is aorist of ξενίζω "entertain as a guest." It derives from a noun meaning "alien," "stranger." This is supplementary predicate participle. In league with ἔλαθον it forms an aorist periphrastic translated, "have entertained unawares. . . ." This is an idiom of classic Greek in which the main idea is carried in the participle.

Verse three contains a compound sentence of two clauses. The subject of each of them ("you") is expanded by participles, probably attributive. συνδεδεμένοι "having been bound" is perfect. The fact that they had at one time "been bound" helped them to identify with "prisoners." The effects of their own imprisonment was still with them.

431

The sentence is a couplet in keeping with poetic form. The second line restates the thought of the first but with variation. "You as (being mistreated) also yourselves in (your) body, (go on remembering) the ones being ill-treated."

In the compound sentence of verse four the verbs in the first two of the three clauses are not expressed. They need to be supplied. It is difficult to decide whether they should be indicative ἐστίν "is" or imperative ἔστω "is to be" or "let be." Either makes sense. Imperative makes them an exhortation in the light of a problem facing the Christian community in a permissive society. The indicative makes a positive assertion to support and encourage a level of moral life befitting redeemed people.

The third of the clauses lays on the conscience a reason that supports the ideas of the first two. "God will judge fornicators and adulterers." κρινεῖ is future indicative active = "will judge." Unless the context gives strong reason future tense is usually punctiliar action. Permissive moral misbehaviour, acceptable among men, doesn't change basic moral realities. God is still God and very much in control. There is to be a point at which judgment will be consummated.

Hebrews 13:5-7

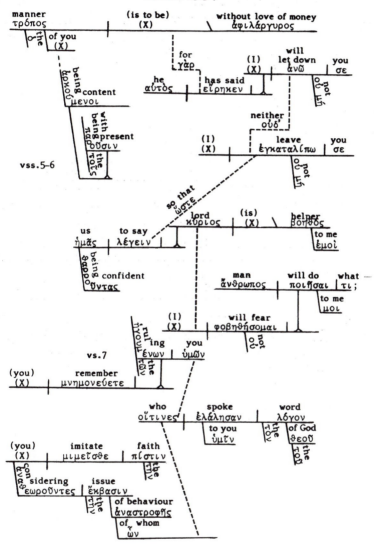

433

THE DIAGRAM OF HEBREWS 13:5-7

The thought of 13:5-6 channels itself through seven clauses besides an infinitive expression and a nominative absolute. With two independent clauses the sentence proves to be compound-complex. The first clause lacks a verb so we supply imperative ἔστω "let be." When the context demands, the definite article may be translated as a possessive. So ὁ with τρόπος may be "your." However the diagram has supplied an "understood" plural "of you" so as to give the unattached nominative participle ἀρχούμενοι "being content" a point of connection. Otherwise it is a nominative absolute. Or it may be used as a finite verb, "you be content. . . ." In that case it would be as another distinct clause. That participle, "being content," has a present participle in instrumental case modifying it, τοῖς παροῦσιν "with the things being present."

The second main clause has pronoun αὐτὸς "he" for a very emphatic subject. The "he" refers to God! εἴρηκεν is perfect tense which indicates that what "he has said" still stands as his pledge. The content of what he has said comes out in two noun clauses, objects of "has said." I will *not* let you down neither will I leave you." Note the emphatic negatives that appear with both object clauses, οὐ μὴ. Note too that one of them is a double negative in combination with conjunction οὐδέ. Literally it would read, ". . . neither will I not leave you. . . . " Greek uses double negative where English rejects it.

ὥστε with infinitive expresses result. ἡμᾶς is accusative of general reference; ". . . so that we, being confident, are saying. . . ." Present tense points up the fact that since God has been lavish in his promise we may *go on saying*." The content of what we say is in two noun clauses, objects of the infinitive. "The Lord (is) helper to me" and "I will not fear. . . ." The verb φοβηθήσομαι "will fear" has for its object a noun clause, "what man will do to me."

Verse seven displays a complex sentence of three clauses. Again the independent idea is an exhortation. "Remember the ones ruling you. . . ." μνημονεύετε "be remembering" is present imperative which insists on unbroken alertness to the task of following leaders. Present participle ἡγουμένων is attributive with article, "the ones ruling" and is genitive after verb of ruling. It also takes the genitive as object. Of special note is the fact that this word translated "rule" is *not* "rule *over*." In fact, the primary idea is not rule at all; that is a later derived meaning. Fundamentally it means to "lead." With our western idea of "rule" as governing it would better communicate the biblical notion by translating it, "remember the ones leading you. . . ." The ὑμῶν "you" is described by an adjective clause, "who spoke to you the word of God." This clause sustains the idea of "rulers" being "leaders" rather than governors. Another adjective clause modifies οἵτινες "who." It is ushered in by relative ὧν "of whom." μιμεῖσθε is present imperative, "go on imitating their faith. . . ." These "rulers" lead by their word of teaching and their faith, not by power of political position.

435

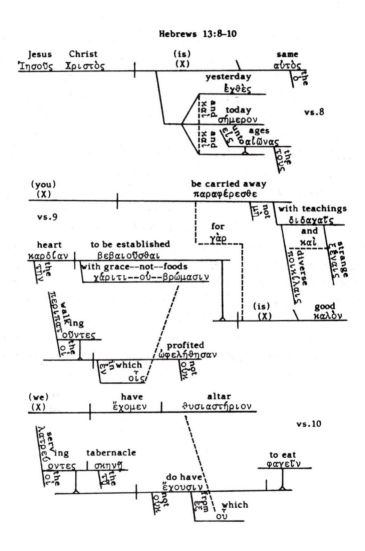

Hebrews 13:8–10

436

THE DIAGRAM OF HEBREWS 13:8-10

Verse eight is a short sharp statement about Jesus. "Jesus Christ (is) the same yesterday, today and unto the ages." It's a simple sentence. The words translated "yesterday," "today" are adverbs. "Unto the ages (forever)" is an adverbial phrase.

The sentence of verse nine is compound complex. παραφέρεσθε is present imperative with negative, "do not be carried away. . . ." διδαχαῖς is instrumental case. The second independent clause has an infinitive phrase for its subject. βεβαιοῦσθαι "to be made stable." καρδίαν is accusative of general reference. Modifying the infinitive is χάριτι "by grace" which is adverbial in function expressing the means by which the heart is to be made stable. The additional negative modifying expression οὐ βρώμασιν "not with foods" could have been placed under a full clause, implied by the context; "(the heart is not established) with foods." But the diagram has abbreviated and placed it together with "grace." An adjective clause springs off βρώμασιν describing these Old Testament ritual "foods" as being ones "in which the ones walking did not profit." There is a finality about the aorist tense when it refers to events that in their actual transaction took place over extended periods of time. ὠφελήθησαν is just such an historical aorist. The fact as fact is the point of emphasis.

Hard upon the profitlessness suggested in verse nine is sounded a note of triumph in the complex sentence of verse ten. "We possess an altar. . . ." That's the declaration of the independent element in this sentence. θυσιαστήριον "altar" is a substantive derived from the verb θυσιάζω "to sacrifice." Nouns such as this ending in τηριον and derived from verbs indicate *place*. An "altar" is the *place* where

437

men sacrifice their offerings of devotion to their God. "We" Christians are not confined to "places" but we do have a spiritual "place" at which we worship God through Jesus Christ.

Describing that altar is an adjective clause attached by ἐξ οὗ "from which." The particular point of description is negative in value. It is an altar "from which the ones serving the tabernacle are not having (an opportunity) to eat." The use of οκηνῇ represents the entire Mosaic-Aaronic system. φαγεῖν is aorist infinitive in accusative case (fixed case form) object of the verb translated "are having."

Hebrews 13:11-12

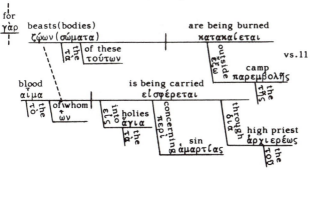

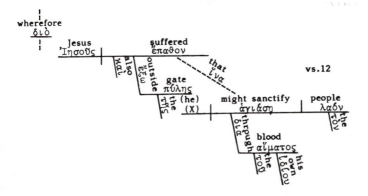

439

THE DIAGRAM OF HEBREWS 13:11-12

The two clauses of verse 11 merge in such a way as to form a complex sentence. But the sentence is not only formally classed as complex it is in fact complicated. ζώων is here genitive plural attracted out of nominative ζῷα into the case of relative ὧν. If we may ignore the Greek forms and grammar for a moment and translate the thought it would read: "Beasts, whose blood is being carried concerning sin into the Holies through the priests, of these the bodies are being burned outside the camp." Thus the sentence begins with the nominative "beasts" as subject. It is then interrupted and the subject described by dependent relative clause ὧν "whose." Then the main clause is resumed by demonstrative pronoun τούτων "of these the bodies are being burned. . . ." σώματα "bodies" which in thought is in apposition to ζώων does not agree with it in case. And that's because "beasts" has been attracted out of its normal nominative into the case of the relative. In order to show the very closest relationship between clauses Greek is capable of attracting a relative out of its expected normal case into the case of its antecedent. Or, as here, of attracting the noun out of its normal case into that of the relative. This explains the genitive plural serving as subject of the independent clause. The author's mind was so animated that he was racing to write the fullness of his idea. His thought was that the beasts' bodies were not eaten (day of atonement sacrifices) but burned outside the camp. The life blood was carried into the Holy of Holies for worship. He had the "of whom" in mind when he started the sentence so he began with his subject in the genitive of the relative. In spite of its being in the genitive it is still subject, the main idea about which he's writing

The verbs in both clauses are present indicatives picturing linear action. κατακαίεται, though singular, is translated plural because neuter plural subjects use singular verbs. "Beasts" and "bodies" are both neuter plurals. In view of the fact that the author clearly has in mind the day of atonement sacrifices the linear action is probably iterative. It pictures the action as being repeated year after year after year. Of course it includes a moving picture of each time the blood was "being carried" and the body was "being burned."

Verse 12 also is a two-clause complex but a good deal less complicated in its arrangement than that of verse 11. It presents the real fulfillment of the pattern as set by the priestly sacrifices of the day of atonement. The independent clause states, "Jesus suffered. . . ." Answering the question as to *where* he suffered is the adverbial prepositional phrase, ". . . outside the gate. . . ." The purpose of his suffering arises in the ἵνα clause; ". . . in order that he might sanctify the people. . . ." The means or agency through which he sanctified them is presented through another prepositional phrase; "through his own blood."

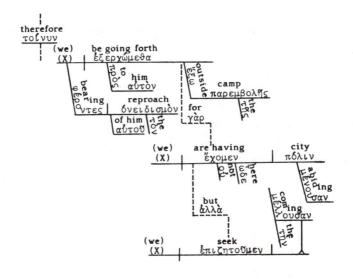

THE DIAGRAM OF HEBREWS 13:13-14

The inferential particle with which the sentence of 13-14 is launched is postpositive in classic Greek. However, in koine times it began to be used as the first word. It is a compound term made of τοί and νῦν. It means "accordingly" or "therefore." In view of that which has been stated in the preceding sentence "therefore" a certain reaction should follow on our part. It introduces the present exhortation as based on the preceding thought. This is a compound sentence of three clauses.

First comes the exhortation, "Let us be going forth. . . ." Present imperative ἐξερχώμεθα is fitting because we must repeat this every time we are summoned to be "bearing his reproach." The present circumstantial participle φέροντε "bearing" is also present as it matches the linear action in the main verb, "going forth." Two adverb phrases tell *where* we are to be "going. . . ." "Outside the camp!" This

442

indicated a total break with Judaism and its outmoded weak covenant. But when we get "outside the camp" it is more than just an isolated place. We go out "to him," our living priest and sacrifice. And we go always "bearing his reproach."

The next two clauses offer supporting reasons for "going to him outside the camp bearing his reproach. . . ." First, "we are not having here an abiding city." Present participle μένουσαν is attributive; it's an "abiding city." Second, ". . . but we are seeking the one coming." The article τὴν with present participle μέλλουσαν guarantees it to be attributive. The present tense of ἐπιζητοῦμεν is descriptive of our present life as Christian believers in Jesus as the Christ. There is no permanent abiding city here but there is such a city somewhere. *That* we "are seeking." The preposition ἐπί on the verb is perfective. We "are seeking it *out*." We are going "all out" in our search.

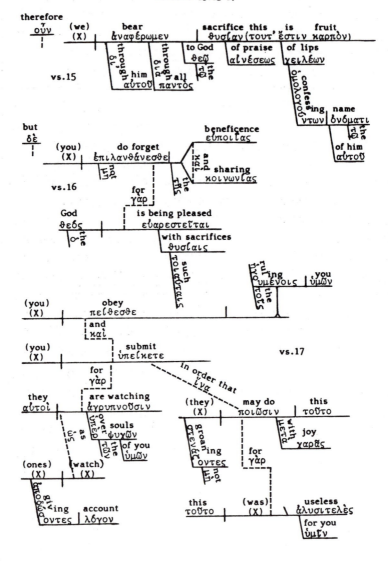

444

.THE DIAGRAM OF HEBREWS 13:15-17

Verse 15 is patterned as a simple sentence, ἀναφέρωμεν is present active volitive subjunctive, ". . . let us keep on offering up. . . ." How are we to do this? "Through him." And *how long* are we to do this? "*Through all,*" that is, continuously through the days and years. *To whom* are we to bear the "sacrifice of praise?" "To God!" The "sacrifice" is defined by the idiomatic phrase "that is, (the) fruit of lips. . . ." χειλέων is genitive characterizing the kind of fruit. To "lips" is added a present circumstantial predicate participle translated "confessing." This phrase describes what kind of praise shall come out of the lips. ὀνόματι is dative as direct object. This is unusual after "confess" but for that reason is to be noted as drawing attention to the *Person* of Jesus. To confess the "name" is to confess the *Person*!

The two clauses of verse 16 develop as a compound sentence. They offer an exhortation and a supporting reason. The adversative sets this admonition, not in opposition to, but in contrasting companionship to that of the preceding. Whereas 16 urged offering the "sacrifice of praise" this says, "don't limit your devotion to words; include some practical service. Don't be forgetting the beneficent (deed) and shared (donation)." Present tense with negative, "forget not . . ." insists on the regular remembering to do and give! The second of the clauses buttresses the advice by declaring, "God is being pleased with such sacrifices." Present linear action of the verb "is being pleased" matches the continuous action of "not forgetting." θυσίαις "with sacrifices" is instrumental case. τοιαύταις is a qualitative demonstrative, "such kind."

445

Six clauses in verse 17 appear as compound-complex. Three are independent and three dependent. The first two independents urge, "Go on obeying . . . and submitting. . . ." Both verbs are presents. As object of "obey" is a present participle ἡγουμένοις "ones ruling. . . ." As with verbs of ruling it has a genitive (ὑμῶν) as object. πείθεσθε "obey" is present middle imperative. The verb means "persuade." When you persuade yourself you obey.

A reason for submissive obedience is advanced in a third independent clause, "they are watching over your souls. . . ." The subject αὐτοὶ is quite emphatic. They are not dictators over your spirits but are "leaders" for your lives. Present tense of "are watching" suggests the constant responsibility that is theirs. The manner in which they are watching is revealed in the ὡς clause, ". . . as (ones watch) who are to give account." Here λόγον is an accounting term. The ἵνα clause is adverb of purpose, . . . in order that they may go on doing this with joy. . . ." The "this" refers to their "ruling" (leading). The manner in which they hope to "do this" is expressed in the circumstantial present participle with negative μὴ στενάζοντες "not groaning."

The final clause is a litotes, a figure of speech in which an understatement is made in order to increase the effect "This (failure to submit to leaders) (is) profitless to you." In other words, to be submissive would be profitable.

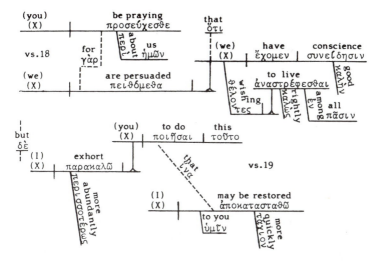

THE DIAGRAM OF HEBREWS 13:18-19

Verse 18 unveils a compound-complex sentence. The first of two independent clauses exhorts, "Be constantly praying concerning us." Present tense of the verb underscores the need for continuing prayer. The remainder of the sentence is a combination of a second independent clause whose verb has for its direct object a noun clause. "We are being persuaded. . . ." Is the independent idea. There seems to have been some reluctance on his part to "be persuaded" but in view of the facts he yielded to persuasive evidence. ὅτι introduces indirect discourse. The noun-object clause reveals the content of what it was about which he needed persuasion. It seems clear that he had been accused by some of living improperly in bad conscience. He had finally been convinced that such accusations were being made about him. Hence a request for persistent prayer. The present circumstantial participle

447

modifying "we" of the noun clause tells how the author felt about himself and his own motives, ". . . wishing to live properly among all." The phrase ἐν πᾶσιν "among all" as translated suggests that he wishes to live *amidst* his peers, especially his Christian brethren, "rightly." But ἐν can be translated "in all respects" or "in all things."

Verse 19 frames a complex sentence. The change from subject "we" in the preceding sentence to "I" in this sentence isn't without significance. Others were obviously associated with the author in this epistle, its teachings, exhortations and personal counsels. And they were associated with the request for prayers in verse 18. But here in 19 he asks that the prayers include a personal need for him in his desires and plan to return to them "more quickly." "I am exhorting . . ." is the bare clause. "More abundantly" is an adverb answering the question as to how much. The object of the verb "exhort" is the infinitive phrase ποιῆσα with an understood accusative of general reference ("you") Demonstrative pronoun "this" has for its antecedent the praying as requested in verse 18. ἵνα inserts a purpose clause, "in order that I may be restored to you more quickly." Why he was restrained from being "restored" as quickly as he might wish isn't clear. Was it sickness, betrayal imprisonment, problems? We do not know. But whatever it might be he believes that their continuing prayers would bring about his return to them "more quickly."

Hebrews 13:20-22

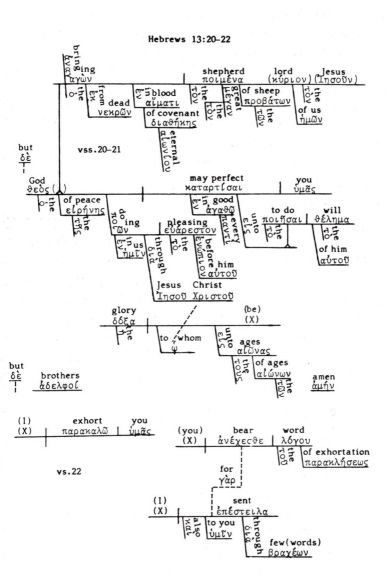

THE DIAGRAM OF HEBREWS 13:20-22

A brief glance at the sentence of verses 20-21 might suggest a rather complicated collection of clauses. But not so! Were it not for an eight-word adjective clause at the close this would be a simple sentence. Disrobed of all modifiers the one main clause expresses a wish about the future "May God perfect you. . . ." καταρτίσαι is aorist active optative. By koine times the optative had faded in use. It appears only 67 times in the New Testament. And in the New Testament a wish about the future is usually expressed by the optative as here. But the most commonly expressed such wish is that found in μὴ γένοιτο "may it not become," (the groundless "God forbid" of some versions).

The subject, θεός, besides being described by genitive "of peace," has a long participial phrase in apposition. The phrase begins with the aorist active articular participle ὁ ἀναγαγὼν "the one bringing. . . ." "From (the) dead" tell from whence; "in blood of eternal covenant" answers the question "how." In function both are adverbial phrases. Object of the verbal is "shepherd" described by the adjective "great" followed by genitive "of the sheep." Finally he is described by appositional "our Lord Jesus."

The subject "God" is further expanded by the circumstantial present participle ποιῶν "doing. . . ." The wish is ". . . may the God perfect you. . . ." This participial phrase informs as to the manner in which "God may perfect. . . ." That is, "accomplishing in us through Jesus Christ the thing pleasing before him." Each modifying phrase carries an important ingredient. Where does he "do" this perfecting? "In us." By what means? "Through Jesus Christ." What does he "do?" "The thing pleasing." And it is done "before him," in whose presence it is impossible to hide behind a sham front. Modifying the main verb, the εἰς phrase voices a purpose idea; literally, "for the to do his will. . . ." Using an understood accusative of general reference with the infinitive it may be rendered, "that you may do his will." The only subordinate clause adds a descriptive idea about "Jesus Christ." It says, ". . . to whom (be) the glory unto the ages of the ages."

As the diagram of verse 22 appears on the page the first clause declares, "I exhort you. . . ." The next two clauses appear separately as though they formed a separate compound sentence. In fact they give the content of his exhortation and may be placed as direct objects of παρακαλῶ. If so the sentence would be complex. ἀνέχεσθε "be bearing" or "be enduring" as present depicts linear action, "Go on tolerating. . . ." The "word of exhortation" refers to the present epistle. ἐπέστειλα "I sent" is an epistolary aorist. It looks at the entire epistle as though already in the hands of the recipients.

Hebrews 13:23–25

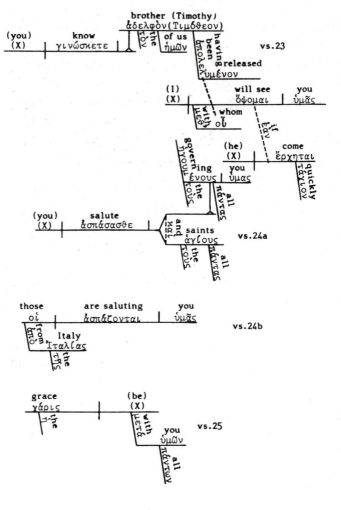

452

THE DIAGRAM OF HEBREWS 13:23-25

Verse 23 reveals a complex sentence. γινώσκετε may be either present indicative or imperative. If indicative the author is reminding his readers of something they already know. If it is imperative he is informing them of something they don't know. Perfect passive participle ἀπολελυμένον "having been set free" is here used in indirect discourse. "You know that our brother Timothy has been set free. . . ." And the perfect indicates that he is still free. The relative clause introduced by μεθ' οὗ "with whom" is adjectival describing Timothy. This adjective clause is also the apodosis of a third class condition. The adverbial "if" clause (ἐὰν) is a condition undetermined but with prospect of determination. "If he come quickly. I'm not sure that he will but he may. But if he does, then I will see you."

Verse 24a is a simple sentence with a compound direct object. ἀσπάσασθε is aorist imperative which is a usual way of extending a salutation. It is a request that the readers express the writer's greeting in his absence. In the object two groups are singled out. First, "all the ones (ruling) leading you." And second, "all the saints." By thus separating them the author gives a subtle reminder that each group has a responsibility toward the other.

Verse 24b is also simple in form. "Those from Italy salute you." οἱ is the demonstrative use of the article and may be translated as demonstrative "those." ἀσπάζονται is present indicative. The linear idea here is possibly distributive. Each separate one from Italy salutes! Whether "from Italy" refers to people with the author in Italy or to people who have come to the author from Italy is open to question. There seems no way to be certain—along with a number of other uncertainties about this epistle.

The final sentence is simple. "The grace (be) with you all." The definite article ἡ refers to a particularly prominent, well-recognized grace, the grace of God revealed in the Lord Jesus Christ. May it be "with (μετὰ) you" as a constant presence.